Effective Department and Team Leaders
A Practical Guide

Effective Department and Team Leaders
A Practical Guide

Rodney J. LaBrecque
Wilbraham and Monson Academy

Christopher-Gordon Publishers, Inc.
Norwood, Massachusetts

Credits

Every effort has been made to contact copyright holders for permission to reproduce borrowed material where necessary. We apologize for any oversights and would be happy to rectify them in future printings.

Reprinted by permission of the publisher from Hyman, R.T., IMPROVING DISCUSSION LEADERSHIP, (New York: Teachers College Press, © 1980 by Teachers College, Columbia University. All rights reserved.), pp. 117, 121.

Figure. Reprinted by permission of the National Board for Professional Teaching Standards, (1998), all rights reserved.

Christopher-Gordon Publishers, Inc.
1502 Providence Highway, Suite #12
Norwood, MA 02062
Tel: 800-934-8322

Copyright 1998 by Christopher-Gordon Publishers, Inc.

Printed in the United States of America

10 9 8 7 6 5 4 3 2   03

ISBN: 0-926842-76-5

To Shirley, Nicole and Christer

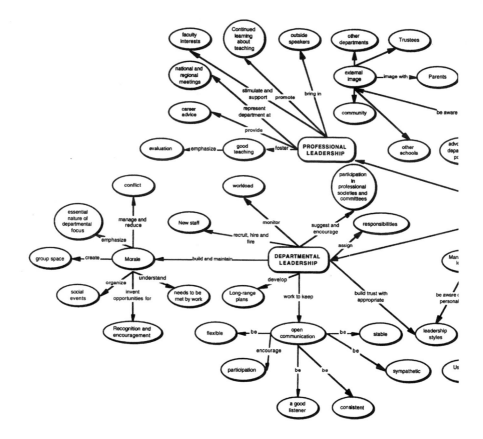

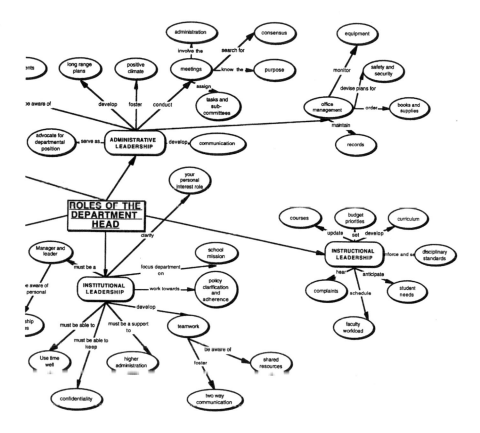

ROLES OF THE DEPARTMENT HEAD

administration

consensus

equipment

involve the — search for

long range plans

positive climate

meetings — know the — purpose

safety and security

monitor

devise plans for

develop — foster — conduct

assign

tasks and sub-committees

office management — order — books and supplies

be aware of

maintain

ADMINISTRATIVE LEADERSHIP

records

advocate for departmental position — serve as

develop — communication

your personal Interest role

Manager and leader

budget priorities

courses — curriculum

clarify

update — set — develop

INSTITUTIONAL LEADERSHIP

must be a

school mission

INSTRUCTIONAL LEADERSHIP

enforce and se — disciplinary standards

be aware of personal

focus department on

policy clarification and adherence

hear — anticipate

work towards

complaints — schedule — student needs

ship es

develop

must be able to — must be a support to

teamwork

faculty workload

must be able to keep

be aware of

Use time well

higher administration

foster — shared resources

confidentiality

two way communication

Contents

Introduction

The department head is the most crucial role that exists in our schools today. Department heads are expected to organize and implement changes in the curriculum; supervise and evaluate teachers; run productive meetings; resolve the inevitable student/teacher/parent conflicts; handle academic problems; order books and supplies; manage the budget effectively; recruit, select, and orient new teachers to the department/school/profession; and deal with the occasional crisis or emergency while maintaining a reputation as one of the department's most effective teachers. And often all of this must be done without release time from full-load teaching.

Is it any wonder that this job is one of the most underappreciated in our schools. However, there is no lack of willingness to take on this challenging task. Unfortunately, there is little in the way of training that exists to prepare teachers to assume this role and be effective. The small amount that has been written is aimed at heading college academic departments.

This book's purpose is to bridge this training gap and provide useful strategies and practices to increase your effectiveness as a department head or team leader. The case studies are culled from real life situations. The materials are designed to be maximally helpful in solving the subtle and sometimes not so subtle problems that crop up daily in a department or team.

It is my hope that this book will serve as a manual to help you anticipate problems before they grow and to anticipate right action. It is designed to give you the big picture of the job, although in reality the major focus of any department head or team leader is interpersonal interaction. Most of the time problems that arise are not clearly delineated and, in fact, are "total messes." And, without training, the department head is left to function in a chaotic environment, flying by the seat of the pants. Those who are perceptive usually learn what they need to know by trial and error. Trial usually doesn't lead to problems, but error can become a major difficulty.

In addition to striving to be as personally effective as possible, the good department head spends a tremendous amount of time helping others reach their potential. The word "administrator" implies service to others. The effective department head builds the department and team into a group that has a special spark of energy and professionalism. Such fine teams and departments are easily recognizable. People in such groups feel the security of professional respect balanced with the courage to grow. They feel the freedom to take the risk that is the necessary essence of artistry. Yet the group, led by the force of an effective leader, remains accountable to high standards.

Department heads and team leaders are indispensable to the functioning of an effective school. Anything that makes such leaders stronger is good for students and education. This book is one small step in that direction.

Wallingford, CT
January 1998

Chapter 1

Walk that Walk, Talk that Talk: Understanding and Defining Your Role

Introduction

Before you can move forward with either the creation or the development of the department or team, you need to have a clear understanding of your leadership roles. What exactly are you expected to do? Often, this can be the hardest part of the job. It may be the first time you consciously have to exhibit behaviors and traits that may not be as natural as those you have exhibited in your teaching. Yet, even though such behavior might seem foreign at first, you should not despair. These new leadership behaviors are not difficult to learn, if you are consciously and systematically attentive to the major areas of your job responsibilities.

As in all leadership behaviors, reliance on common sense is paramount. There isn't any extraordinary skill or magical power that underlies quality leadership. Instead, a major factor in good leadership behavior is paying close attention to your behavior and making sure you do what feels right. A somewhat worn, but no less appropriate, cliché about leadership is: "*Managers* do things right, and *Leaders* do the right thing"(Bennis and Nanus, 1985). For example, choosing to read this book is one step on the journey toward leadership excellence. While doing "things right" can be improved through proper training, doing the "right thing" is more closely connected to your common sense. If you let that inner voice be your guide, there is great likelihood that you will be successful as a leader. Stephen Covey in his book *First Things First* makes the point that following the dictates of our conscience connects us to the wisdom of the ages and, in doing so, supports us in defining and reaching our goals.

To be an effective leader, you must understand and expand your leadership behavior in five major areas: Instructional, Departmental, Profes-

Don's Case

Two years ago Don was asked by the principal to become the head of the history department. This was a position Don had always wanted to attain, and he accepted the offer immediately. He had been working at St. Michael's for nine years and had taught the full range of courses in the department from Ancient History to US History to departmental electives devoted to special topics such as "The Workings of Government" and "History of the Wild West." He had a reputation as one of the department's better teachers; students repeatedly commented positively upon his ability to be spontaneous in the classroom. And parents saw his efforts at individualized instruction as a breath of fresh air in a somewhat traditional department.

Don had watched the previous department head work diligently to develop the elective program, and he felt he could continue to expand it. He also had seen the former department head thwarted in attempts to develop courses of integrated studies with the English department. Don figured that he might be able to make some progress in this area because he had been an American Studies major in college and was therefore comfortable with English as well as history.

Now, two years later, Don looked back and was puzzled by all that had happened. His disillusion with the position was palpable. Soon after he began heading the department, he put together a proposal to the English department to begin some integrated studies courses. The English department did not agree to this plan and cited the lack of intensive writing as the primary reason not to move in this direction. In fact, what Don discovered was that his own department wasn't all that excited about these courses either. Don was amazed, because he had studied other schools where such courses were given, and the faculty in those schools seemed quite happy with such innovation.

Don also was confused by the tension he often felt as the department head. It was a feeling that did not exist when he was one of the teaching staff. It seemed that he would regularly have to convey new policies or initiatives from the administration to the department and in so doing felt that the department was resistant to these initiatives with no strong basis upon which this resistance was formed. Don saw these initiatives as not a big deal in the overall workings of the school, but nevertheless his history colleagues gave him a hard time. When two additional days were added to the yearly calendar, Don remembered that the department members balked and complained that he was not doing his job as the department head. They wanted to know how he could have "rolled over" so easily on this added burden. Don felt distinctly on the other side of the issue from his department and understood the administrative thrust to increase class time, but he could not, for the life of himself, convince his staff that this was not the beginning of the slippery slope.

Don continued to be frustrated in his attempts to implement the faculty evaluation system, which had been devised under the guidance of a special faculty committee. There just didn't seem to be enough time in the day or week to get to all nine members of the department and do a thorough job on the evaluation. Besides, Don also heard through the grapevine that several members of his department had doubts about his ability to evaluate their teaching. When he heard this, he was shocked because he felt that having been a fellow teacher with these folks for such a long time would automatically bring him credibility as an astute judge of fine teaching. After all, he was still primarily a teacher, receiving but one class of relief time in exchange for being the department head. He, more than most, understood how difficult it was to be a good teacher.

Finally, Don was embarrassed by the fact that he had erred in placing the book order last spring and school had opened in the fall with one class missing their texts. The teacher of this course had been very angry about this mistake and Don didn't understand why the teacher had made such a big deal out of it. After all, he had apologized to the teacher involved and then reminded the entire department that paperwork was not necessarily his strength. Creative curriculum-building was where he felt skilled and enjoyed devoting his time and energy.

So now, Don is looking at the next three years of his tenure as the department head stretching out before him and is wondering why he had thought this position was so desirable in the first place.

Think about:

1. What has changed for Don in moving from a multi-talented teaching slot to the department head position?
2. What should be the first item of business for Don when school begins again in September?
3. In what distinct roles has Don failed to perform adequately?
4. What advice would you give Don if you were his principal?

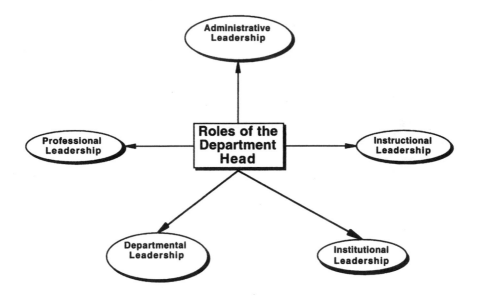

sional, Institutional, and Administrative Leadership. This chapter is designed to lead you through all of these areas and to help you build a personalized job description focused on realistic goals—goals tailor-made for your individual situation.

I. Instructional Leadership

One of the most important areas of the department head's or team leader's job is that of **Instructional Leadership**. After all, the reason for doing anything in a school should be to improve learning and, therefore, teaching. Emphasizing learning doesn't mean adult needs can be ignored. Certainly, if basic adult needs are not met, there will not be effective instruction. But the prime area for your special attention is the area of instruction and its effectiveness.

Making sure the curriculum offered has appropriate content, is continually updated, and is being taught with effective methods and materials must be high on your list of concerns. It will take time to do this effectively, but it is time well spent. In a department where there is a range of courses taught, such as a language department or science department, you may not be skilled in all the content areas. This gives you the opportunity to share leadership with another department member. Having another person to monitor and keep abreast of current pedagogical practices is a powerful method of instructional leadership. As the department head, you can set the tone for curricular development by always being aware of instructional quality in your dealings with all the members of the staff.

For example, when talking with members of your department it would be effective to focus your remarks on their classroom work. Everyone wants and needs feedback on his or her work. Spending your time talking with your staff about their teaching, rather than other possible conversation topics, will bring educational benefits. Remember the old adage "The best fertilizer is the footsteps of the farmer."

One of the most important aspects of instructional leadership is that of faculty supervision. In Chapter 9 you will be introduced to some specific methods for developmental supervision. It is crucial that you develop a sense among the staff that such supervision is a key component in their work and yours. Again, only through effective supervision can teaching and learning improve.

Today, there are many new forms of student assessment, and you will need to help your team ferret out those that make sense in the context of your institution. It is not easy to know which method will be most effective. You need to encourage your team always to be investigating the latest mousetrap, so to speak. It is in this constant tinkering and experimentation that advances are made in instruction. It will not work to force faculty to adopt an assessment method if they do not believe in it. It is the slow and steady development of new methods that wins the day. Leading by example is one sure fire method to instill a sense of trust in your staff along with a sense of experimentation. If you are willing to try new methods (and even fail sometimes in the attempt), then your staff will be encouraged to also try new teaching techniques and alternative methods of assessment.

Consider how you might introduce articles about other educational programs using new methodology in an effective manner. Such reading might serve to effect change or to bolster something with which a member of your staff might be experimenting. Perhaps a colleague from a neighboring school district might attend a department meeting and provide a first-hand account of some pedagogical innovation that was tried at his or her school. Cross-fertilization is a powerful means of stimulation. Just as the triathlete uses cross-training to improve all aspects of performance, cross-fertilization of educational ideas serves to strengthen all areas of teaching.

Courses and Curriculum

A key ingredient in making sure you have the right curriculum is to pay attention to the national standards set by the various professional societies in your discipline or area. This does not mean you should slavishly follow every guideline to the last degree. It does mean helping everyone to be aware of what others in the field have carefully thought about and have recommended as "good." Making these standards part of your departmental discussions is a common-sense way to foster curricular development. In addition, it prevents the department from spending time reinventing the wheel—and saving time is a basic desire for teachers with busy personal and professional lives. Chapter 6 will provide an extensive treatment of ways to make best use of the limited resource—time.

If one thinks of the course as the major unit of curricular currency, then the number of students in a class can be thought of as the effect of inflation of that currency. To a certain degree, the more students there are per class, the less the course currency is worth. It may be the best use of teacher power to offer more sections of a particular course, in order to keep the student-to-teacher ratio low, than it is to offer another new course. Every institution has guidelines about maximum and minimum levels of enrollment, but there is little agreement on what serves as the optimum ratio. In general, it makes sense to work towards providing classes where the number of students is not much higher than the minimum. It should be a departmental focus that the first order of business is class size and the second order is variety of offerings. Variety might have to be curtailed in order to keep class size small. Again, this is an example of common-sense leadership in action.

While you may be powerless to change class size, you can always be the voice for quality education. Reduced class size may not lead to increased national test scores, but everyone knows that reduced class size allows for more student-teacher interaction. That interaction provides the influence to change the direction of many students who otherwise would drift through school.

It is also important that the department protect itself from the over-development of "boutique courses." Such courses are those that can only be taught by a particular person. You can recognize a boutique course by asking yourself this question: "If the teacher of this course should leave the school, who would teach it?" If the answer is *No one*, then that is a boutique course. Notice, I didn't say that boutique course should be avoided at all costs. That is not true. Providing faculty members with the opportunity to follow an area of study that is near and dear to their hearts can be a very motivating strategy. However, the number of such courses must not grow so large that the basic curriculum is in danger should something happen to the teachers of those courses. You can imagine the chaos that would ensue, should such teachers become ill. What could you do to ensure that the course would still be given? Could you do *anything* to ensure this? Could you even hire a replacement to teach the course. Keep all of this in mind (and help the department keep it in their collective mind) as you work together to develop the departmental program.

For example, it may be prudent when developing courses to have several teachers involved in their development. Even if all the teachers will not be teaching the course immediately, you will be developing a stable of qualified teachers. Much as the bull pen provides emergency relief to the starting pitcher, the extra teachers who were involved with the course development can serve as back-up in case on an unanticipated problem.

This is an important consideration with which your department needs to wrestle. They should feel they are developing a departmental program, not a collection of individual programs. Developing a departmental program means that personal needs and wants are overridden by the needs of the group. A good department head does everything possible to make courses both departmentally and individually valued.

Serving Student Needs

In creating the department program, you need to help everyone see that the offerings must serve a range of students. This means that all courses, not just new courses, should be in process of continual development. Given the advanced state of our understanding of how students learn, it is your responsibility to incorporate such learning theory into the fabric of courses. One of the best ways to do this is to continue to have an experimental course or two always in operation. It is in such pilot projects that teachers can attend to how different learning styles are addressed more effectively, how students with learning differences can be accommodated, how new materials can be used, or how alternate assessment methods can be applied.

All the while, attention must be paid to student needs. Does your department provide opportunities for students to be "experts" in an area? Are you ever alert to the student who is gifted in your area and can serve as a department model, or even departmental advocate, within the student body? Are you developing a cadre of students whose love of the discipline needs to be nourished? How does your department help students excel in venues external to the school? Are there competitions you help them enter? Does anyone take them to conferences to see the subject in action? Do you provide the opportunity for them to see how a discipline is used in the world of work? How do you advise and counsel students who are interested in your discipline? How do you identify those who might be interested? All of these questions, when addressed, will serve the department well by helping students realize their maximum potential.

In today's society, the driving force behind all service organizations as well as businesses is the need to provide the products and services that meet the individual needs of the clients or customers. In the world of school, the best schools and the best departments will have figured out how to provide a varied program that meets the individual needs of the students and their parents.

One of the most powerful ways to serve student needs is to make sure the department "reeks" of student work (Levine). This seems to be more common at the elementary level than at any other level. In fact, as the educational ladder is climbed, one clear practice is apparent. The higher up you go, the less likely that student work will be publicly displayed and, when it is, it will be viewed by fewer and fewer observers. The Ph.D. recipient publishes his or her work for a narrow segment of the educational community, while the first-grader's painting is hung in the main entrance to the school for any and all visitors to see and enjoy. Why not change this? Why not make sure papers written by seniors in English or history are publicly displayed? Isn't this a form of assessment and a way to instill self-esteem in students? Isn't this a way to say publicly that in this work the educational values of the department are visible?

Faculty Workload and Complaints

Closely allied with developing a departmental program is paying close attention to faculty workload. You must make sure that your staff are not overloaded with responsibilities outside the classroom. When this happens, less attention is paid to preparation and student engagement. This will mean that learning will not be as effective as it could be. Paying attention to faculty workload often means protecting the teachers from themselves. Teachers commonly have a hard time saying NO. It is one of your jobs to help them do so. You have to help them walk the fine line between appearing to be recalcitrant and being taken advantage of.

For example, talking with your staff in some in-depth ways will help you discover what energizes them and provides them with motivation. You can then act to structure their work around such energizing activities. There is some truth to the idea that the happier a staff you will have and the better your department will be. Again, this is nothing more than applying common sense.

Finally, an important area of instructional leadership will be your ability to deal with complaints when they occur. And occur they will. There
will be disagreements among staff, students will complain about teachers,
parents will complain about teachers. You'll need to be understanding and
even-handed in dealing with such complaints. Chapter 4 explores in more
depth the difficult topic of giving information the listener would rather not
hear and the giver would rather not give. What you need to remember is
that some parental and student complaints are indeed valid. But it is imperative that you never give the impression that you are not supportive of your
staff. Your support must be realistic, however. You must let the teachers
know that you will be thorough in investigating any complaint and you will
be completely honest with them whenever a complaint surfaces.

II. Departmental Leadership

Teacher Morale

"From the artisan's logic, I would rather look to the department as the unit
of collaborative planning and execution in a secondary school. This is
where people have concrete things to tell one another and concrete institutional help to provide one another . . . where the contexts of instruction

Figure 1.1 Departmental Leadership

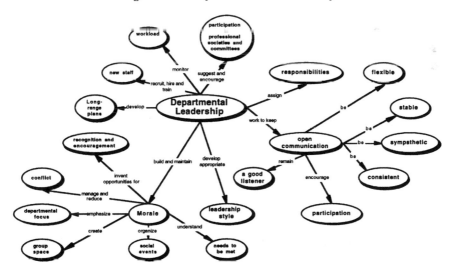

actually overlap" (Huberman, 1994). If you accept that logic, then **Departmental Leadership** is probably the next most important leadership behavior after **Instructional Leadership**. And first among your goals in this area should be the development of strong, positive morale.

Motivating and helping your department members to reach their full potential as teachers brings you another step closer toward the goal of increased learning for students. Good teaching is essential if there is to be "good" learning. The primary locus of attention for your department is, obviously, the department itself. By paying attention to certain details of physical and psychological needs, you can create the conditions for better morale and foster an atmosphere of togetherness.

For example, you can discover some of their needs simply by asking direct questions of your staff such as:

- "Do you need any supplies?"
- "How can I help you reach your goals?"
- "What would you like to see us do as a group to improve our performance?"

Every department should continually review its own goals and objectives. Chapter 3 contains many specific activities that a department can engage in as a way to develop goals or monitor progress towards goals. An effective department head knows that team behavior needs to be actively fostered. Making departmental goals specific and concrete is essential. Once the goals have been identified, an interesting way to use them for motivation is to turn them into a poster-sized display. Post these goals prominently for all to see. A simple action such as this can keep a department focused on what is important. Such a public display also emphasizes the group nature of the goals. The best educational goals are those that the department can realize *only by working and striving together*.

For example, a goal focused on the need for students to participate in a multidisciplinary course as a culmination to their schooling means that each course in the sequence leading up to the culmination is crucial. All the teachers must be involved in making sure they point students toward this culminating experience. If any individual teacher fails in his or her task, then all fail, because the departmental goal cannot be met.

When looking at the needs of your department, you might want to do so very systematically. Exhibit 1.1 gives a chart that might allow you to look at the needs of those who work in the department. Understanding, and then acting to help team members fulfill, their needs is an essential part of a successful department head's or team leader's job. It may not be possible for you to fulfill every need. Sometimes only the person himself or herself

---

Exhibit 1.1 Know Your Staff

Basic Needs *Names*

Need for status
Need for feeling accomplishment
Need to be loyal
Need for high standards
Need for adherence to authority
Need to be recognized as an individual
Need to excel
Need to create
Need to cooperate
Need for independence
Need for leader approval
Need for privacy
Need to separate work and non-work

---

can do so. But you can create the conditions where such fulfillment is more likely to happen.

In building better morale, one aspect of department life that cannot be overlooked is tradition. Every school has traditions that are school based, but this may not be true of individual departments. Yet the place teachers call home is more likely to be the department than the school. Even though they may see themselves as important cogs in the school machine, the larger organization is not as concrete as the department. In fact, it is more likely to be true that math and science departments in different schools have more in common with one another than math and history departments in the same school. Thus, by creating or observing departmental traditions, you are providing, at the local level, a context for community building that can be translated into school loyalty. If you do not have clearly discernible traditions, then start some. The sooner you do so, the sooner your team will feel more connectedness to one another. It is probably going overboard to say that there should be a "cult" feeling within the department, but some level of shared camaraderie is not terribly off base.

For example, bringing special snacks to the department space every Friday might be a simple message to the teachers that you've appreciated a week of work well-done. Consider instituting a monthly TGIF time. Or make sure the daily local paper or the New York Times is available for reading. Every department has one or two creative minds who would leap at the chance to help you develop some welcomed traditions. Developing traditions can also be tremendous fun, and whenever fun can be made the central emotion of a task or event, the chance of failure is very low.

Creating the Work Space

For people to work together, they must communicate clearly with one another. One of the best ways to accomplish this is to arrange a physical space where the group continually interacts. If you have a large room that all department members can call their home base, you will be well on your way to ensuring closer contact. A group space needn't be especially fancy. It may be that a spare classroom can be used. By consolidating the schedule during the day, it might be possible to free up a classroom. In this space, you'd need a large table or set of study carrels. A carrel arrangement allows each member of the department to have personal work space and still interact in the larger shared space.

If you can also bring to this area mailboxes, bulletin boards and message boards, faculty course files, copying machines, computers, telephone, and the all-important coffee pot, you will have created a place where people can get work done and can socialize. If there is anything that teachers have in common, it's the need to talk, and such a group space gives them the opportunity to do this.

Creating individual offices is the best way to ensure that you will not have close communication. Even though teachers might like to have an office for privacy, as well as status, I would encourage you to not provide them. In departments where offices are the order of the day, isolation and fragmentation are the main outcomes. Teaching is already well-known as one of the more isolating professions. Encouraging such isolation will definitely work to your disadvantage in trying to build a team, and your role as department leader will be compromised.

What you want to create is a hothouse of teacher talk. Not for the kind of grousing that can be the staple of faculty room discussions, but rather for discussions about pedagogy and successful teaching strategies. If there is a department room close to the work spaces or classrooms of the teachers and team members, the chance that they will engage in conversation about teaching is high. When a teacher finishes a lesson that worked especially well, he or she wants to talk about that lesson. The teacher wants to continue to feel that feeling of success. Such talk will motivate others either to try a similar method or at least be uplifted by the enthusiasm of a colleague. Furthermore, as such talk becomes routine, teachers will also talk about their failures and frustrations. In such an atmosphere of trust and mutual understanding, the inevitable advice-giving and support from colleagues will also serve as the motivation to persevere. To make teaching work is difficult, exhausting and often times frustrating. Spreading such hard work among many people lessens the burden.

Finally, as teachers learn new methods of teaching, especially using computers, the department space can serve as a "safe zone" for colleagues to teach one another. It can be considered a "safe zone" because only in a supportive departmental atmosphere can teachers let down their defenses to admit that there are areas of weakness in their teaching. It is in such a group physical space that they might be more willing to ask for and receive help.

For example, most teachers are not skilled in the subtleties of computers. By practicing in the department space, they can learn techniques and procedures that only more experienced teachers might know. Reading the manual to determine what to do when the computer freezes, we all know, can be an exercise in futility. But learning how to address this problem from a colleague is a way to develop confidence and skill with the new technologies.

Often, however, faculty will argue for individual spaces, not necessarily offices, but certainly classrooms. "I have to have a classroom I can call my own." "I can't get any work done if I have to sit in a room with other people. I need an office or my own classroom if you expect me to be a really good teacher." "I need a place to work with students in private, so this kind of group work space won't help me get my job done." Don't listen to such talk. If you give in, the likelihood that the teacher will spend time in the departmental space will be very much diminished. There are plenty of spaces in a school where a teacher can go to be alone and get work done. The library is one such space. A study hall might be another (not to mention that added adult presence in such a space could be helpful). There are almost always empty classrooms where a teacher can meet one-on-one with a student or set of parents. The only need for a private space might be the need to make confidential telephone calls.

As a department head, you will need to think carefully about how you use your office, if you have one. You need to be careful not to isolate yourself from the department. Perhaps your office is the place to make available to all faculty when they might make those private telephone calls to parents or to hold confidential conferences with students. Remember, you need to be out with the team as much as possible and serve as a role model for teacher talk.

Praise

Morale can be improved by paying attention to what people have done, and all the members of your staff have done *something* this year that is worthy of praise. A short, heartfelt written note is all that is needed to make that person feel important and essential. The value of written communication over verbal communication is that it lasts so much longer. People tend to keep their written correspondence and can take it out to read over and over again. This kind of private praise is a definite motivator, although, as in all praise, you must be sincere, and it must be for real accomplishment.

Sometimes public praise is more effective than private praise. This can be done via school-wide or community-wide publications. It can be something mentioned at a faculty meeting or even a department meeting. Whatever the occasion, there is a time and place for public recognition. Nominating a member of your department for external competitions and awards is one way to combine public and private recognition. If the person wins the competition, the news will be public. If not, then the effort is a private one between you and the staff member. However, that staff member now feels better because of your willingness to support and recognize his or her work and effort. Again, this is extremely motivating for the staff member, and it gets you to be more connected with their teaching.

Figure 1.2 shows the familiar hierarchy of needs as described by Maslow. While you may not be personally able to help with the fulfillment of the lower order needs, your institution must be in the position to do so. Your function as a leader is to help with the higher order tasks. Your goal should be to develop structures that allow each person the autonomy to make decisions about their work. You have to provide tasks that truly matter. In doing so, you will provide the opportunity for growth and advancement that all adults need.

For example, pairing the experienced veteran with the raw rookie in a mentoring relationship is one way to help teachers fulfill self-esteem needs and to find a sense of meaning in their work. In addition, you can praise teachers, who have done exceptional work, in either departmental meetings or full faculty meetings.

It should be mentioned that most administrators operate from a weak position in the area of Safety Needs. This is primarily due to the public nature of the position. Everyone is free to criticize, especially the Monday-morning quarterback. This leads to a sense that one is not safe from such criticism. And there is fear that one will be attacked at any time. However, it is also true that most administrators also work with great strength in the area of self-esteem. Perhaps this strength needs to be there, or the leader

Figure 1.2 MASLOW'S HIERARCHY OF NEEDS

NEED FOR SELF-ACTUALIZATION
Self-mastery, desire to help others,
ability to direct one's own life, rich
emotional experiences, a sense of real
meaning to one's life.

ESTEEM NEEDS
Self-esteem, esteem of others, achievement,
recognition, dignity, appreciation, self-
confidence, mastery of one's self and
one's environment.

BELONGINGNESS AND LOVE NEEDS
Love, affection, belongingness; need for family, friends,
group, clan, territorial imperative, community.

SAFETY NEEDS
Security, stability, dependency, protection; freedom from fear,
anxiety chaos; need for structure, order, limits, etc.

PHYSIOLOGICAL NEEDS
Homeostasis; specific hungers: sex, food, water, air, shelter and
general survival.

would not be able to endure the inevitable criticism that comes with leadership.

It is very important for each staff member to see that he or she is valued as a part of a winning team. Winning can mean many things and should be defined in your own context. However, you can see how important this aspect of work is when you look to professional sports. Many top players, when given the opportunity to be traded, look for programs that are winners. Corporations work very diligently to keep up the winning image, not just for financial reasons, but for worker-motivation reasons.

In further developing morale, finding the time for socializing is important. While creating a group space can serve as a socializing agent, more formal social events are also important. Such events can be simple affairs such as a pot-luck supper on a Friday evening. Alhough an occasional dinner, where you take on all the work, gives the message that you value each person's contribution to the team and you want to reward everyone. This will be a treat to the group and well worth the effort on your part.

Paying Attention to Teacher Workload

Because one fundamental characteristic of good teaching is the desire to help others, it is very difficult for many teachers to say no when asked to do a task. While these extra tasks are essential for the operation of a good school and every teacher should do some, teachers need to be protected from themselves. For some teachers, serving on committees, working at after-school events, driving students to community service sites, coaching teams, advising clubs and providing sundry other work, is neither rewarding nor motivating. As a good department head, you can help those individuals say no to those things for which they have little interest or skill and, instead, search out those opportunities for productive, rewarding work.

Holding private discussions with each team member at the opening of the year to discuss what might lie ahead and what the teacher wants to accomplish can help that teacher create a plan of action to address any duties outside of the classroom. Sometimes, you should encourage the teacher to attempt something new. This can be exciting and enjoyable as long as it is not too far beyond the edge of the teacher's competency. As a skillful department head, you will recognize each person's key attributes and talents; you can help them put to work their ability as an organizer, personal supporter, mentor, beautifier, student connector, or Pied Piper.

Sometimes the tasks that are important to the school and the department member lie outside the school boundaries. Urging participation in local, state, and national professional societies builds self-esteem, and through sharing can bring new ideas and current thinking back to the department and school. Usually, it takes no more effort to be part of such organizations than to volunteer for service. Such groups are always looking for new blood and will readily provide membership to that volunteer. In addition to personal growth, such activity signals the rest of the school that your department is committed to pedagogical excellence and is working to be part of a teaching community larger that the school itself.

Workload issues are especially crucial for new teachers. They definitely feel they cannot say *no* to anyone, lest they look less than enthusiastic. You are the only one who can protect them. Letting them know what the departmental and institutional expectations are for work outside of the classroom is an important first step in getting them acclimated to the school culture. You should continually give new teachers the message that the most important portion of their job is classroom performance. They should not expect to be as active in external school affairs as the ten-year veteran teacher. You need to help them sequester time to spend on the development of their teaching methods and course content.

While each new teacher should have a veteran teacher as an official mentor, you should also remain close. They need your encouragement, and they need to know from you that they are doing a good job. (They also need to know when they are not doing a good job, and the details on such feedback can be found in Chapter 4.) Working with the new teachers to acclimate them to their new culture is one nonthreatening way you can interact with them. Often, they will view the department head somewhat warily because they will feel your power as the instructional leader and immediate administrative force in their lives. Spending some time with the new teachers talking about aspects of their school work, both in and out of the classroom will go a long way toward making you a more accessible figure.

Long-Range Planning

Every department should develop and use a long-range plan. Such a plan provides a department with coherent views of how they should be acting and developing. In addition, as the department adheres to a long-range plan, progress can be charted and measured. In fact, such progress should be actively recognized.

Displaying the long-range plan publicly in the department space, will serve as a daily reminder of what has been agreed upon as important. Every teacher can measure his or her personal efforts of that day or week against the goals for the future. Public awareness of target goals is a dependable way to ensure that progress will be made. The old saw that "If you don't know where you're going, then any road will take you there" is applicable when you do not make the departmental and institutional goals part of everyday reality.

Likewise, your team's long range plan also will serve as *your* road map to success. You should have that road map constantly at your side. Print the plan on a single sheet of paper and laminate it. Then place that plan on your desk, so that every time you sit down to work, you will see where the group wants to go. Awareness of the goal will help you decide how to use your precious time.

Another way to keep goals in mind is to use a portion of every department meeting to remind the members of the team that there are goals to be reached and that you expect everyone to be working to attain them. There is not enough talk about goal attainment with most school groups. Somehow it seems to be resisted because it smacks of the business world, and yet there is no more motivating activity than looking back at the road traveled while attaining a particular goal.

Communicating Openly

Every department depends upon the leader to get things accomplished. The members assume that you will represent their interests to the administration in their stead. They, therefore, need to be kept informed of all your interactions with upper-level administrators. The first step in being a good communicator is to be a good listener. You need to hear what your staff is saying when they make requests. There is always meaning between the lines, and you need to be sensitive in picking up those tacit messages. It has been said that not only is a good listener often popular, but that he or she actually knows something after awhile. In listening, you will be learning—and you will be popular.

A good listener always know how to be sympathetic to the speaker. Often, what the person you're talking to wants most is not advice, but rather a certain amount of agreement and understanding. In fact, you are best served in not giving advice unless directly asked.

For example, if a member of your staff starts complaining about the fact that the students did not do their reading last night, don't spew forth several methods on how to get them to do assignments, even though that may be your first inclination. (After all, department heads are often selected because they are good problem solvers.) You'll be more effective by responding sympathetically. You can agree that sometimes it can be very disheartening when students don't do the reading because then the teacher task is exponentially more difficult. You want to signal that you have also had classes where students didn't do the assignment, and you sent them away to read the material. You had stopped the class and, without anger, said that everyone was to spend the next ten minutes reading the assignment beginning at the beginning. This is a very indirect way to give support when the teacher needs it.

For your staff to develop trust in your ability as a leader, you have to be consistent in your action and message. Such consistency should be broadened to describe your emotional dealings with the staff. You do not want your team to be worried about whether "the boss is in a bad mood" today or not. They are counting on you to be the positive source of energy. You should think of yourself as the eye of the hurricane. When all around you is whirling crazily, you remain focused and calm.

Another metaphor you should to keep in mind is an image often connected with former President of the United States, Ronald Reagan. Sometimes he was described as the "Teflon™ Man." No criticism was able to stick. Whatever he had done, somehow the criticism directed at him was ineffective and rarely did the public associate negative outcomes with his leadership.

When the inevitable departmental disagreement crops up, if you think of yourself as coated in Teflon™, where any and all critical comments merely slide off your surface, you will be able to remain calm. No parent, student or staff member can cause you to become unglued, because you are Teflon™ coated. Maintaining your composure is an essential element in being a top-notch communicator. Chapter 4 provides in-depth examples of how you can communicate without causing turmoil.

III. Administrative Leadership

If there is anything that is unsettling or radically different about being the department head or team leader, it's that you will now be viewed differently by your former colleagues. Most new department heads do not think this will happen to them. But experienced department heads know that being a leader means that you have to exhibit certain leadership traits. These traits, surprisingly, may not be the same traits that you used to become a successful teacher. As the leader, your staff expects that you will be active in setting agendas for work, that you will be helping them achieve important goals, that you will be spending time working on their behalf. Whereas before you worked for the betterment of your students, now you will have to work for the betterment of your adult staff.

In his book *Servant Leadership,* Robert Greenleaf makes the case that the best leaders are those who look at leadership as service to others. The Latin roots of administration give us its true meaning: *Ad ministrarae* "to minister unto," that is to serve others. If you take this view as your raison d'être, you will have made an important first step on the path toward excellence as a leader. Your most important job is to help your staff become the best teachers they can be. All your actions should be devoted to that task. Every time you have a choice of doing this thing or doing that thing, you should weigh each option by how much each one improves instruction. If you can rate one action higher than another in terms of how it will

FIGURE 1.3 Adminstrative Leadership

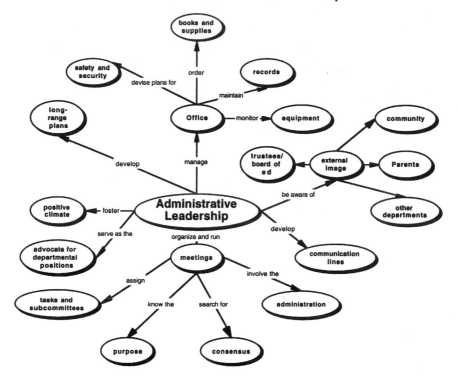

affect learning, then you should act in the manner that improves instruction.

In mentioning communication, the previous section discussed dealing with a member of your staff. However, that is not the only line of communication you must master. You need to be able to communicate to the administration the needs of your staff. Correspondingly, you need to communicate the needs of the administration to your staff. You must continually concentrate your staff's focus on the larger picture. It is too easy for department members to be so immersed in their own world, that they miss the important needs of other departments. They also may not see that when one department suffer, all departments suffer, since the school as a whole is affected by mediocre performances in any area.

One venue for such formal focus is the constructive and useful meeting. (See Chapter 8). Meetings should have a purpose, and when an action is agreed to, there should be a reasonable chance of accomplishing the task at hand. Whenever possible, consensus decision making is a better choice for coming to agreement that voting. Voting may make decision making appear to be easier, but usually, it only serves to drive alternative positions underground.

One way to stimulate big-picture thinking is to invite upper-level administrators to your meetings. Get them to explain their view of your department, in the context of the overall school picture. This somewhat more formal contact will serve all the department members well. In addition, the senior administrators will become more knowledgeable about your staff, your program, and your departmental vision.

Serving also means making sure everyone has teaching tools in sufficient supply and working order. One major service role you will play is to make sure the inevitable paper work that accompanies administrative positions is completed on time. Your staff expects you to be an efficient office manager. You must maintain accurate records of purchases, as well as policies relating to student issues. Ordering supplies on time, making sure all equipment is in working order, or has been sent out for repair if it is not working, creating a supply of back-up material are all important tasks for you to complete. You may need to be the one to insist on using some meeting time to train faculty on equipment use. Above all, it is your responsibility to make sure that your department areas are safe. Students and faculty need to know that help is readily available in the event of an emergency.

I suggest you create a file of all policies in your department and make a note whenever a policy is invoked. If you do not do this, confusion will almost definitely visit your actions at one time or another. What happened to Tom Smith five years ago when he removed magnesium from the lab bench may be a murky memory now that Mary Jones has done the same thing. Also, there are always exceptions to any policy and these need to be recorded so that consistency of action is clear.

Another major way you serve your department is to cultivate its image continually. You will be the public spokesperson for your department at many gatherings, both formal and informal. There will be invitations to present information about your program to parents and other community members, to give speeches and workshops for colleagues in other schools, and to give progress reports to your school administration or the Board of Trustees or Board of Education. To do this well means that you might need to work on your public speaking skills, as well as your writing skills. Seek out the speech teacher or other skilled colleague in your school. Too often, we seek help elsewhere when it is right at hand. If there is an especially skilled department member who could help with public presentations, etc., then this might be an excellent shared activity.

Proceeding in such a service manner allows you to help the department develop and maintain a healthy voice in the community. It is this voice that is essential in creating recognizable differences among departments in a school. Such differences are healthy, as long as there is an underlying core of commonality of educational belief—the stated school mission—among departments.

IV. Institutional Leadership

You and your team are part of a much larger team. It is important, if you expect to work smoothly with the senior administration of a school, to keep this thought at the forefront of all that you do. Sometimes being a part of a larger team will force you to behave somewhat paradoxically.

While the typical vision of the department leader is one of being a good problem solver, it may be that to do a fine job you really must be a problem maker. Problem makers do not sit back and take care of a pro-

FIGURE 1.4 Institutional Leadership

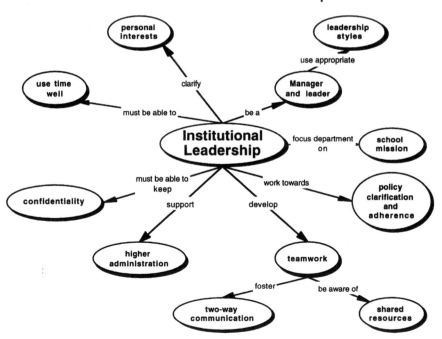

gram. They consciously act to change the status quo, whenever that status quo is below the departmental and school expectations of excellence in promoting learning.

At first, playing the role of a problem maker might seem confusing. Aren't you, as a good department head, supposed to make things work smoothly and not generate problems? The answer is usually YES, but sometimes it is most emphatically NO. For example, you may see the need for a particular teacher to have an extra section of a course. This will either cost the school more money or will require that the teacher's workload in another area be reduced. This is going to be a problem for the senior administrator in charge of compensation. However, if such problems are set in the context of reaching stated school goals, it can often serve the program best when you attempt to solve them. Thus, while you might have created a problem, it was not an unhealthy problem to have created.

One painful dilemma you will face, with regards to institutional leadership, is that your classroom teaching will probably not be as good as it was before you became the department head. This is only logical, as you will be spending a good deal of time working with adults, rather than with students. You will need to decide how much of your effort will go into departmental leadership and how much will remain in your teaching.

This dilemma is even more poignant for those who do not get release time to do the job of department heading or team leading. You should be getting release time. If not, the administration may not understand the full scope of the department head's job nor the important contribution your leadership can make towards creating an excellent school. If you do receive release time, you need to be sure to sequester that time for department related tasks; otherwise you will fritter away valuable time without even knowing it. You should write down how you plan to spend your week and then *follow that plan*. That plan should be focused on achieving your major goals. (See Chapter 6, "Using Time to Work Smarter, Not Harder")

While it is a given that everyone must know the departmental mission, you also must make sure that your department members understand and obey all the rules of the school. You need to help teachers strengthen their grasp of the big picture of the school. They should feel accountable not only for the academic program in their own departments, but also for the programs and offerings of other departments. Lortie discovered that teachers are more concerned with matters directly affecting their classroom than with those that affect the school organization as a whole. (Lortie, 1975) Thus, to ask them to focus on what other departments are doing is not an easy task. And yet such an understanding of other departments develops an overall understanding of how the departments fit together to create a synergistic learning environment.

You will need to help teachers see the congruence between their personal goals, the departmental goals and the institutional goals. Developmental supervision is one way to accomplish this. (There is much more about such supervision in Chapter 9). Publicly posting a copy of the school mission statement gives a clear message about what is important for the group. Spending a bit of regular meeting time on how teachers are reaching these goals is also a good use of time.

All schools are complex institutions. As the leader of a school team, there is no doubt that you must serve as a member of a larger administrative team. You will need to decide what you wish your role to be in that group. Are you an advice giver? the voice of reason? the voice of the faculty? the devil's advocate? the educational literature guru? Is there a role the senior administration wants you to play in the group? By spending some time talking as part of this group, you may be able to have the group define the role of each department head. In this way, there will be no confusion about actions and responsibilities. Whatever your role is, be sure to remain free of behavioral expectations that paint you into an operational corner from which there is no escape.

In working with such an administrative group, you should set your sights high. Work toward creating something special, even if it means stepping out of the safe zone, the area where there is little risk but little accomplishment. To work at the edge of greatness is to work at the edge of failure. Being bold, within commonsense limitations, is leadership in action.

As a person privy to institutional thinking and policy making, there will be times when confidentiality is essential. And sometimes keeping such confidentiality can make your job very difficult. For example, you know the real reason why Mr. Topper took early retirement. His teaching had deteriorated in the last year or two because he was preoccupied with the fact that his adult son was struggling with AIDS. But Mr. Topper has sworn you to secrecy about his son. Thus, it may appear to others that Mr. Topper was pushed out of the profession without due cause. You'd like to be able to explain all that you know to avoid blame, but that is not going to be possible. This is one of the painful consequences of leadership.

Sometimes, you are also going to be called upon to support administrative initiatives, even when they don't necessarily serve your department (as many in the department are only to quick to point out). You will have to work your hardest to help your staff see the reasoning behind such administrative decisions. You cannot undercut that decision without risking your status as a professional. Being the department head does carry along some amount of advocacy for the department, but it cannot always be in opposition to the administrative necessities. There will be times when you will be working with the larger group of department heads to come to agreement on new policies or adherence to old ones. This may mean that you will have to compromise the position you know your department favors. You will have to be able to go back to your team and explain why your decision to act, in a direction not

---

Exhibit 1.2 Department Head Job Description

Qualifications: Five years teaching experience, good organizational skills, strong desire and demonstrated ability to work with adults, reputation as a strong teacher.

Reports To: The School Principal.

Term of Office: Five years with the option for re-selection two times for three year periods. Total consecutive time in the position could be eleven years.

Overall Goal: The department head must work effectively alongside department members to achieve school-defined and department-defined objectives, making best use of the resources of the school. The department head must work as a facilitator to help others in the department reach their individual professional potential and attain career goals.

Evaluation: Evaluation will be performed by the Dean of Academic Affairs and the Dean of Faculty through a process to be devised by the Committee of Department Heads.

1. **INSTRUCTIONAL TASKS AND GOALS**
   a. Lead the department in setting instructional goals that focus on improving the quality of learning.
   b. Determine with department members course offerings and their sequencing. In addition, help department members develop new courses so that teachers feel they own the departmental program and are professionally stimulated by developing new courses.
   c. Work with the Dean of Academic Affairs to create catalog materials that fully and accurately describe the program of the department so that students and parents can make informed course choices.
   d. Ensure that department members understand and adhere to the academic regulations and policies of the school so that they speak with one voice to the students and parents and work fairly in an overall school context with the other departments.

e. Determine the quality of courses taken by students at other schools (including summer schools) in order to place students correctly and give credit where credit is due.

f. Oversee an effective procedure for covering classes in the event of faculty absences so that students receive the maximum amount of contact time with teachers.

2. DEPARTMENTAL TASKS AND GOALS

a. Build a healthy climate within the department to improve working conditions connected with the need for adult control over such condtions.

b. Help the department function together as a smoothly working team in order to promote collegiality, to improve working conditions and to motivate every adult member to strive for excellence.

c. Resolve conflict when it arises in order to keep the team functioning smoothly and cooperatively.

d. Trustfully handle confidential information to ensure that a professional level of behavior is maintained.

e. Oversee the timely selection and ordering of textbooks, teaching materials and supplies. In addition, help with the selection of audiovisual materials, technological hardware and software, and library books such that the appropriate concrete materials needed for quality instruction and learning are provided to the right teachers for the right students at the right time.

3. ADMINISTRATIVE TASKS AND GOALS

a. Meet regularly as a member of the committee of department heads for the purpose of maintaining effective interdepartmental communication and developing skills pertinent to successfully functioning as the department head.

b. Function as part of the administrative team to ensure unified understanding and communication of school operation and decision making to all constituencies.

c. Know policies and procedures of the school and help all department members adhere to those stated policies and regulations, both academic and social, to create and maintain a school where order and fairness prevail.

d. Assign/rotate/balance the teaching responsibilities of each department member, at all times keeping the best interests of students and faculty in mind for the purpose of maintaining equitable workloads among all departmental faculty and of maintaining a motivating and stimulating job assignment for each faculty member.

4. INSTITUTIONAL TASKS AND GOALS
   a. Develop and be responsible for annual and long-term balanced budgets to guarantee fiscal responsibility at all levels of school operation.
   b. Oversee the physical needs of the department classrooms and offices, including ensuring the security of departmental facilities and equipment so that our facilities are safe, clean, and in good repair.
   c. Provide information about the department to others in the school so that everyone understands department operation, policy and need as part of a whole-school context.
   d. Hold effective, regularly scheduled meetings of the entire department for the purpose of involving all department members in the business of the department and the school.
   e. Serve as a liaison between the department and the school administration in order to serve both as an advocate for the department and as an advocate for the administration.

5. PROFESSIONAL TASKS AND GOALS
   a. Serve as a role model for good teaching practices, for involvement with professional organizations relevant to teaching and for continued personal professional development in order to inspire and lead departmental faculty.
   b. Remain current about new national curricular initiatives in departmental disciplines and help department members do the same in order to incorporate the best educational thinking into the academic program.
   c. Take responsibility for professional growth of both the department as a whole and faculty as individuals in order to help all teachers reach their stated professional goals.
   d. Help recruit and hire staff, being ever vigilant for potential new faculty for the department in order to attract the best teachers to the school and, hence, improve the quality of learning.
   e. Encourage and coordinate curriculum development by faculty, supporting innovation where appropriate in order to increase faculty job satisfaction and student achievement.
   f. Consider and supervise appropriate teaching methods to ensure students are provided the best possible learning environment.
   g. Supervise and evaluate teachers in a supportive and developmental fashion according to the guidelines in the Faculty Handbook such that faculty continue to improve the quality of student learning.

perfectly in congruence with their wishes, was a good idea. This is a duty that has to be met by any institutionally effective department head.

Your role as an institutional leader should be clearly defined in your job description. If you school does not have a job description, then create one. Exhibit 1.2 shows an example of a Department Head job description.

Note how each task is stated so that it has a goal attached to it. It is not enough to say, for example, that as the department head you have to develop teaching assignments. There has to be a reason for doing so—a reasonable way for you to show that you have accomplished the task—and a clear understanding that each action you take serves the educational needs of the students and teachers. Each year you should selectively concentrate on a few items from the job description. While it is true you may have to be involved with all the items in the job description, you should devote major blocks of time and attention to only a few of them each year, as part of your desire to

---

Exhibit 1.3

GOALS 1997–1998: Science Department Head

During the next academic year it is my goal to

1. encourage the design and implementation of effective programs of study and support teaching methodologies appropriate to accomplish such programs

in order to insure

that the academic needs of our students are met in effective, productive and imaginative ways, that the professional, motivational and socio-emotional needs of our faculty are met, that our school remain a "learning organization," and that we continue to be recognized as a leader in academic circles
by

   a. working closely with the other department heads on departmental reviews,
   b. helping the curriculum committee produce a final report on curriculum renewal,
   c. putting into place at the appropriate time a daily schedule that meets the needs of the new curriculum,
   d. producing a self-study report that clearly describes the science department,
   e. developing plans to implement the technology strategy developed during 1996–97, and meeting with small groups of students each week for lunch.

2. bring to fruition plans for the complete renovation of the Science Library

for the purpose of
providing the most useful facility both for student and faculty acquisition and construction of knowledge
by
   a. working with the Director of the school library and the library consultant,
   b. creating Ad Hoc Faculty, Student and Trustee committees to provide advice in the rendering of preliminary architectural sketches.

3. continue to build an effective working team among the department members
                        in order to guarantee
better communication about and understanding of individual and institutional goals
by
   a. holding both separate and group meetings on an as-needed basis,
   b. spending time with each member of the department in his or her own space, and
   c. listening closely to requests for both support and understanding and acting, when possible, on such requests.

4. devote reasonable time to reflection and reading concerning educational issues
                        so that
the science faculty are informed about new developments in teaching and learning and, thus, can improve the quality of learning students exhibit
by
      devoting Wednesday afternoon to such a purpose.

5. serve as a role model for professional behavior and development
                        in order to
stimulate professional behaviors in other members of the community
by
      serving on professional committees outside of the school, giving workshops and seminars to outside groups and publishing at least one scholarly article.

---

accomplish major goals. Exhibit 1.3 shows how several goals for the year are developed utilizing "purpose" statements and action items. Such a format helps you know exactly why you are concentrating on those goals along with how you plan to accomplish those goals. All that would remain is to design a method to gather feedback on whether those particular goals were attained.

Finally, as an administrator, your time is very valuable. You will have many demands that spring up fortuitously throughout your day, week, and months. These demands may be as simple as suddenly dealing with a backed-up toilet or as complex as dealing with a team member who has a heart attack and will be out of school for the last four months of the year. You have to be resourceful when it comes to sequestering time for all of the demands so far discussed. One good way to begin is to follow the suggestions in Chapter 6, "Work Smarter Not Harder: Understanding and Using Time." Suffice it to say that you need to know at the outset that there will be moments when you feel your life is out of control. At those moments, you need to have a reserve plan for getting it back into control and for completing all the tasks that need to be done. If you have been concentrating on goals that serve the higher purposes of learning, such a temporary imbalance will be easy to endure.

V. Professional Leadership

A professional is anyone who engages in a specific activity as a source of livelihood. Thus, anyone can be deemed a professional, if singularly engaged in an activity. We all understand what is meant by a professional actor or a professional golfer as opposed to an amateur. In the teaching

FIGURE 1.5. Professional Leadership

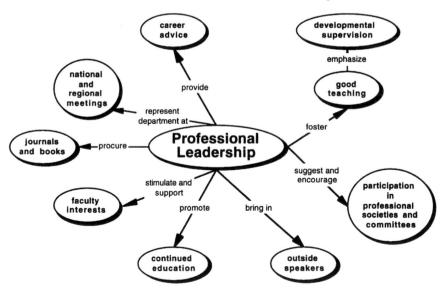

world, it is hard to be anything other than a professional. Has anyone ever heard of an amateur teacher? Novice, maybe, but not amateur. From the outset, it is clear that professional development is the appropriate term for ongoing study about teaching and learning. For your staff to grow as professionals connected with the singular activity of teaching, you are going to have to continually help them become ever more skillful teachers.

However, professional development can be interpreted on a much larger context. It can be viewed as much larger than individual growth and development. Maybe a better term for what you, as the department head, will be doing is "profession" development. A profession does have a specific definition. It is connected with activities requiring training in the liberal arts or the sciences and advanced study in a particular field. Each of the members of your department, by virtue of their undergraduate or graduate training, will have met this requirement. Your goal is to simultaneously improve the professionals in your group and the profession in which they work.

Primarily, this means making sure good teaching is the order of the day, every day. It is not any easy task to define good teaching. Even to paraphrase a famous Supreme Court Justice by saying "you'll know it when you see it," does not do justice to the difficulty in developing good teaching. There are some simple steps you can take to make sure everyone knows that the department stands for excellence in teaching. First, make sure you praise and recognize all pedagogical styles that are applied in a competent manner. Most research has supported the fact that it is not necessarily the style that is important in producing effective learning. In the hands of the right person and under the right circumstances, a great lecture can help students learn more than any other type of pedagogy. Howovor, even the best methods and materials will fail miserably in the hands of the incompetent teacher.

Your task is to help teachers discover their "ideal" style and to help them share their success with others. One way this can be accomplished if there is a supervisory system that emphasizes developmental progress. Not many teachers initially recognize supervision as a means to further their professional development. But under the careful development of a trustworthy method and consistent practice, this notion can quickly change. (See Chapter 9 on supervision.)

As the department head you need to think not only about individual evaluation, but also departmental evaluation. Research has shown that people relate and function in an organization in ways not necessarily connected to the formal organizational chart. You may need help from objective outsiders to determine the actual patterns of behavior in your group. The department members may be so steeped in their own culture that they cannot see damaging behavioral and operational actions. They may not be able to see that they have not been following the accepted and expected norms and channels of operation. Thus, you must be on guard to make sure that the actual working of the group is clearly understood by all.

If sharing is one important way to help these patterns of behavior become more clear, then having an "open-door" policy is an important factor to create venues for sharing. If every faculty member felt free to pop in and sit, for even ten minutes, in a colleague's class, the level of professional discourse would triple in a week. There are many venues besides the open classroom to develop that sense of shared goals and vision. Having a shared space such as a department room or creating a specific time during departmental meetings—both will work fine. Whatever the technique, it is essential that teachers share what they do.

As you find yourself working more and more as a professional with other professionals, the talk will eventually get around to careers. Members of your department might see you as someone who can help them develop their careers. For those teachers who haven't thought of their daily and yearly work as part of a career, you need to help them discover that aspect of their lives. Helping them reach their desired goals is one of the most satisfying roles for a team leader

Be aware of the positions to which some on your staff may wish to aspire. In fact, while they may not even know they have the talent to do certain jobs, you should. Helping each member of the staff create a career is part of building the profession of teaching Unfortunately, this kind of professional development sometimes means that you will lose a very good teacher. In the long run, this is good for everyone involved: the teacher, the department and the profession. Sometimes you can help a member of your staff move to a new position within the school. This will keep that good teacher working in your institution while allowing that person a chance to grow.

But being aware of career needs of your staff doesn't mean that they necessarily will be looking for other kinds of work. Being the very best physics teacher in the school can be every bit as motivating as being asked to become the department head at a new school. By holding career discussions with each member of the department each year, you will be well-positioned to help them move forward.

Since there is a chance that some members of your department will leave in any given year, you should always be on the lookout for promising teachers. You should maintain contact with a cadre of teachers who might be very good in your school. This may give some readers pause because it sounds like a policy of "raiding" the faculties of colleague schools. That is not the intent at all. The intent is to create a professional environment where faculty who have reached a certain level of development in one school will be primed and ready to grow in another school, especially if they cannot do so in their present situation. Over the long run, such exchanges among schools will even out. For example, the day-school life may look very attractive to a boarding-school faculty member, while, at the same time, the opposite may be true for a day-school teacher. Or, to many, the suburban high school will appear much more exciting that the urban high school.

Providing professional development opportunities external to your institution is the most common form of professional development. And yet you can pursue effective professional development within the confines of the department. Think about the many concrete and inexpensive actions you can take within the department to foster a professional atmosphere.

First, you can create a library of professional journals for the faculty to read. Setting up a space for these readings in the department room is simple and will lead to teacher talk—one of your desired goals. In fact, you could assign a short article for common reading and then begin the department meeting with a short discussion of the article. Over the summer, you could send everyone a particular book to read and use this reading as an on-going part of department meetings for the year.

You could bring in a "speaker" from another department in the school. For example, what does the English department have to say about the level of writing found in lab reports? This would make for an interesting meeting. Or you could assign a member of the department the task of reading about particular learning styles or pedagogy, and give a report to the department. You could use a portion of a meeting for faculty to convey any new and unusual assignments they have created during the term.

Above all, effective professional development must be connected with the personal interests of individual faculty. You need to be aware of these personal interests. The more you can make use of these interests in developing the departmental program, the happier each team member will be and the richer your program. But it is not enough to simply know what their interests are. You need to take action to develop those interests. You may have to be creative with release time in order to develop a system for freeing faculty from their teaching responsibilities.

For example, it might be that each year two faculty members agree to teach an extra course for a term. This would probably be half a load of a full-time teacher. Thus, a teacher in the department could have two sections of time free from teaching commitments. If the understanding was that these extra workload courses would be rotated and that everyone would get a term or a semester to have 50 percent of their time available for curriculum development, the department would soon have a very powerful professional development ethic, not to mention, a bevy of newly energized teaching fellows.

A common, but often surprisingly underutilized, method of helping your staff to develop professionally is to send them off to conferences and symposiums. That is because, it is often hard for teachers to manage all the logistics of being away from the school. If your department has no easy system for hiring substitute teachers or for sharing responsibility, teachers will be reluctant to ask colleagues to cover for them. You have to develop a system that makes it easy for them to leave their classes for a day or two. You have to make it attractive for them to leave. Helping your staff be away from school might even create more work for you. You might have to cover their classes. Serving as the leader often will mean more work and that you must serve through personal sacrifice. But, in the long run, your department will improve, if not in substance, then in spirit. There is nothing more energizing for teachers than getting away for a day to clear the cobwebs and experience a change of pace.

Summary

You must consciously attend to these five major areas of leadership: Instructional, Departmental, Administrative, Institutional, and Professional. Otherwise, the department or team will grow lopsidedly or not at all. The department will come to resemble the withered and nutrient-deficient scrub growth of the outback. But with your careful attention as the master forester, your department can develop the elegance and symmetry of the stately elm.

Thus, the job of the department head and team leader is incredibly complex and demanding. It takes dedication and a spirit of adventure to do this job. But the rewards that accompany success more than make up for the hard work. As the team leader, you possess what Stephen Covey calls *response-ability*. Your response as a leader is under your control and is connected to your desire and ability to accomplish good in the lives of students and faculty.

References and Bibliography

Bennis, Warren and Nanus, Burt (1985). *Leaders: The strategies for taking charge.* New York: Harper and Row.

Gardner, John W. (1978). *Morale.* New York: W. W. Norton and Company, Inc.

Levine, Sarah (1989). *Promoting adult growth in schools*: *The promise of professional development.* Boston: Allyn and Bacon.

Lortie, Dan C. (1975). *Schoolteacher: A sociological study.* Chicago: The University Press of Chicago.

Mallery, David (1975). *The strengths of a good school: Notes on evaluation, growth, and professional partnership of teachers.* Boston: National Association of Independent Schools.

Schein, Edgar (1978). *Career dynamics: Matching individual and organizational needs.* Reading, MA: Addison-Wesley.

Sergiovanni, Thomas J. (1984). *Handbook for effective department leadership: Concepts and practices in today's secondary schools*, 2nd ed., Boston: Allyn and Bacon.

Chapter 2

Developing Your Leadership Style:
What Works When and With Whom

Introduction

Understanding leadership has become a very popular topic of books and articles in the last few decades. The bookstores are filled with leadership biographies, autobiographies, and a plethora of "how to" books. And yet we seem to be focused in many groups on the skills and talents that the leadership at the time appears to lack. This may be the result of some confusion that exists between "leadership" and "management." All groups want to be led—but not overly managed. The task for the department head and team leader is to exert the correct amount of pressure to manage the group while at the same time leading them to new visions of what they might become, collectively and individually.

Before launching into the practical matters of leadership, it is important that you take stock of what you have experienced in the groups in which you have participated. Everyone has vast experience with groups and teams and everyone has stories to tell about the success or failure of such groups. By thinking carefully about the characteristics of both successful and not so successful groups, you will create a context in which to learn more about how your behavior is intimately connected with your success and a leader. Spend some time with Reflection 2.1 below before you continue with Chapter 2.

Reflection 2.1

Think of some of the organizations or groups in which you have worked.

1. List as many words as you can which describe the best groups in which you have worked.

a.   b.   c.

d.   e.   f.

g.   h.   i.
j.   k.   l.
m.   n.   o.

2. List as many words or phrases which describe the worst groups in which
   you have worked.
   a.   b.   c.
   d.   e.   f.
   g.   h.   i.
   j.   k.   l.
   m.   n.   o.

Some of the words that come to most people's minds when they describe the best groups in which they have worked are the following:

Humor	Trust	Produce a good product
Work toward common goal	Calm	Provide time for fun
Mutual respect	Diverse talents	Respect
Synergy	Risk Taking	Outcome clear
Brainstorming	Leader delegates	Welcomes change
Energizing	Committed to the task	Openness
Criticism, but no rancor	Works hard	Clear expectations

On the other hand, words that come to mind when people recall the worst groups in which they have worked are the following:

Sarcastic	Apathetic	Closed
Selfish	Unclear goals	Personal agendas
Decision only by the leader	Open hostility	Disorganized
No Decisiveness	Too big	Poor leadership
Mistrust	Arguing	Under delegation
Goals change in mid-stream	Deceitfulness	Isolated
Suspicious of motives	Time constrained	Big egos

Your list probably closely mirrored the words and phrases above, because groups have characteristics in common when they work well or work poorly. As you ponder these lists I hope you will notice that there are two major areas where the leader must exert influence. There are (1) tasks and jobs to be done, and there are (2) relationships to be maintained.

Every group has some reason for forming or for being formed. There is an expectation that something will happen in a group; that there will be a tangible outcome, be it some product or conclusion. At the same time, the members of the groups expect to be happy in the group and expect to find working in the group an enjoyable experience. Meeting these two expectations can be a tall order for any department head or team leader.

There are four major areas of relationships in school life where team collaboration and community work together to improve the climate of the school (Vesey, 1996, 31–34). These relationship areas are administrator/counselor, teacher-to-teacher. teacher-to-student, and student-to-student. As the department leader, you can see that your role naturally brings you into three of these four relationships, and good practice by the teaching staff can lead to improvement in the fourth.

While the conditions surrounding the formation of the group influences, to a large degree, whether the group has the chance to be successful, such conditions alone do not automatically ensure success or failure. Rather, the leadership of the group is more important than the surrounding environment. As you will see in the rest of this chapter, your understanding of the characteristics of the group and your ability to respond to that understanding will determine whether the participants in your group will come away from that experience with a positive or negative impression.

Definition of Leadership and a Leader

There probably has not been any one topic more widely written about than leadership. There as many definitions of leadership as there are leaders—and writers of books on leadership. However, it is important to think about leadership in the context of a school. Most books on leadership are written from the standpoint of business. While there are many commonalties between schools and businesses, they are also worlds apart. Dealing with students, parents, and teachers is much messier than dealing with the production of a fine carpet. The number of variables that present themselves to a department head or team leader on any one day vastly outnumber the variables that affect the building of a better window sash, for example.

In schools, the definition of leadership must take into account the position of authority of the leader, which is often not greatly different from that of the people the leader is leading. It takes a special skill and understanding to define leadership among peers. In Chapter 1, I stressed the importance for the leader to realize that he or she is no longer at the same level of importance or responsibility as the nonleader. In every group, there must be some kind of leadership, even if that role rotates to many people at different times. Groups need leaders just as much as they need followers, or those willing or agreeing to be led.

James MacGregor Burns' book *Leadership* is a seminal work in leadership studies. In this work, Burns describes leadership as follows: "I define leadership as leaders inducing followers to act for certain goals that represent values and motivations . . . the wants and needs, the aspirations and expectations . . . of both leaders and followers." While there is much in this definition with which to agree, I do not think that groups that have been induced to act in a certain way are necessarily the most happy of groups.

To induce action is to act in such a way as to influence and convince the group. However, what might be the means of such inducement? Gentle prodding, convincing argument, the production of irrefutable data, or can it mean threatening behavior? Actions designed to evoke action that is actually against the will of the followers? Actions that depend upon the positional power of the leader? It is unlikely that such leadership behavior will ultimately be successful. This isn't to say that such behavior doesn't necessarily have a place in the repertoire of team leader behaviors. Indeed, there may be a situation that demands such behavior. But in the general school atmosphere, I think there needs to be an emphasis of the desires of the led more than on the desires of the leader.

A definition of a leader that is more appropriate for the school setting is found in Max Depree's book *Leadership is an Art*. "Leaders . . . foster environments and work processes within which people can develop high-quality relationships . . . relationships with each other . . . relationships with the group with which they work." If nothing else is true about school work, it is essentially a business of people working with people. The more firm and supportive relationships between people are, the easier it is to accomplish the complex tasks involved in teaching. The question that needs to be answered is how do you develop these relationships. See Reflection 2.2 for some ways to think about this skill.

Not all relationships are equal. The leader of a group is bound to have some relationships that do not reach the depth of understanding (nor do they need to) as some other relationships. Leaders often fill the gaps in the complexity of organizational design. The organizational chart of any school or department is only a theoretical construct. Within the construct, there is always space for the leader to exert influence and authority. But often there is a situation that is not necessarily covered under the organizational chart. Only the informal organization will suffice to create the space for action.

Reflection 2.2

1. Who creates the "energy" on your team? Do they know you think this way about them? Can you tell them?
2. How do you let people know that you want them to succeed?
3. Can you improve your team by asking for small incremental improvements? If every task, that currently constitutes the business of your team, were to be improved by just 1 percent, you could have a major improvement in the working of the team. Make a list of all of these tasks and how you would accomplish a 1 percent improvement.
4. What do you think of when you picture the ideal team with you leading the way? What do you have to do to make that a reality?
5. Do you think you are currently acting as a leader? What do you need to do to bring your ideal of what a leader does and what you do into congruence?

In other instances the changing conditions of the workplace demand that the leader act in such a way to manage the change or respond to the crisis. On any given day, the phone can bring incredibly disruptive news. Faculty become ill or even die unexpectedly. Students complain to parents about alleged wrongs and slights that teachers have made or that other students have inflicted upon them. New curricula are approved by the Board of Education and handed to the school to implement with little notice.

The dynamic nature of departments demands that there be a leader in charge who can respond quickly and intelligently to all of these demands. It demands a leader who can devote time and bring a substantial understanding of group processes to the relationships that will need to be maintained and developed.

Some Useful Theories about Leadership

Trait Theory

One of the earliest "theories" about leadership and one that still generates discussion today is the Great Man versus the Great Event. In this theory, great men were born not made. Leadership ability was inherited, especially by people from the upper class. The debate raged over whether men were great because of their personalities or because of the events in which they found themselves immersed. Unfortunately, the work was done primarily in the time when the only leaders deemed worthy of study were men of the past—Caesar, Charlemagne, Washington, Lincoln, Grant, Hitler, Eisenhower, for example. In addition, the great leaders were almost always military leaders. The conclusions of this debate was that there was little evidence to objectively or scientifically come to any end point. It was impossible to tear the behavior of these men from the events they managed. The question was one that did not allow for reasoned study, because it one could never pull the two intertwined important theses apart.

However, these Great Man/Great Event debates did launch a study of the traits that characterize leaders. In the first half of the century, researchers tried to determine the LQ, Leadership Quotient, much as the IQ used standardized tests to determine the Intelligence Quota of people. The research was abandoned in the late 1940s, but not before coming to the conclusion that there was not a demonstrable relationship between physical, emotional, intellectual, or social characteristics and successful leadership. Even recently, there has been speculation about height as a key to leadership ability, as the average height of a member of the US Senate is greater than that of the average US citizen.

There has also been a resurgence in trait theory research. Evidence shows that there are some traits that do matter, though they are more akin to characteristics, which can be developed rather than attributes, which are inherited. Figure 2.1 gives these six leadership traits. These traits alone however, do not mean success. Possessing some of these traits may make being a leader easier, but it doesn't mean that the person who possesses these traits will necessarily become a leader any more than having large hands means that the person will become a great guitar or piano player.

Regardless of the outcome of the discussion about whether a leader becomes a leader because he or she has learned the behaviors that matter or because leadership is a skill given at conception, it is clear that leaders are

Figure 2.1 Leadership Traits

1. Drive; in terms of ambition, achievement, energy, tenacity and initiative.
2. Leadership motivation:
   a. Personal drive for power and authority as an end in itself.
   b. Social drive to other achieve a personal vision or goal.
3. Honesty and Integrity.
4. Self-confidence, including emotional stability.
5. Cognitive ability.
6. Technical expertise.

different from other people. Just as the Tom Wolfe book, *The Right Stuff*, pointed out the characteristics astronaut candidates had to have in order to be successful, leaders also need the "right stuff" to become leaders and continue in leadership roles.

Three Early Leadership Styles

In the early 1900s Kurt Lewin founded the school of thought that has become known as social psychology. As part of his studies, he investigated the relationship between leadership behavior and group accomplishment and functioning. In his study, Lewin assigned people three different leadership behaviors: Authoritarian/Autocratic, Democratic, and Laissez-Faire. Researchers studied all three styles in connection with leading a group of young boys in the task of building model airplanes.

In the *Authoritarian* model, the leader dictated every step of the process. The leader assigned the tasks to each boy and was very personal in his criticism and praise. Nothing was left to the boy's decision. In these groups, the boys were both more aggressive and more passive than the other groups. When the leader was absent, work stopped and aggression increased, but, by a small margin, this group was the most productive of the three.

In the *Democratic* model, the leader held discussions and let the group set policy and procedure together. The group designed the techniques and methods for arriving at a finished product. Only after discussion were tasks assigned. The leader used fact-oriented and objective comments when working with the boys. In these groups, there was a friendly atmosphere and praise was frequent. Though slightly less productive than the Authoritarian led group, the work was more original and creative.

In the *Lassez-Faire* model, the group was free to set its own policies. The leader did not participate in any way. In fact, the leader gave help and interacted with the group only when asked to do so. The leader made no attempt to criticize or praise. In these groups, the work was of poor quality, and there was less of it. The boys spent most of their time in playing with the tools and the materials rather than trying to build models. These boys also expressed the most dissatisfaction with their group.

Unfortunately, the most commonly held conclusion to these studies is that the Authoritarian model must be "bad," and the Democratic model must be "good." This would also imply a kind of linear continuum with poor leadership on one end and good leadership at the other. Figure 2.2 shows such a continuum.

Figure 2.2 Linear Leadership Continuum

Task   *Relationship*

Autocratic _____ Democratic
Leadership   Leadership
Leader disliked   Leader liked

In present society, the democratic model has reached an apex with the Total Quality Management (TQM) movement founded by Edward Deming just after World War Two in Japanese industry. Further studies have shown that there are situations where the best method is certainly not a democratic model. The task often defines the leadership style that needs to be exhibited.

Situational Leadership

This brings us to the refinement of such a linear model. This refinement was carried out through research conducted at the Ohio State University in 1957. This study emphasizes the first notion that tasks and relationships are the two most important dimensions of leadership. Figure 2.3 shows the Ohio State Study Leadership Grid. It has two dimensions and four quadrants. The term *Initiating Structure* can be interpreted as the task to be performed and *Consideration* as the relationship to be developed. In these studies, effective leadership style was associated with high Initiating Structure and high Consideration ratings.

However, in meta-analyses of such "best" management style research, it was discovered that there was no best leadership style for all situations. In other words, the best style must fit the situation at hand. Since situations differ, leadership style must differ. Paul Hersey and Kenneth Blanchard in-

Figure 2-3 Leadership Study Grid

High Consideration and Low Structure	High Consideration and High Structure
Low Consideration and Low Structure	Low Consideration and High Structure

troduced the notion of group maturity or "readiness" as a way to explain why a leader must adapt his or her style to the situation. Not surprisingly, their leadership model is termed the Situational Leadership Model and I think it is the most useful for understanding school groups. What has lately become clear is that success does not automatically happen because groups are used and led. Instead, leading and using those groups correctly is what matters. (Trimble and Miller, 1996)

Hersey and Blanchard defined readiness as both the ability and willingness to perform a particular task. In their model as shown in Figure 2.4, there are four readiness levels, which combine the willingness and ability

Figure 2.4 Hersey and Blanchard

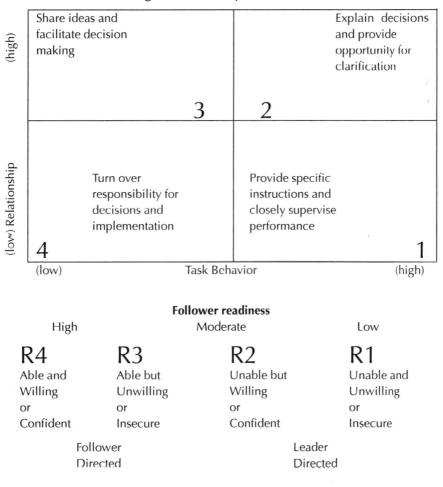

of the group. When these readiness levels are projected onto the two dimensional leadership grid, the leader now has a picture of the kind of leadership style that might better suit the needs of the situation. Depending upon the level of maturity of the group, the situation leader uses one of the four combinations of task and relationship.

For a department head, this understanding can bring clarity of approach when dealing with different constituencies. Blanchard and Hersey give the four modes of leadership style the catchy terms, *Telling, Selling, Participating,* and *Delegating.* For example, when dealing with new teachers, the **Telling Mode** is probably the best style to use. In this situation, the team leader, usually, is dealing with followers who are in a very low level of readiness. In this situation the new teachers *want* to be told what to do and preferably exactly how to do it. The situation demands that the department head be very specific in directions to the young teachers. It is here that one-way communication dominates the interactions. You'll know when it's time to move from the telling Mode to the selling Mode when the members of the group start asking, "Why do we do this way?"

Neophyte faculty need to be given detailed information about what is expected from them in almost every aspect of the job. Too often, the young teacher is thrown into the classroom with the instructions "Don't smile until Thanksgiving," and "If you need anything, you know where my office is."

The new teacher to a school, even though she or he may have plenty of classroom experience, still needs to understand the day to day workings of the department or team. This means that the department head cannot assume that this cohort of teachers can fend for themselves. If you buy the idea that they are basically an immature or unready group, the will need leadership in nearly equal amounts to the teacher with zero experience.

In the **Selling Mode,** the department head is working with group members who, while willing and confident, are still not technically proficient to be set loose. In this situation, your task as the department head is to provide the conditions for good two-way communication, yet still control decision making. Your group members need to be supported until they have the confidence and enthusiasm necessary for continued success.

To demonstrate one possible scenario in which such a style might be needed, consider the following case. Members of your department or team approach you with ideas for how they might alter their teaching to be more effective. You recognize that the method they are espousing will ultimately cause chaos and confusion. You listen to their idea and then carefully sell them on changes of method that incorporate some of what they have suggested, but not all. You use your practical knowledge from years of teaching to help them see that the road to ruin was hidden within their proposal. Unfortunately, Selling to many people feels like a form of manipulation. It is not. It is a way for the leader to incorporate ideas of the group into sound decisions and direction.

As the group gains maturity, the leader can move into a more **Participating Mode.** In this style, control shifts from leader only to leader and followers together. The leader spends time listening, facilitating problem solving, and helping the group make the decisions that need to be made. The reason a group in this stage may be unwilling or insecure is that their motivation is somewhat lacking. As an example, consider the faculty member who has spent much of the semester learning to use HTML programming language to build webpages. This person has the technical ability to be successful, but may not want to spend the summer working on the departmental webpage. However, if the department head can provide some summer curriculum development funds or provide a period of non-assignment for the next term, that faculty member may become very eager and willing to attack the task. As the leader, your major responsibility is to provide the right kind of leadership to motivate the faculty member to tackle the task.

In the **Delegating Mode,** the leader's responsibility is to totally delegate responsibility for decisions to the group. The group is now mature enough to take responsibility for "running their own show." In fact, they are ready to handle quite a bit of responsibility. The group will continue to need the attention of the leader, but in a more consultative, rather than directive, role. It may be that you use the time, which used to be devoted to close inspection, for expansive thinking about the next possible goals and roles for the team.

The Delegating Mode is by far the leadership style that is hardest to achieve. This is not because groups do not reach sufficient levels of maturity to function alone. It is because leaders find it difficult to imagine the group being able to accomplish a task nearly independent of their help. Understanding this basic fact is one of the subtle points of mature leadership. Yet this shouldn't surprise anyone.

Teachers often feel similarly about the classes they teach. They worry about letting students fly on their own. They wonder, "Can I let a group of students work on a project without my constant supervision." And yet they can and do. It takes a certain leap of faith to sit back and let such behavior manifest itself.

Even though this model of leadership makes plenty of sense, there is some criticism of the Situation Leadership. Many experts feel that human behavior is too complicated, and sometimes fixed, for people to truly change their styles in different situations. I do not believe that such criticism bears out in reality. It may be true that deeply held beliefs are hard, if not impossible, to change. The leader who believes that a third-year teacher could never be the leader of an adult group is certainly not going to put that faculty member in charge of a curriculum study subcommittee. The department head who feels that teachers with the greatest seniority deserve the most academically able classes is not going to give the decision-making power for course assignments to the department faculty as a group. The team leader who believes that democracy rules and puts every decision before the entire group will certainly not be able to use the telling mode in dealing with the ordering of supplies. Developing a feel for leadership is as much a seat of the pants activity as it is one of study and contemplation.

What we can learn from these theories is that there is no one best leadership style. Your leadership success is intimately tied to the needs of your followers. The needs of your followers are tied to the environment in which they, and you, work. Whether or not you are effective is a somewhat relative concept. The demands of the task at hand, the time in which it must be accomplished, the skills of the members of the group, and the motivation of the group to accept the task, all influence your ultimate effectiveness regardless of the style of leadership you exhibit. When considering how you will act with the group, probably the most important factor to ponder is the needs of the group.

Followership and Motivation

Why should anyone follow a leader? This basic question has many answers, though not all are satisfying. If the answer is simply that he or she is in a position of authority, this may not be rewarding to the group members. A platoon must obey and follow its sergeant, but the members may not find any intrinsic pleasure in so doing. In this kind of leadership situation, the members follow because of possible negative personal outcomes: demotion, lack of pay increase, the brig, or even firing. In such cases, what we have is not followership, but subordination. This is not commitment, but merely, compliance.

But if, as the leader, you capture the hearts and minds of the group, then true followership can occur. In every group, at one time or another, everyone leads and everyone follows. As paradoxical as this may sound, being a good follower is one way to lead. But in any situation where people must act together, there are three different sources of motivation: extrinsic, intrinsic, and overarching. Sergiovanni makes a point of detailed investigation of these three sources in his book *Moral Leadership.*

Extrinsic motivation can most easily be summed up by the sentence, "What is **rewarded** gets done." Many followers find that working diligently is worth all the long hours because there will be a bonus at the end of the job. The reward is tangible and public. People always feel good about themselves when their efforts and actions are recognized publicly, especially by their peers. Good leaders know when to use this method of motivation. However, praise must be genuinely heart-felt and must be for authentic accomplishments. Yet rewards alone are somewhat empty as motivators. They deny the person a sense of self-motivation and self-management. They move the locus of control away from the individual. It does not take much time for rewards alone to become ineffective for personal or group motivation.

Intrinsic motivation can most easily be summed up by the sentence, "What is **rewarding** gets done." For example, the department or school that chooses to emphasize learning over teaching is one where intrinsic motivation dominates. In such an environment, it doesn't matter what model of teaching is used; it doesn't matter what tradition dictates. What matters is that the children learn and that this very fact is rewarding to the teachers. Unfortunately, what is rewarding can be very different for different individuals. The definition of learning is a relative concept in many teachers' opinions. For many teachers, the act of teaching overshadows learning. They believe that the teacher is skilled in a particular method, the children will learn. It is not the method that needs to be questioned, but the person practicing the method.

However, in a community, where shared values are evident, motivation can be summed up in the sentence, "What is **good** gets done." The good consists of the values, the beliefs, the core commitments, the morals of the community. In this kind of environment, being committed to learning would mean that each teacher would continually monitor his or her performance every year, month, week, day, even, hour when working with the students. When everyone understands the mission and internalizes such community values, the highest form of motivation exists. These actions constitute a kind of moral behavior.

Actions that are moral come from a sense of duty, and duty implies what must be done because it is right. In the Gilbert and Sullivan light opera, *The Pirates of Penzance,* the subtitle is "The Slave of Duty." The hero can not act dishonorably because he is a "slave" of duty. He must do the right thing. In a commonly espoused aphorism, the effective manager does things right, but the effective leader does the right thing.

Reflection 2.3

Complete the following sentences and then share them with another member of your team.

1. Over the long term, I would like to be remembered for . . .

2. If my children could attend any school, I would like that school to be . . .

3. If I were to look for employment in another school, that school would have to have . . .

Adapted from R. Barth, *Improving Schools from Within.* San Francisco: Jossey-Bass, Inc., 1990.

Thus, the leader must concern him or herself with, not only the conditions of work, but also with the work itself. The work must be challenging and interesting, it must be recognized as the right thing to do and give each teacher a sense of inner fulfillment. But more importantly, it must be work that is valued by the community and meet that community's standards. Reflection 2.3 is one way to determine what, not only individual teachers

Reflection 2.4

1. What roles do you think your team members expect you to assume as the group leader?
2. What roles do you think your principal or immediate supervisor expects you will assume?
3. Are there any leadership roles you will have to assume that you feel are in conflict?
4. Do all team leaders have the same amount of positional authority in your school? Will this cause you any problems?
5. How comfortable are you with the idea that your are viewed as a person with a certain amount of power?
6. In which specific areas do you have authority to take action?
   a. Hiring?
   b. Firing?
   c. Evaluating?
   d. Work assignments?
   e. Professional travel?
7. How will you lead when you and your department or team are on one side of an issue and your principal is on the other?

Table 2-1
Attributes of the Effective College Department Head

1. Guides the development of sound procedures for assessing faculty performance.
2. Recognizes and rewards faculty in accordance to contributions to the department.
3. Guides the development of sound organizational plan and accomplishes faculty goals.
4. Arranges effective and equitable allocation of faculty responsibilities.
5. Takes the lead in recruiting new faculty to the department.
6. Fosters good teaching
7. Stimulates research and scholarly activities.
8. Guides curriculum development.
9. Maintains faculty morale by reducing, resolving, or preventing conflicts.
10. Fosters development of each faculty member's special talents.
11. Understands and communicates school expectations to the faculty.
12. Effectively communicates department needs to the administration.
13. Improves the departmental image in the total school community.

think is the right thing to do, but, when used as a group exercise, can give information about the feelings of the entire group. Reflection 2.4 is designed to help you answer questions that might be posed about your leadership. How would you answer them?

Summary

In an extensive study of 458 college department heads by 5830 faculty members in 65 colleges, thirteen attributes were characterized as essential for effective department leadership. You will notice the two major themes: people concerns and task concerns. Knowing yourself is still the key to any effective leader's ability to lead. Just as you are going to ask your team to be reflective about their work, you must also be reflective about your work. However, this is not always as easy as it sounds.

The is an old story that makes this message clear. At the end of the Second World War, a rabbi was walking to the synagogue and was stopped by a soldier who asked, "Who are you and what are you doing here?" The rabbi stopped and asked the soldier, "How much do they pay you to do this?" The soldier replied, "About 12 rubles." The rabbi then said, "I'll pay you 20 rubles if you stop me here everyday and ask me those two questions."

When thinking about your leadership, it might be beneficial to determine your motivation for taking the position in the first place. Did you sign on because you wanted to correct some problem that existed? Or did you wish to be a creative force for change? Did you wish to assist others in reaching their goals, a form of servant leadership? Or did you simply wish to avoid serving under someone else?

Whether or not your motivation was one of the above, knowing who you are and knowing what you are doing in the place where you are will pay enormous dividends in terms of leadership effectiveness. But there is no substitute for action. Most of leadership cannot be learned from a book. It can only be learned by doing the thing. Leadership is not necessarily brain surgery or rocket science. Much can be learned, for sure. But you learn most when you begin to lead.

References and Bibliography

Bennis, Warren and Townsend, Robert (1995). *Reinventing leadership, Strategies to empower the organization*, New York: William Morrow.

Blanchard, Kenneth, and Hersey, Paul (1995). "Situational leadership. In *The leader's companion.* Ed. J. Thomas Wren. New York: The Free Press.

Burns, James MacGregor (1978). *Leadership.* New York: Harper Collins.

DePree, Max (1989). *Leadership is an art.* New York: Dell.

DePree, Max (1992). *Leadership jazz* (1992). New York: Doubleday.

Hesselbein, Frances, Goldsmith, Marshall, and Beckhard, Richard (eds.) (1996). *The leader of the future: New visions, strategies and practices for the next era.* San Francisco: Jossey-Bass.

Hoyt, D. P. (1976). *Interpreting faculty ratings of academic chairpersons/heads*, 2nd ed. Manhattan, NY: Office of Educational Resources, Kansas State University.

Nanus, Burt (1992). *Visionary leadership, Creating a compelling sense of direction in your organization.* San Francisco: Jossey Bass.

Patterson, Jerry L. (1992). *Leadership for tomorrow's schools.* Alexandria, VA: ASCD.

Sergiovanni, Thomas J. (1996). *Leadership for the classroom.* San Francisco: Jossey-Bass.

———. (1992) *Moral leadership, Getting to the heart of school improvement.* San Francisco: Jossey-Bass.

———. (1990). *Value-added leadership, How to get extraordinary performance in schools*, San Diego: Harcourt Brace Jovanovich.

Sheive, Linda T., and Schoenheit, Marian B. (eds.), (1987) *Leadership: Examining the elusive.* Alexandria, VA: ASCD.

Stogdill, Roger M., and Coons, Alvin E. (1957). *Leader behavior: Its description and measurement.* Research Monograph #88, Bureau of Business Research, Ohio State University.

Trimble, Susan, and Miller, John. (1996). Creating, investigating and sustaining effective teams. *NASSP Bulletin, 80,* #584, 35–40.

Valentine, Jerry W. et al. (1993). *Leadership in middle level education.* Reston, VA: NASSP.

Vesey, Jack, (1996). Team collaboration leads to a sense of community. *NASSP Bulletin, 80,* 31–34.

Chapter 3

The Basics of Team Building:
All for One and One for All

Helen's Case: Initial Analysis

If you were to make a list of characteristics that describe an effective team, you might arrive at most of the following: everyone works well together with common goals; trust is evident; there is competition to get on the team; there is a spirit of enthusiasm, uniformity, cooperation, honesty, dependability, shared responsibility; communication is constructive; and there is an elevating vision. You could probably add many similar characteristics. As you look at this list, note that many of these characteristics demand the influence, direction, and intervention of the leader. Much of what is implied in this list deals with both the general departmental tone, as well as the procedures for working together.

It is the leader's responsibility to make sure the group is accomplishing its work. Helen might be too close to the situation to see how to clearly express her feelings of frustration with the lack of focus and direction of the department. Ideally, this is why team building should occur *before there are problems*, rather than after they happen. To create a team-like atmosphere, it is essential that the department head or team leader not behave in ways that will surely lead to divisiveness, rather than cooperation. If the team leader is arrogant, insensitive to the needs of the staff, political, covers up problems, cannot act independently, or cannot think globally, then it will be very difficult to create a team-player environment.

In a word, the team leader must have the respect of the staff. This is the first fundamental of team building. Garnering this respect may take many months and many individual actions by the team leader. Unfortunately, it is often easy, in a single moment of poor judgment, to undo months of work through an injudicious comment or an overlooked opportunity for praise.

Helen's Case

Helen is finishing her second year as the English department head and is in her eighth year of teaching at the seventy-five-year-old Shoreside Preparatory School, a ninth- through twelfth-grade day school of four hundred students. She was selected to replace the retiring department head by a majority of teachers in her department, by the Dean of Faculty, and by the Head of the School. The Dean of Faculty, at the time of her selection, said the major factors in her appointment were her agreeable personality, her intelligence, and her initiative as a teacher in creating interesting English classes.

At the conclusion of her first year as the department head, Helen thought everything had gone well. The tone was the same as it had always been; people were friendly, but not overly so; students (and administrators) were still the main topic of discussion in the department room. While Helen had wanted to place the stamp of her personality on the department, she also did not want to move too quickly. Not only had she heard that it was best not to rock the boat during your first year of leadership, she also decided it was only considerate to act temporarily as a care taker for her predecessor's programs and projects. So, she patiently sat back and did very little that first year.

During the second year, Helen began to encounter clear difficulties as the department struggled with several changes. "The department seemed to run itself last year," she thought. "All I had to do was communicate to them information from our weekly department heads' meeting with the Dean of Faculty and make sure everyone's student reports and grades were turned in on time. But now, everyone is whining and complaining." That thought triggered in her mind a depressing picture of some of her less than uplifting dealings with each of the four department members during the last few months.

Helen had noticed that Bob, a twenty-five-year veteran teacher and long-time varsity boys' lacrosse coach, was more challenging and vocal than at any time during her tenure at Shoreside. She knew Bob had a reputation for holding high performance expectations for his students, players, and colleagues. Specifically, she had heard him voice his opinions many times that "the newer teachers are too soft on the students, especially the seniors!" and "the new teachers act more like the students' pals than they do teachers."

She knew Bob was especially critical of Adam, who had come to Shoreside two years ago, immediately after earning an M.Ed. from

Harvard. Adam, in turn, was intimidated by Bob and tried to avoid him whenever possible. He felt that Bob had never been friendly to him. Helen knew it had hurt Adam to find out that Bob had complained to the Dean of Faculty that Adam had an unorthodox teaching style and should be reined in. It seemed that Adam consistently arranged individual project deadlines for student work, and, while there were no rules to prohibit this, it had never been done this way before.

Adam was a person to whom the students related and they spent a great deal of time after school at his apartment. He had also initiated a weekly activity for juniors and seniors he called R.E.A.D. (Read, Explain And Discuss). The students, however, referred to this meeting as Read Everything Adults Don't, because of the unusual nature of the readings.

In department meetings, Bob and Adam weren't noticeably uncivil towards one another, but they did disagree whenever the topic of what type and how much reading a student should do arose. When Helen tried to find out what two other members of the department, Carole and Diane, had to say about these discussions, each suggested that maybe there should be fewer department meetings.

Carole, who had spent her entire six-year teaching career at Shoreside, said little in these meetings and even less in general faculty meetings. But Helen knew that when Carole spoke, she usually said the right thing. "She is the most intuitive person in the department, a person who is always willing to cooperate and who works behind the scenes as a 'fence mender.' However, I am concerned about her teaching," thought Helen. "Unfortunately, as much as I love her, her teaching is both uninspired and uninspiring. But she's valuable to have here because she keeps a much more even keel than the rest of us. She's never hypercritical of administrative decisions. In fact, she's rarely critical of any decision or policy."

Helen remembered one talk when Carole said, "I feel best when everyone is smiling. Life is too short to waste on squabbles. I'd rather do what everyone else wants to do than try to force my opinion on others. In fact, I often feel that I don't know what's best for our students, even though I've been teaching here for a long time. Someone like Bob really knows the pulse of the school and is much better at determining what the students need than I am. I think we probably ought to listen to him more. Besides, he's so adamant in his beliefs."

When addressing parent and alumni groups, Helen most praised Diane. Diane had spent seven years teaching at Shoreside's cross-town rival and now was finishing her eighth year at Shoreside. Helen admired Diane's willingness to try new, even unconventional, ideas. Her enthusiasm for bringing new approaches and authors to the department was unparalleled. Helen knew that Bob held Diane's teaching in great respect, especially her ability to motivate weaker students. However, in the last department meeting, Bob had said to Diane, "Diane you spend too much time going to meetings and conferences. We really need to have you here, working with students and making a real difference. We have a quality program now, and the changes you keep suggesting won't lead to any more papers getting written. In fact, I can't see swapping perfectly good, respected authors for some new author, just because some college professor thinks the world of her."

In her conversations with Diane, Helen noted how disappointed and disheartened Diane had been with the lack of enthusiasm she had gotten from both the English and history faculty for her proposal of an interdisciplinary course. "How can we call ourselves teachers, if we're not constantly evolving, learning, and searching for new ways to open up the world of ideas to our students? It takes so long to get anything done around here. Helen, I'm hoping you and Mark (the history department head) will push to have this course included in next year's course booklet. At least, we have some new readings in the Senior English program. I don't know what I would have done if we hadn't decided last year to alter that syllabus to include more women authors."

Helen clearly remembered that Bob was away at a make-up lacrosse game and couldn't attend the scheduled department meeting the day they made those changes. He was somewhat irked that the decision had been made in his absence, but Helen felt that if he had strong objections, he could have said something to her before the meeting and registered his vote. That he had not done so, she took as a sign that he didn't have a strong opinion on the matter.

Finally, Helen remembered what she had said in her department head selection interview. "I want the English department at Shoreside to be one of the best in the country, one that is dedicated to developing the skills of our students using up-to-date curriculum, technology, and methodology. Above all, I want the staff to be intellectually stimulated, to feel appreciated, and to be happy."

Reflection 3.1

While your first inclination might be to give Helen advice on how she might act, override that impulse. Instead, focus on defining the problem or problems with this department. Try to be as detailed as possible in your description of these problems. Include problems that Helen at best made worse and at worst created.

Do the problems sound familiar? Do you encounter similar difficulties in your department. The remainder of this chapter is devoted to an analysis of this case with applications that you can adapt to begin team building with your department or team.

Team building is a skill that can be learned, and while it is a process of tremendous complexity that often defies being reduced to a systematic formula, team building does have concrete, manageable elements. There are a series of behaviors and actions whose purpose, when well thought out and practiced, can help to achieve maximal effect. It is a way of acting with people that does not come easily to everyone, but when consistently employed, can create an atmosphere of empowerment, energy, and excitement.

Helen's department functions as many groups function. Each person has his or her individual mindscape of what makes up great teaching and effective learning. Each member of the group is not necessarily thinking about a group identity, but rather about individual identity as a great teacher. It takes work to get a group of teachers to recognize that the old adage, "the whole is greater than the sum of its parts," is indeed true.

In Helen's department, it seems clear that most of the teachers are at least average classroom teachers and, perhaps, even better than that. Only Carole is noted for uninspiring classes. From the conversations with Helen, each teacher is acting out of his or her notion of what it means to be a good teacher. Each of them is concerned with effective learning defined from their individual reference point. The question of whether their individual actions are actually having a uniform effect on student learning does not seem to be one they are asking—but it should be.

Each member of the department has a slightly different vision of how to accomplish the goal of effective learning. All the members are crying out for the others to listen to them, but since all of them are asking, no one is listening. If they listened closely, they would hear the same song being sung.

Helen wishes for more cohesion from the group, but she hasn't placed her "stamp" upon them. She is afraid that if she leans on them there will be the appearance that she is forcing her will upon the group. She knows there are very few leaders who can behave autocratically and still have a follow-ership, at least in a school setting. In fact, this may be one of the biggest problems Helen faces. How much should she stifle her wishes in order to fulfill the wishes of the group? We will explore the answer to this later in the chapter.

So how can Helen act to encourage a group mentality, a department vision, an educational force field, where all the vectors are pointing in the same direction? What can the members in the group do to make things work more smoothly? Why should they work at building group coherence? What makes using precious time for team building a worthwhile goal?

The central answer to these questions is that educational teams that work well together improve the quality of teaching and learning. That's what all educational team building must always keep as the goal. All actions of each department member and the department head must ultimately be measured relative to their effect on improved learning. While it is important to understand adult behavior and satisfaction needs, it is more important to focus on the effect of teacher actions to improve the level of student learning.

What Does It Mean to Be a Team?

The work of schooling is often done by adults working somewhat alone with groups of children. Given this set-up of solitary behavior, it isn't any wonder that getting adults to work together is difficult. But we all know that positive adult interaction can have positive effects upon learning. Positive interaction can stem from a common set of goals and assumptions. In such a working group, commitment, rather than compliance, is the watchword. Collegiality replaces congeniality. To paraphrase a well-worn slogan (Bennis and Nanus, 1985), effective teams pay more attention to doing the right thing than doing things right.

It is instructive to understand the difference between a group of adults who function as just that—a group of adults—and a group of adults who function as a team. To create a team requires overt, explicit organization and attention by the leader. In order to move groups into a team mentality, they must be trained to think of themselves as interdependent. When it is understood that each person's unique talents and skills augment the effectiveness of the entire group, then the group has taken the first step toward working together to get things done.

The leader of the group does not so much tell them what to do, as help them establish goals and priorities that they deem important. The group should feel, palpably, the encouragement of the leader to own the tasks in which they choose to engage and, also, to feel full responsibility for the successful outcome of such tasks. One way to begin this process is to develop a charter document (Grier, 1996, 96–102). Such a document is a leader-defined set of goals, outcomes, processes, resource needs, and decision making guidelines. A charter gives the group a locus to begin discussion. However, you must be ready to let the group substantially alter the charter if you expect optimal group participation.

Figure 3.1A provides a graphical representation of how one might picture one type of working relationship between adults. In this situation, the leader exhibits an autocratic style and employs a one-way relationship style. Individuals in such groups become accustomed to taking orders and rarely develop into a creative team.

Figure 3.1B illustrates a group where individuals work easily with the leader, but have trouble, or no interest or incentive, in working with one another. In such individually interactive groups, there can be a certain kind of satisfaction and, even, effectiveness. However, in time of stress or when resources are in short supply, this group will experience difficulty setting priorities that call for self-sacrifice. This is often the kind of group that develops in the upper administrative structures of many schools. The Dean of Faculty, Academic Dean, Assistant Head, Vice-Principal, Principal, or Head of School work with Department Heads who tend to protect their turf

FIGURE 3.1A The Autocratic Leader

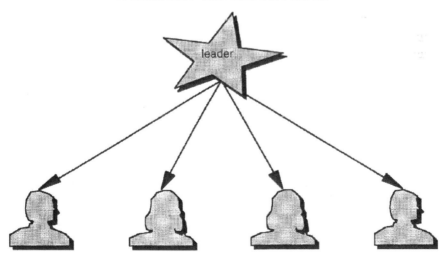

leader

Figure 3.1B The Interactive Leader

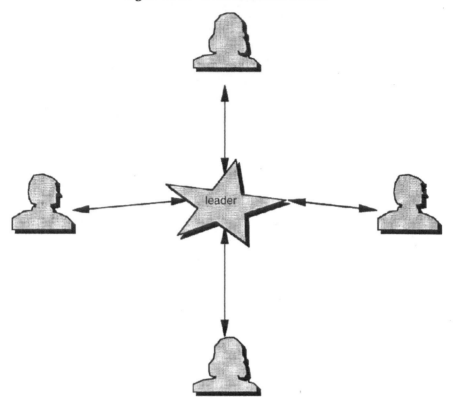

and expect attention and consideration within a one-on-one relationship with such senior administrators. Such arrangements do not make use of the potential effectiveness that is available.

Figure 3.1C shows how a maximally effective team structure can be pictured. The leader, while still labeled as such, fades a bit into the background and can function as one of the group. The interactions do not all have to pass through the group leader. In fact, there are relationships that the group leader may not even know exist. This type of arrangement can create the environment for a team atmosphere to develop, where every member of the team understands and interacts with every other member. In such groups, success is considered relative to the degree that each member attains his or her goals. Such groups function best when the leader creates an environment for open discussion, interpersonal cooperation, and mutual dependence.

Figure 3.1C The Interactive Team

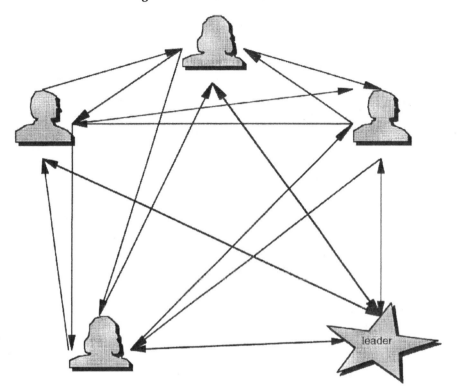

The Sports Metaphor

The most common image of a team in America is the sports team. This metaphor allows for wide interpretation, as there are several types of teams. There are football teams, where each player has a very special role to play and must execute that role from the same initiation point each time—the huddle. There is little room for freelance behavior, at least at the beginning of the play.

There are basketball teams on which all the team members are asked to perform identical and overlapping tasks. Everyone must play both offense and defense. Everyone must score, as well as prevent scoring. The sixth player off the bench must fit into the team as a hand fits into a familiar glove.

Finally, there is cycling, where team members must all support the leader, who may or may not be the strongest cyclist. The role of the cycling team member is to do all in his or her power to ensure that the leader wins the race. Each team member is expected to sacrifice personal glory for the sake of the strongest member.

Yet, while the sports metaphor for teams is a strong one in America, there are other types and functions of teams. Think about the ultimately stubborn team, the twenty-mule team. These teams of mules hauled borax out of the desert one hundred years ago and were created not only for their strength, but also for their ability to endure harsh environments. One can only imagine what keeping those mules in line must have been like. Of course, every leader has days when it feels as if he or she is leading a team of mules—stubborn and uncooperative beasts.

At times, teams are formed spontaneously and serve to inspire the rest of the group. Those soldiers who came together to raise the flag on Mt. Surabachi served such a purpose. They inspired the American troops on the bloody beaches below to keep fighting. Because the high ground was now in American hands, it was clear that victory was inevitable. To be an inspiration for others is to be an inspiration for one's self. An inspired team provides natural internal feedback, which can serve as the basis for continued growth.

At one time or another, groups of teachers in departments exhibit all of these different types of team behavior. Whatever the type of team, there are commonalties: organization and commitment to a goal. Also common to all these successful teams is the fact that there was some kind of training, which took place to help the members of the team function together. But in our schools and departments, we expect people to work in teams without any prior training and, often, towards unspoken, and certainly, unwritten goals. Teachers and administrators are supposed to simply and magically know what they need to do and how to do it. Sadly, this is simply not so.

While there might be common behaviors for all effective teams, there is also a common refrain on all poorly functioning teams. "It's no fun working with these people. They're only interested in their own agenda. It's a power struggle to see who's going to get their way," or "There are some people I work with whom I really like and enjoy, but there are others who bother me. We just don't get along. I find it easier to avoid them or to get things done with as little interaction as possible." or "I don't like department meetings. Nothing ever gets done. We have to sit there and listen to X drone on and on."

Whenever there is hostility, griping, and complaining, general low-level conflict, ineffective meetings or minimal effort or interest by the members of the group, there is a need for conscious team building. Usually, we are not aware that team building should be a planned and orchestrated activity. Many department heads think that talking about teamwork is for the Knute Rocknes of the world, not for the sophisticated environs of the adult work place in schools. They think that if you just get the "right" people together, you'll have a good team. "Bad" teams arise because the "wrong" people are on them. While it is true that there can be better and poorer groupings of adults, there is much that the leader can do to foster good teamwork. Any team can improve its performance.

In the 1930s, Elton Mayo of Harvard University studied the effect of lighting intensity on productivity in making telephone relay switches at the Western Electric plant in Hawthorne, Illinois. By increasing the intensity of the lighting, he found that productivity increased, a result that did not surprise him. What was not expected was that when the lighting intensity was decreased, production *also increased*. Mayo realized the increased productivity had to have been caused by something other than lighting intensity.

What he discovered was that several actions by the group leader were essential in making the group function better. For example, the leader took personal interest in each person's performance. The leader also took pride in the record of the group and posted feedback on their performance. In addition, when changes in procedure were contemplated, the leader consulted the group and often modified the changes based upon the suggestions of the group.

These work groups responded to this trust and developed a sense of themselves as a social unit. They made changes because they felt it was the "right" thing to do, not simply a response to external pressure. The group developed an unusual sense of openness and candor amongst themselves. They also took pride in their performance as a group (Lickert, 1960).

These conclusions now seem somewhat less than revolutionary. Perhaps, it's because they have been woven into the practice of so many groups in the sixty years since this research was done. These principles seem to be the "givens" for good group dynamics. It is important to note that the leader plays an unusually large part in helping the group function well.

The Seven C's

The characteristics of a successful work team can be described by what I call "the Seven Cs": Common Goals, Cooperation, Consensus, Camaraderie, Communication, Creative Conflict, and Care. The question each leader needs to ask is, "How will I infuse these Seven Cs into the daily workings of my group?" The effort it takes fully to develop these traits in a group will be well worth your time. Team building exercises, as described in the remainder of this chapter, can be used to create a productive, hardworking, and positive team.

Common Goals

Every school in the country has a set of goals or purposes—a mission statement—that seeks to communicate to the outside world, and to the internal inhabitants, exactly what that school is about. However, these goals are often somewhat generic in character and make many schools sound like any number of other schools. And, what's worse, schools may not choose to follow their own goal statements.

This need not be true at the departmental level. By discussing the question, "For what purpose does this department exist?" departments can embark on the quest for what Peter Senge (Senge, 1990) calls "a shared vision." "A shared vision is the first step in allowing people who mistrust each other to begin to work together. It creates a common identity."

Motivational psychologists such as Abraham Maslow have found that having goals to which everyone has a commitment is one source of great job satisfaction. Sergiovanni (Sergiovanni, 1992) also points out the educational and motivational power of a "covenant of shared values." Even though a department may be made up of teachers with vastly different teaching styles and personalities, when each person defines and identifies with the mission of education set forth by the group, the synergistic benefits to the school are large.

One way to begin the necessary conversation about shared vision is to describe concrete behaviors that presently exist within the department. Using the following three questions as a springboard for discussion, there will naturally emerge a pattern of behaviors and a set of commonly held beliefs that characterize the group.

1. As a department, what are we doing well that we should continue doing?
2. As a department, what are we not doing well that we should cease or, at least, change?
3. As a department, what have we not thought about and should begin doing?

Using the concrete answers to these questions, the group can construct philosophical vision statements. See Exhibit 3.1 for some typical answers to these questions.

Because the answers to the above set of questions are usually not very people-specific, answering them does not pose interpersonal problems in even the most dysfunctional of groups. The set or responses shown in Exhibit 3.1 gives a good picture of the tone and substance of this team-building exercise. Getting the team talking to one another is the essential task of this first exercise.

Exhibit 3.1 Getting Started with Team Building

The following is the response of a science department, when it was asked to answer the three questions below.

1. As a department, what are we doing well that should continue?
   - We support each other.
   - We have a high level of energy.
   - We respect differences among ourselves.
   - We support individual students through extra help, etc.
   - We provide the appropriate level of challenge to students.
   - We offer a program designed to meet the needs of a wide variety of students.
   - We have an active laboratory program that encourages questioning and open-ended work.
   - We responsibly provide a safe environment for our students and ourselves.
   - We keep current in our fields and discuss with one another not only our subject areas, but also our teaching.

2. As a department, what are we not doing well that we should cease doing or at least change?
   - We need to find more *time* to serve students better.
   - We need to encourage more women, African-Americans, and Latin-Americans to attempt upper-level courses.
   - We need to tone down the friendly teasing of students that takes place in the faculty room.
   - We need to improve the general tidiness of all areas in the building. This includes the faculty workroom.
   - We should integrate computer work into our lab assignments.
   - We need to inform the school's tour guides about the nature of the independent activities that take place in the building.
   - We need to leave notes stating that we've taken specific equipment and the time frame for which we will be using it.

3. As a department, what should we begin doing that we are not presently doing?
   - We need to examine how students select courses of study and how we can help them make appropriate choices.
   - We need to review the ninth-grade curricular options.
   - We need to begin more systematic professional visits to other schools.
   - We need to begin a general equipment upgrade.
   - We need to begin requiring all upper-class students to word process their lab reports using up-to-date software tools.
   - We need to work on our public image both with the immediate school community and with parents and alumni.

Having common goals leads to a feeling of both support and commitment. You'll be amazed at what commitment, as opposed to compliance, will do for a department. There will be a stronger desire to teach well and to share with others the result of some well-managed pedagogical exercise. As you develop your goal statements, I suggest you post them in a visible place. Remember that the group needs to take pride in overall group accomplishment, and the first major accomplishment will be the development of departmental goals. You do not have to wait until all goals are developed to make reference to work being well-done by the team.

One ancillary benefit to carrying out this kind of exercise is that the meetings that you hold, while developing this exercise, will focus on items meaningful to the individuals in your department. If there is any one thing that fosters a positive tone, it is attending meetings that are meaningful, where important issues are discussed, and where the outcomes will result in significant responsibilities for those involved.

There is an apocryphal story of three brick layers working on an urban project. When the first was asked what he was doing, he said, "I'm laying bricks." When the second was asked the same question, she said, "I'm building a wall." But when the third was asked what he was doing, he said, "I'm part of a team building the largest discount store in the state. Over four hundred new jobs are going to be created, and I'm glad to say I'm part of this." It's clear which worker understood the team goals.

One of the most effective actions a team can engage in together is to consciously reflect upon the level of importance of the goal and the urgency behind action. Figure 3.2 portrays an Action Grid, which shows the four quadrants of action priorities. The horizontal axis depicts the level of urgency of an action while the vertical axis portrays the level of importance of an action. Research has shown that in most teams, 80% of the group's time and effort is devoted to quadrants III and IV. Only 20% is devoted to quadrants I and II. In fact, of the 20% spent in these two quadrants, 78% is spent in quadrant II. The shouldn't be surprising. Dealing first with tasks that are the most enjoyable and the easiest to accomplish, though not necessarily urgent, is natural. Unfortunately, being natural and being effective are not synonymous terms.

In Helen's department, a common goal exists, though it is never overtly stated. Each teacher is genuinely interested in creating an environment that promotes learning, though each has idiosyncratic ideas of exactly what such an environment looks like. If only they would sit down and talk about their goals, they would see that, given a typical student body

Figure 3.2 Action Grid

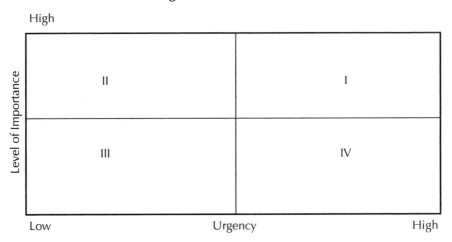

with a multitude of learning styles, varied individual teacher approaches can have synergistic effects.

For example, the students in the department are exposed to the one-on-one emphasis of Bob, as well as Adam's individual deadline system. Awareness of the entire range of teaching styles can only have beneficial consequences when clearly understood, appreciated, and celebrated by the group. The likelihood of such a group sitting down spontaneously and voluntarily is low. Helen needs to be make this discussion happen.

If Helen were thinking in a team-building context, she would devote the next department meeting to creating a list of completions to the statement: "I promote a maximally effective learning environment by . . ." By displaying these lists in a commonly used area so that everyone could read them (posted on large newsprint), the group would have a starting point to discuss how each teaching style reaches different students. In addition, the group could identify the level of similarity of each person's teaching goals to his or her colleague's goals.

Such discussion could result in the formulation of concrete policies. For example, the department might decide that there needs to be a minimum number of words written or pages read each week. They might decide that 50 percent of the material in a course should be based upon the teachers' own interests and skills, but that other 50 percent must come from a common core. In other words, the meeting question, designed and proposed to the team by the department head, can have an enormous affect upon helping the group recognize their clear, common goals.

Cooperation

Getting people to cooperate is at the heart of teamwork and should be the first priority in building an effective team. Cooperation can mean everything from working out mutually beneficial schedules for classroom use to sharing supplies and teaching materials. When people cooperate, it's often because they understand the role each person plays within the department. Often, when people refuse to cooperate, one reason is that they do not see that cooperation will be in their best interests. Particularly effective teams emerge when the members of the team understand what is expected of them, as well as what they can expect of every other team player.

But in order for cooperation to become one of the automatic behaviors of team members, they have to understand one another. While it isn't necessary to delve too deeply into co-workers' psyches, it is necessary to know what they appreciate, what they respect and what aggravates them. One way to promote better interpersonal understanding is to structure a discussion around the following three questions.

1. What are some behaviors or characteristics I admire in others?
2. What are some behaviors or characteristics I try to develop in myself?
3. What are some behaviors or situations that frustrate or aggravate me?

For two-thirds of such a set of questions, the focus is on positive attribution. When such an exercise is used, groups often discover that they have much more in common with their colleagues than they thought they had. Again, the nonthreatening nature of the questions provides the possibility that members of the department will alter their behavior simply because they now know that such behaviors have been explicitly denoted as either admirable or aggravating by their colleagues.

Exhibit 3.2 details some responses from a department when these questions were posed. Notice that the behaviors the teachers admired in others were often mirrored as behaviors valued in themselves. Transformation is a key component of adult growth and development. Tennant and Pogson (1995) note that "the task is not discovering who one truly is, but inventing, imposing, and creating who one can be."

Recent studies have pointed to the fact that shared dialogue may be more useful for successful collaboration than is shared work. Teachers involved in school/university collaborations have cited newfound understanding of the necessity for dissemination of experiences and an awakening of their sense of professional responsibility in so doing. They

---

Exhibit 3.2 Interpersonal Understanding Results

Person #1

I admire in others:
Humor, authenticity, personal warmth, compassion, kindness, perspective

I admire in myself:
Authenticity, humor, long-range vision, person-centeredness, growth and all its consequences

I get frustrated:
hearing students bad-mouthed, being surrounded by mess (especially chemical mess), being overloaded with expectations (my own and others)

Person #2

I admire in others:
sincerity, humor, commitment to work, compassion

I admire in myself:
humor, loyalty, kindness, ethics, interest in others, hard work

I get frustrated:
when there is undue anger, with people with excessive egos, by prejudice, by my own impatience

Person #3

I admire in others:
caring for students, sharing, patience, sense of humor, sense of responsibility

I admire in myself:
willingness to help students, organization, warmth for students, willingness to learn

I get frustrated by:
those who leave a mess for others to clean up, those who patronize students, those who expect others to do their jobs for them

---

see dialogue as a process to create opportunities for reflection on practice, engagement in critique of practice, and support for one another in making professional choices and change (Clark et al., 1996).

In fact, it is not uncommon for such changes to occur because most people can behave in a multitude of manners that are equally satisfying to them. I can either take the mail out first thing in the morning or at lunch. It really doesn't matter. Yet, if I know that it matters to people in my department, I can alter my behavior so that they are satisfied. Since I have no preference in the matter at hand, I am happier because I have been cooperative and have acted to serve my staff.

One departmental discussion in which I participated sounded like this.

Person A: "You admire a sense of humor in others? I thought you were so serious."
Person B: "You did?"
Person A: "Yes. I mean you don't laugh at the jokes we tell."
Person B: "You know, you're right. I don't often laugh, but it takes a lot to make me laugh. I still appreciate the joke, even though I may not be laughing when I do."
Person A: " That's important for me to know, because I thought you sort of didn't like joking, and I've actually been aware that I haven't told you a story I've heard because I just thought you'd think it was dumb."

Untested assumptions about the motives behind another person's actions is one of the greatest universal impediments to cooperation and communication. In this scenario, you can see how Person B would tend to feel somewhat isolated because he or she wasn't part of the storytelling/joking portion of the department. Such isolation would, over time, present itself as an unspoken barrier to better cooperation.

If Helen were to attempt this exercise with her department, it would offer her an additional benefit. She would have the opportunity to voice her frustration about not having put forth her desires for the department during the last two years. She might be able to speak about her increasing fear that the department was coming apart at the seams. She'd be able to say that it frustrates her that she felt somewhat hostage to the former department head's ideals and programs and that she hadn't reached out to the department with her own ideas. This would be a strong step for Helen toward acting the part of the leader. As mentioned in Chapter 1, as the leader you have to "walk that walk and talk that talk."

The exercise would allow Bob to state that he admires teachers who devote their time to students, giving them direct support and encouragement. In hearing Bob state this, Adam might discover that Bob has nearly identical goals to his, though both use different methods to achieve those ends. Adam and Bob have more in common that they realize.

In many groups, just the opposite of cooperation occurs: competition. From the 1940s to the 1990s, Morton Deutsch (1949, 1990) has been one of the most long-term, influential thinkers concerning competition and cooperation. For him, competition arises in teams when individual members of the team see their goals connected in a negative way with the goals of others. In other words, when other members of my group successfully reach their goals, then my goals cannot be reached. In a cooperative group, the goals of individuals are congruent with the goals of the group, and every success of a single group member is experienced as a success for all.

Competition is all too common in our schools, especially among college-bound students. Many of those students feel it is in their own best interests not to help others. By helping another person to score higher on particular tests, the helped person might be perceived as the stronger candidate for competitive college admissions and thereby reduce the helper's chances for admission. Such thinking and action inhibits community building.

Faculty are sometimes placed in similar situations, especially where salary increases are based upon merit performance. Such compensation structures can be seriously flawed, when they set up rewards based upon competition rather than cooperation. Additionally, when faculty work for their own best interests, you can be assured that in the long run students will suffer. Faculty need to be continuously reminded that schools exist for students and not for faculty.

One of the hallmarks of the Japanese schooling system is the honor and prestige that accrues to the teachers when an entire class does well. The focus is on group achievement, not individual performance. While this may be viewed as a cultural norm that doesn't exist in the United States, it is not unusual to hear professional athletes extol the value of the experience of being a part of a successful team, more than they value individual accomplishments. There is a certain ennobling experience when everyone contributes to overall success. Though there is no solid research to suggest that such a value is hard-wired into our DNA sequencing, it seems to be common sense that there are deep psychological reasons why teamwork is rewarding. To go further, many top athletes have clauses in their contracts allowing them to choose which teams they might be traded to, seeking to negate a trade to a losing team and agree to a trade to a winner. Everyone wants to be part of a winner. If one concludes that we could have survived as a species only through teamwork, it is clear why the "team" is a common element in all human societies.

One possible reason for the apparent competition in Helen's department might be the unconscious attempt for approval from the group leader. Dean Tjosvold (Tjosvold, 1986) calls this the "need to be the most able member of the group." This character trait is often most recognizable in children born first in the birth order. Even the passage of time, as the child becomes the adult, may not sublimate this trait. In Helen's department, Diane seems to be the most likely competitor for Helen's approval. Helen can help the situation by telling Diane she admires her talents as a teacher, but that Diane must also use them to bring Bob into the fold. Helen needs to help Diane understand that if she wants to create unusual curricula, she'll need to convince the others why such new curricula are important. Diane must be made aware that simply presenting an idea does not mean it won't be challenged. However, presenting an idea is an act that Helen values. Thus, Diane will come to understand that curriculum development work must be a cooperative venture.

Another tactic that Helen could take, would be to put into operation a simple idea from the founder of Mary Kay Cosmetics, Mary Kay Ash (Ash, 1984, 15). She says "Whenever I meet someone, I try to imagine him or her wearing an invisible button that says: MAKE ME FEEL IMPORTANT!" This means acting, not in a manipulative manner, but in a way that shows care and interest. If Helen had that slogan tucked into the back of her mind, she would be able to ensure that not only would Diane feel appreciated, but so would every member of the department.

All people want to feel loved. In fact, many followerships are solely based upon the feelings followers have for the leader. As the leader of a group, you need to set the tone for cooperation by making each person feel important and loved. Your actions and behaviors will do more to create a cooperative tone that you can imagine. Remember people love others for how they make them feel. Make me feel good, and I will follow you to the ends of the earth. Make me feel bad, and I won't follow you across the street.

Another important factor in getting cooperation is the degree of physical interaction within the group. When a group spends more time together, the chances for cooperative behavior increase. Arranging for a single space, that can serve as the departmental work area, provides constant contact and opportunities for spontaneous cooperation. The use of common space allows teachers to spend more time talking about the actual craft of teaching. Common space allows you to have more intimate contact with all of your staff. It provides you with the opportunity to give information about your hopes and dreams, and for you to voice support for each person.

Max Depree (DePree, 1997) believes that trust is important for leadership success, and developing quality personal relationships is crucial to developing that trust. In addition, he feels the successful leader knows how to affect the context of a situation. Development and use of the common space gives the leader the place where context can be influenced most easily.

By not creating the need to work together, Helen is certainly missing an opportunity to create a sense of teamwork. A department that has a task to accomplish, preferably a task where there is some question as to whether the group can complete the task successfully, will tend to function much more cooperatively. Providing challenging and interesting work is a hallmark of vital organizations. Helen needs to bring the group together around some pressing problems. Those problems may focus on elevating the level of writing that students produce or on increasing the number of books they are able to read in a term. Whatever the task, Helen needs to be the person who defines that task and sets the initial criteria for successful completion. Over time, the group can modify such criteria.

For Helen, the task of determining just what would characterize "the best English department" might keep this group focused for the entire year. See Exhibit 3.3 for a sample departmental review format that can serve as a model for a productive departmental task. This task serves to help the group understand the congruity, or lack thereof, among their individual goals, the departmental goals, and the school's goals. You might look upon this task as setting forward not only the vision, but also the strategic plan of the department.

When the group has such a task before them, they will find ways of working together, rather than looking for ways to isolate themselves. This will be especially true if the task results in some specific effect upon students. Bob and Adam would be ideal members of a subcommittee charged with developing a plan to increase student recreational reading. In putting these two men together (and Helen should be directive in creating the subcommittee), Helen would be affecting the context for possible understanding and cooperation. Again, the key to success will be Helen's careful definition of the task.

If Helen does not structure the tasks of the department so that the goals of each individual are seen as mutually supportive, this group will continue to have members who act independently. It will remain a group whose major activities are designed to thwart the efforts of others in the group. That is, this group will continue to act out of individual self-interests. Such lack of interest in others' goals is a sure-fire recipe for conflict. Creative conflict is addressed a little bit later in this chapter.

Collaboration

Collaboration, while similar to cooperation, is significantly different. When members of the group collaborate, they must work in close connectedness with one another. One of the most striking examples of collaboration is that between two scientists at the Southwest Medical School in Dallas, Michael Brown and Joseph Goldstein, Nobel Laureates in Medi-

---

Exhibit 3.3 DEPARTMENTAL REVIEWS

I. **Step One: Internal Analysis**
A. **Curriculum**
1. Provide a statement of departmental educational philosophy and highlight areas of congruence with school philosophy. The school mission statement should be your primary guide here.
2. Describe how the academic initiatives of your school's long-range plan are being addressed by the department. (Use only those initiatives that apply to your department.)
3. Describe how the department addressed the recommendations made by previous visiting teams such as the ten-year accrediting review or any other such professional body.
4. Highlight and describe areas of the program that are especially vibrant, thriving, or in ascendance. Note areas where the program needs to be supported/changed.
5. Describe the role new technology is playing in departmental offerings.
6. Describe how all levels of student ability and interest are attended to both within the departmental offerings and within each classroom. Describe the department's approach to AP/achievement testing.
7. a. How does the department determine if its program is educationally effective?
    b. Provide feedback on departmental effectiveness from students, parents, and alumni. (This needs only be a random survey of a small number of people from each group, not an exhaustive analysis.)
8. Describe how the departmental facilities augment/detract from effectiveness of the program.
9. Determine if there are any enrollment patterns (gender/race/subject areas) that should be recognized.

B. **Personnel**
1. Provide a professional biography of each department member (prose or CV style) addressing the following:
    a. personal teaching goals;
    b. professional development history (teaching history, summer study, seminars/workshops attended, etc.);
    c. accomplishments (seminars/workshops given, books/articles published, unique curricular materials developed, etc.);
    d. courses taught/areas of teaching proficiency;
    e. membership in professional societies, educational committees, etc.

2. Provide a complete faculty workload profile.

C. Accomplishments
1. Highlight programs that are unique or areas of a course that are special, e.g. field trips, regular outside speakers/experts, etc.
2. Describe any interdepartmental initiatives.
3. Note any program recognition from outside sources (visits from other schools, national awards, etc.).
4. Provide information about special student distinctions/awards/ activities/participation.
5. Describe special departmental programs such as math team, debate team, gallery exhibits, district music festival participation, etc.

II.   Step Two: External Review
A. Outside Experts
1. Invite two or three outside experts to review the departmental analysis. Reviewers will be chosen by both the Department Head and the Dean of Academic Affairs.
Format
2. Begin with dinner including all department members, the Dean of Academic Affairs and the reviewers. Purpose: to set the context, provide for some initial questions to be answered, acquaint reviewers with department members.
3. Day-long visitation/attend classes/interview department members/overnight stay.
4. Continue visitation and end with an oral report to the department on preliminary findings.
5. The visiting team will submit a final written report, within one month, to the Dean of Academic Affairs and the Department Head.

III. Step Three: Review Analysis Response (Department): Provide a written response to the review analysis to the Dean of Academic Affairs within a month of receiving the visiting team's analysis.

IV. Step Four: Administrative Sharing (Senior Administration)
A.   The Dean of Academic Affairs shares the reports with the Senior Administration.
B.   The Dean of Academic Affairs meets with Department Head to discuss the review and develop responses that might need to be initiated.

cine in 1984. Their offices are connected by a set of double doors, which they often keep open, so that they will instantly be able to communicate ideas to one another as they are divined. In addition, their experimental technique is so collaborative that, in looking at their laboratory notebooks, one cannot tell where the efforts of the one ends and those of the other begins. Their understanding of each other is so complete, that they literally know what the other is thinking.

It is possible, even common, for members of the group to be cooperative, but never work closely with each other. Carol can be expected to be a very cooperative member of Helen's department, and yet it is unlikely that she would be asked to be a collaborator by anyone in the department.

Collaboration should be thought of as a goals-directed process (Parker, 1990), where people are willing to work outside their well-defined roles and have no problem sharing the spotlight with others. Collaborators are able to see the "big" picture. Such group members focus broadly on what is good for the school, not narrowly on what is good for the department or for themselves.

While denying self-interest may be an ideal that very few individuals, let alone departments, ever attain, it is possible to create contexts for this kind of intense collaboration for any group. Pursuing departmental policies that necessitate close contact will foster a collaborative spirit that will enhance the morale of the group. Carefully structured practices and strategies can go a long way toward promoting an environment in which collaboration is essential to success. Creation of common term examinations; construction of core curricula in multiple-sectioned courses; group design of class, activity, or lab schedules; understanding the needs of subsequent courses in a sequence can all foster a spirit of collaboration.

Working in an environment where teachers must work out course details together and share ideas, not only creates positive collaborative spirit, but also helps relieve the isolation many teachers feel. It is all too common for teachers in multi-sectioned courses to balk at such collaborative efforts, stating that any system that emphasizes uniformity is a threat to teacher autonomy. Such ideas are simply misplaced. Collaboration does not have to come at the expense of autonomy. Arguments that rely upon "teacher autonomy" often stem from teacher insecurity.

Leavitt and Lipman-Blumen (1995) describe the formation of a "hot group" as one way to promote collaboration. Such groups are usually small and begin in an environment where there is an individual who is excited about an idea. If the idea involves a significant challenge and is intrinsically meaningful, there is a very good chance that for a short period of time, a group will form, focused on the task of bringing the idea to reality. The nature of such groups is that they become totally preoccupied with the task at hand. Csikszentmihalyi (1990) calls this the experience of "flow" and has determined that this is the state in which the most effective learning can occur. When a group of people are learning and creating, their capacity for developing close relationships increases.

The formation of a "hot group" is not that far-fetched for Helen's department. The incubation necessary for such a group to gel can lead to a period of intensive interaction, when the members of the group begin to feel differently about one another. The chance to partake in a shared experience, as one way to promote team bonding, must not be taken lightly. It has long been common practice for business firms to take the senior executives for a week-long Outward Bound experience as one way to promote team bonding.

Diane seems to be the one individual who, if paired with Adam, might transmit her passion for interdisciplinary studies to others in the department and in the school. By working as part of a pair, rather than as an individual, Diane is less vulnerable to criticism. Realizing that it is much easier to make changes on a small scale, Diane and Adam could act in concert. Indeed, the likelihood of creating an educationally impressive course is heightened, especially if Helen serves as the motivational force, acting unobtrusively in the background.

The problem is that Helen hasn't tapped the creative power of her position as the team leader. She hasn't explicitly tried to make things happen. As Maeroff (1993) notes, teachers need to be urged to interact whenever there is the possibility of change. They also have to be mentored and supported by the leader.

In creating a need for collaboration, Helen does not have to have all members working together. It is enough for members to work as pairs or trios. The trick is to make sure that these smaller groups are creating programmatic structures that are connected to the main goals of the department. This will create the need for sharing information about such structures with the rest of the department. See Exhibit 3.4 for an example of a departmental collaborative task. Richl and Sipple (1996) showed that teacher commitment was improved when schedules were designed that were not considered onerous by the teachers.

Consensus

The most prevalent example of consensus decision-making lies in the American justice system. Trial juries come to their conclusions via the

---

Exhibit 3.4 Developing a Departmental Course Assignment Schedule

Having a say about the conditions of one's work is one of the principles discovered by Lickert and reemphasized by Hackman and Oldham (Hackman and Oldham 1976). For example, one could allow teachers an opportunity to design the staffing of departmental courses for the next year. In February, begin the "Wish List."

Place a large poster board in the department workroom with open spaces for each course that must be filled in the next year. By keeping careful enrollment records from year to year, these predictions became quite easy. Announce that each person should take a "Post-It"™ note and place it with his or her name in the course slots he or she wants to teach. It doesn't matter if more teachers place their names in courses than the number that are needed to teach all the proposed sections. Remember, this is a "wish list." Invariably, there will be some course slots that remain empty. Do not panic. Rather, go to the department and encourage them to work with one another to come up with a completely staffed program. Emphasize that this is a departmental program and everyone has an obligation to figure out the appropriate staffing. Don't feel that you must have a finished slate of assignments at this early date.

---

method of consensus. If all members cannot agree, then they are ordered by the judge to continue working until they can agree. The difference between a jury and a department is that, ultimately, the jury can agree that they cannot reach consensus and the trial ends with a hung jury. In department work, such an outcome is unacceptable, because the department must continue to function. Having a "hung" department is not an option.

The word consensus comes from the Latin root word "consentire," which means "to feel together." The department head works with the group members searching for the feeling of agreement. This search should not be limited to formal meetings, but pervade every aspect of leading the department.

Consider how the department head might go about creating the conditions for consensus decision making in Reflection 3.2.

Resolving the Impasse

The central dilemma for the department head to resolve in Reflection 3.2 is how to encourage new curricular emphases without alienating veteran faculty members. With a group that has been working together for some

---

Reflection 3.2

In a language department, Pilar, an excellent Spanish teacher has felt, for a long time, that the final examination in third-year Spanish should be more heavily weighted toward oral response. The rest of the teachers in the department favor the present arrangement, which emphasizes reading comprehension and the interpretation of literature. Each of these teachers has been to see the department head to complain about what they view as Pilar's unreasonable demands for a change in exam emphasis. Pilar has also been to the department head to explain that the nature of college expectations in Spanish has changed and that oral ability is much more important these days.

1. Describe the dilemma the department head faces with Pilar and the other teachers. Focus on being as detailed in your description as you can.
2. What should be the nature of the interaction the department head has with Pilar? with the other department members?
3. What level of intrusiveness is acceptable? You might want to review the material from Chapter 2 on Leadership Styles, especially the models of situational leadership of Blanchard and Hersey.

---

time, it would be appropriate for the department head to ask the group to contact several college Spanish departments, and then determine if more oral response work is needed. By searching out reasons to change, the group will discover either that Pilar is correct and the teaching methodology of the department is somewhat dated, or that Pilar is mistaken and is acting out of her own interest in oral expression. Whatever the outcome, gathering and analyzing objective data is one good technique to help groups arrive at consensus.

So often, the department head's primary complaint is that "my department just won't work together. There's always at least one person who refuses to go along with the group. We can never decide on anything." The "stubborn single" is present in almost every group. It is the department head's task to set the discussion and the problem, to bring these rogue members into the fold. That is, they must come at least far enough into the fold to agree that the decisions agreed to by the majority of the department are ones with which they can live. Consensus does not imply that everyone is totally committed to an idea or decision. Instead, it is a means to surface strong feelings about an item and to deal with those feelings. Consensus is the pathway towards open communication and mutual understanding. The leader who chooses not to seek consensus is sure to have a short tenure.

In any decision made through a consensus mechanism, it is essential that all points of view make their way into the decision. The term "compromise" is sometimes thought to be synonymous with "consensus," but it is not. To compromise is somehow to accept less than what was wanted. In a consensus decision, the results are somewhat tentative, and there is the possibility that more than was expected can result.

Some people are uncomfortable with the informality of a consensus decision-making style. They would prefer the rigid Robert's Rules of Order be applied, thinking that this structure will lead to less chaos. Unfortunately, what is true about such a decision-making process is that motions can get passed that no one really supports. And decisions can emerge that have no majority support.

Peter Senge (1990) describes two types of consensus: "focusing down" and "opening up." In "focusing down" consensus, the group members take their positions and focus on what common ground exists among each member. This is the search for the common denominator. For Helen's department, this might be the fact that all members want to have the students excel at English.

In "opening up" consensus, each individual's views are studied with an eye to how they fit into a larger picture. Each member of the group tries to envision his or her goals through the eyes of another. In Helen's department, this might mean focusing on the future needs of students or on the link between departmental goals and school goals.

Consensus decision making can take more time than voting or top-down edicts, but it is worth taking this precious time. There is no better way to promote a feeling of unanimity than by reaching decisions with everyone in support of an idea. Gathering support and searching for the "feeling" certainly means that discussions will take longer. The department head must plan meetings with an eye towards possible conflict that must be resolved and allow more time for discussion. If the members of the group can view one another as working for common goals, the apparent "stubbornness" or "rigidity" of another in the group might be more positively viewed as that person's "concern" or "personal integrity." Those who disagree should be looked at as helpful in bringing more views to the attention of the group. However, the dissenter must also be astute enough to realize when his or her dissent is not well-founded. It is not helpful to persist in trying to clarify a direction that is all too clear to all others in the group. It is at that point that the dissenter must search for the common ground between the opinions and wishes of the many and those of the dissenting few. There is nothing worse than when a group has to endure what Spiro Agnew termed the "nattering nabobs of negativism."

Voting and Not Voting

In a very small group, one of the most damaging methods for making decisions can be voting. Voting can leave a taste of failure in the mouths of the minority. And failure does not breed positive mental attitudes. Secret ballot voting of the nonbinding, straw-poll variety can be an intermediary step towards full consensus decision making. Such voting allows the department head to know the degree of difference and to decide which plan of action to take. Ideally, the department head can lead the group in an open dialogue about the issue. While it is true that decisions can be reached faster by voting than by reaching consensus, successful implementation of decisions reached this way can take much longer.

If voting must occur, there is a method of voting that can be less divisive. It is called "approval voting." In such voting, everyone can vote for as many candidates (positions, alternatives, options, whatever the issue is) as they wish. The option with the most votes is declared "the sense of the group," and it is from this place that further discussion can begin. In this manner, the group has expressed its "approval" of the item at hand.

Peter Senge (1990) cites the distinction David Bohm (a contemporary physicist, who has recently been very influential in the area of teamwork) makes between dialogue and discussion. Discussion is more closely related to words like percussion and concussion. The outcome of a discussion usually means one side wins and the other loses, even though there has been a back and forth exchange. On the other hand, dialogue is most closely connected to the exchange of meaning. *Logos*, word, and *dia-*, through, come together literally as "through the word." Understanding occurs through the *meaning* we give to ideas. It is understanding the meaning of others that results in group learning and, thus, progress in thinking and action.

To create the conditions for an open dialogue, the department head must appeal to the group to suspend its usual approach to talking with one another. They must now come at the task, not as if it were a discussion, but rather with a suspension of beliefs. Each participant must try to make meaning out of what every other person is saying. Only then will the department be able to move forward with any degree of consensus. This takes skill and practice, but can be accomplished if you are willing to spend time structuring the ground rules for the group meeting. When each person makes it a priority to restate the position of others, as a way of checking his or her own understanding, meetings will be infinitely more productive and the likelihood of reaching consensus greater.

It is useful to be careful in questioning the thinking of group members. Some ways of question asking can be very combative and judgmental. When asking for a person's thinking on an issue, it is best to ask him or her "how" he or she arrived at this belief or "what lead you" to this belief. It is not helpful to ask "why" this belief is held. "Why" puts the person on the spot to justify his or her thinking.

However, it is a good practice to ask "why not?" This question allows the respondent to be somewhat critical of the other's views and, in so doing, bring to the surface ideas and feelings that can be clarified by the rest of the group. Sometimes the "why not?" leads to a much more candid response and an opening up of the beliefs of the dissenter. For example, if the issue is one of expanding the number of honors courses in a department, the question might be, "Why is it not a good idea for our students to have more honors courses from which to choose?" That is to say, a productive type of question is on the order of "What's wrong with doing X?" Again, since people find it easy to criticize, the talk is likely to bring to the surface hidden thoughts and beliefs previously unstated.

Of course, the bottom line is to bring the department to consensus. One way to do this is to ask, after some time of dialogue and discussion has passed, "What can we do to bring about some agreement on this point? How can we leave this room all feeling as if we are on the same page?" This puts both factions of a group into the position of holding a stake in a positive outcome. If there is no consensus at that point, it is best to end the discussion, reiterate that the group needs to come to agreement on the issues, and then resume at a later time, when all members have had a further chance to think about the issues.

Camaraderie

"All for one and one for all." This rallying cry of Dumas' Three Musketeers is probably the most widely known slogan epitomizing camaraderie. In a department where people act for the common good in a collegial manner, there will almost always be an element of camaraderie. In such departments, teachers enjoy working with one another. They have respect for one another and understand what others do to contribute to the whole. A department with a high level of camaraderie does not hesitate to each lunch together.

Research has shown (Katzenbach and Smith, 1993) the importance for teams to spend a lot of time together. It is the department head's task to find ways for the group to do this. As mentioned earlier, one of the most effective ways to do this is to make sure the team has a central place to work. A department staff room is ideal for this purpose.

Many times a building is built along the lines of the college model, with all faculty members having an office or a classroom where they, and only they, work. It is advisable to do away with these spaces as places where faculty can primarily be found. If it means eliminating a classroom to create a departmental or team office space, then do it. It will be the best use of space you've ever made. You are trying to get people to meet both formally and informally. You want the talk of teaching to be always present. Again, this is part of affecting the context for interaction.

At this point, let me say a word about the more common role of the faculty room in a school. The faculty room can be a node of negativity, where people gather to talk about what's wrong with the school, the kids, the world. This doesn't have to be the case in your department room. If you spend as much time as you can in your department room and continually bring up topics dealing with teaching and learning, you will lessen the negative conversations that occur there. As your department grows in its team spirit, there will be more focus on the goals and positive aspirations of the team and less emphasis on what drags the group down.

Senge (1990) has noted that there is always the tension between a person's or a group's ideals and current reality. There will always be a gap between those two. However, a spirit of camaraderie can lessen the chance that current reality will pull down the ideal. Instead, the ideal can lift up current reality to meet the ideal.

Another way to foster camaraderie is to hold regular meetings. These meetings should be about substantial topics. There is nothing worse that having to attend a meeting where nothing happens. In fact, it is more damaging to team spirit to hold this kind of meeting than it is to hold no meeting at all. For more on specifics of running an effective meeting see Chapter 8.

It is beneficial for the leader, continually, to think of the team as a collection of individuals whose actions are synergistic. Emphasize in writing and in talk that there is a special spirit that the group has that is essential to maintaining an excellent and effective department.

Exhibit 3.5 What We Accomplished Last Year

I look back on the 1996–1997 school year and feel good about our accomplishments as a department and as individuals. I think it's important to begin the 1997–1998 school year by reviewing some of those accomplishments, contributions, and efforts that make the science department a great place to work and our relationships with one another so unique. We have an intangible, invaluable team spirit that should be recognized.

We were blessed with the serendipitous presence of Deb Terst, who so ably substituted for Frank. (Frank brought recognition and honor to our department as one of twelve independent school teachers nationwide to be selected as a Klingenstein Fellow.) We found two new (to us) excellent teachers, Dave and George. Dave has been a ball of fire and, as the teacher closest in age to our students, bridges an important gap in attracting certain students into the department. George brings to us his wealth of knowledge and dedication to middle-school students, as well as his gift of gab. Tom, as an alumnus intern, has served us well and shown that the science education he received here was top rated.

This isn't to say the veteran teachers haven't done their share. Skip and Ralph brought new ideas from their graduate studies and reminded us that the life of a student is never easy. Ralph, with Skip's help, rebuilt all the shelves in the chemical storage area, making it a much safer and functional space. Skip was selected as a participant in a special program at Johns Hopkins and published some book reviews in the physics teaching journal.

Marge refined the chemistry lab program and worked very hard to bring us interesting speakers from BU and MIT. Andy showed his commitment to field studies by showing slides of his Whale Watch trip in the Baja to the entire faculty and served well as Tom's mentor.

Sally, in her quiet and modest way, raised the environmental consciousness of the whole school through her role as advisor to LORAX and was a key person in getting Senator Kerry to kick off Earth Week. In addition, she was recognized as an influential teacher in the development of Presidential Scholar Cindy Stark. "A teacher knows not where 'her' influence ends," to paraphrase Henry Adams.

Pete almost single-handedly organized and oversaw the hordes in Honors Physics. Luckily, we were able to make the right arrangements for his continued stay here.

Nancy served on more than her share of committees, reviewed a new textbook as an editor of sorts, served on an NSTA task force for Gifted and Talented education, and took the job of Head of House for Marling dormitory.

I served on several school committees, acted as a Master Teacher for the AISNE New Teacher Workshop, gave several papers on the use of the Nobel Prize in teaching science, and co-directed the Leadership Workshop for Department Heads.

We instituted very successful term courses that resulted in many more students choosing to further their education in the sciences. We received a $40,000 grant from the Ford Foundation to complete the new observatory and refurbish the Alvin Clark telescope. Students have had good things to say about their experiences in our department and feel challenged and excited by our offerings. We have tried to emphasize the importance of the Freshman course and have modified our hours of availability to be more sensitive to student needs.

We have also weathered some fairly rough times during the selection process for the next department head. In retrospect, the process opened up better communication among all of us. I know I'm looking forward to serving you as best I can during the next five years and will be actively seeking your help, comments, ideas, and support.

During the coming year we will certainly not be at a loss for important things to do. We need to examine our open lab program, consider where we ought to go with semester courses, investigate how we can better serve all students, redouble our efforts to develop a multicultural understanding of students, stay abreast of national developments in science education, make science learning an active process, and be ready for the new, the unexpected, even the unpredictable, which will surely happen this year.

By any standard, this aggregate of individual talents has come together to create a powerful team. This year we can have an even greater positive effect on our students, other faculty, and ourselves by keeping in mind the Seven Cs: Common Goals, Communication, Cooperation, Collaboration, Creative Conflict, Consensus, and Camaraderie. Congratulations on a most productive year!

In Exhibit 3.5, you will see an example of a letter to a department that makes a special point of publicly noting the accomplishments of each person in the group. The letter also demonstrates how the leader can use positive imagery to develop a spirit of togetherness. You will see that there is direct reference to the "rough times" during selection of the new department head. This was a time when personal competition caused some cracks in the team structure. If not for the specific concentrated efforts on team building, the department surely would have become fractured. This letter was very effective at keeping the conversation honest and lines of communication open. You cannot build camaraderie by sweeping problems and issues under the rug.

Another common way to build camaraderie is to build in social time. Create a social time with refreshments before the departmental meetings. Hold pot-luck dinners, or even take the group out for pizza. It does not have to be lavish. It does have to be heartfelt.

Communication

One of the biggest problems Helen faces with her department is the lack of clear communication among the members of the group. Of course, that is not unusual. The usual manner for people to work together (Argyris and Schon, 1989) is one where much of what is thought about another person or a situation is hidden from view. It is mostly hidden from the view of those who could have an effect upon the situation, but there may be things that are deeply held and serve as background to the context for action.

In Argyris's model there are four "governing variables" that provide the background to the way we all act:

1. People unilaterally define goals and try to achieve them.
2. People act in ways to maximize winning and minimize losing.
3. People act to minimize the generation or expression of negative feelings.
4. People above all else try to act rationally.

In following their natural modes of behavior, you can be sure that people will ascribe motives to another's actions, but will not publicly test their beliefs. This is the single greatest cause for poor communication and relations within groups. Members of Helen's department exhibit all of the above behaviors. They are certainly attributing motives to the behavior of other department members, with none of them bothering to test their hidden assumptions.

Bob feels that Diane is going to conferences to avoid dealing with students. In his belief system, the only good teacher is the one who stays home and works with the students. However, he doesn't test this assumption with Diane. He doesn't ask what her motivation might be. Diane urges Helen to make an important curricular decision without Bob present, because she thinks Bob won't want to go along with the new readings. Diane acts rationally to say that the meeting was scheduled and that Bob had his chance to be there, but chose not to do so. Of course, she forgets that Bob also must be at the lacrosse game for which he is the head coach. Now, it may be that Bob would not wish to go along, but this is never made explicit.

Carol's whole existence is focused upon acting in a unilateral manner to keep everyone happy. She doesn't want any conflict to occur and suggests the department hold fewer meetings. Fewer meetings will ensure worse communication and guarantee a longer period of time before this group is fully functional.

Helen may not really know the reason why she has been avoiding taking action with her department. She has said it was to honor the past practices of the former department head, but that may be only a rationalization. Subconscious motivation to avoid leading might be the actual basis for Helen's inaction. Only careful reflection on her part can uncover this. And,

---

Exhibit 3.6A Department Head Feedback

Just as students need feedback on their work in order to feel positively reinforced, as well as to know where and how to improve, I need your comments upon my work as your department head. In the past, your remarks have helped me a great deal and I hope my responses to those remarks have resulted in my being better able to serve you.

Please comment upon the following:

Behaviors, actions, areas where you would like me to continue unchanged:

Behaviors, actions, areas where you would like me to cease acting as I am presently:

Behaviors, actions, areas where you would like me to begin acting:

Exhibit 3.6B Department Head Evaluation Form

Please respond to the following descriptions by circling the appropriate numbers. Note that for each item there are two columns in which to place a response: the first column asks you to judge how much you value the task; the second then asks you to rate my performance while doing the task. "1" is the worst rating, "4" is the best rating. If you have no basis for judgment, leave the response blank.

		Importance				*Performance*			
1.	Performance in handling routine affairs of the department	1	2	3	4	1	2	3	4
2.	Consideration of faculty views in dealing with important departmental policies and issues	1	2	3	4	1	2	3	4
3.	Contribution to improving and maintaining the reputation of the department	1	2	3	4	1	2	3	4
4.	Demonstrates a clearly defined philosophy of administration	1	2	3	4	1	2	3	4
5.	Promotes informed discussion of issues	1	2	3	4	1	2	3	4
6.	Makes clear his or her position on the issues facing the faculty	1	2	3	4	1	2	3	4
7.	Listens well	1	2	3	4	1	2	3	4
8.	Remains in close contact with all teachers in the department	1	2	3	4	1	2	3	4
9.	Effectively solves conflicts between students and teachers	1	2	3	4	1	2	3	4
10.	Makes decisions effectively	1	2	3	4	1	2	3	4
11.	Makes decisions fairly	1	2	3	4	1	2	3	4
12.	Remains open to change and new ideas	1	2	3	4	1	2	3	4
13.	Encourages faculty to attend conferences and meetings	1	2	3	4	1	2	3	4
14.	Secures time for attendance at such conferences and meetings	1	2	3	4	1	2	3	4
15.	Maintains coherent and understandable grading standards in the department	1	2	3	4	1	2	3	4
16.	Encourages future thinking in curriculum development	1	2	3	4	1	2	3	4
17.	Encourages department members to be an effective working group	1	2	3	4	1	2	3	4
18.	Allocates funds in a fair and judicious manner	1	2	3	4	1	2	3	4

it may be that no amount of self-reflection will help. Only direct input from her department might allow her to uncover her true motivations.

One sure fire way to create the climate for open communications is to ask for it by having the department members comment upon her work. Exhibit 3.6A and 3.6B provide two ways to get this communication started. Notice that Exhibit 3.6A is a general request for feedback while 3.6B is a very detailed request for information about specific department head behaviors. Open feedback on your work is the lifeblood of leadership.

So what can be done to improve communication? First, as was mentioned before in the section on camaraderie, having a common space where teachers work together is one way. In such a space, informal discussions inevitably bring talk around to sensitive issues and allow people to explain themselves more fully. But a more important action is a formal and direct focus on open and complete communication directed by the department head.

Communication improvement needs to be an explicitly stated goal of the department. If Helen were to ask direct questions such as " Bob, when you told Diane that she was spending too much time going to conferences, was it was because you believe that going to conferences takes time away from students?" or " Carol, do you think Bob has the best ideas about teaching or are you saying that because he's the senior member of the department?" she would be modeling the testing of assumptions. Such mod-

---

Exhibit 3.7 Teambuilding and Communication Activity

It always helps to think about a challenging interaction BEFORE it occurs. This activity is structured to help you do that.

1. Think about the interaction you are about to encounter.
2. Try to describe the feelings you have right now about that interaction. Are you confident, nervous, upset, worried, etc. Try to describe exatly what outcome you hope to emerge from the interaction.
3. Take a sheet of paper and divide it into two halfs from top to bottom. On left side write out what you think the dialogue will be. On the right side write out what you are thinking when you created the dialogue.
4. Can you discover any tacit beliefs that you harbor after reading this analysis of the dialogue? Will these beliefs interfere with the interaction? How will you work to avoid bringing those beliefs to the interaction?

(Adapted from Chris Argyris and Donald Schon, *Theory in Practice: Increasing Professional Effectiveness* (San Francisco: Jossey-Bass, 1974).

eling would help the department members understand how they too might test their unspoken assumptions. It is amazing what this kind of open questioning does to "set the truth free." Such a practice provides respondents the opportunity to state more clearly what they really meant.

An exercise that is especially helpful for the department head to engage in before bringing an important topic to the group or to an individual is outlined in Exhibit 3.7. In carrying out this exercise, it is important to be as honest as possible in creating both sides of the dialogue. This activity should not be entered into with the thought that in completing the activity, you will be able to manipulate the interaction. Such an approach would be a severe perversion of the team-building mentality. This exercise should only be used to help you clarify your position and thinking and, perhaps, to breakthrough the barriers to open communication.

Another possibility for improving communication is to have the group read something specifically about communication. Two interesting books by Deborah Tannen (1990, 1994) are wonderful sources of topics for this kind of discussion. A discussion focused around the statements "Women do not view men as being helpful when they immediately offer solutions to problems women bring up," or "Women have this mistaken notion that when men saying nothing, it means they are thinking nothing," can serve as good openers for department meetings. You must remember to keep such discussions short and introduce them only in a sincere effort to improve communications. As usual, common sense and good judgment must be the order of the day. You must choose questions that will not provoke personal animosity among the participants.

Finally, the leader needs too make sure that everyone is privy to as much information as possible. Being an information hog may make the leader feel more powerful, but it will be at the expense of making everyone else feel less powerful. This will not build a climate of openness.

Creative Conflict

Bob and Adam disagree on some fundamental pedagogical issues. Diane and Bob don't see eye to eye on the nature of the modern English curriculum. Carole is intimidated by Bob's strong advocacy and directness. Diane can't get the cooperation of others for the curricular innovations she seeks. And Helen can't count on any of them to help her develop a smoothly functioning team.

It seems that their disagreements are causing the fabric of the department, somewhat tattered to begin with, to rip apart at the seams. If this behavior is allowed to continue for much longer, the likelihood of having a staff that is "intellectually stimulated, appreciated and happy" is nil. Instead, Helen will have to deal with a bitter group of workers whose irritation with one another will shatter any dream she might have harbored of creating "one of the best English departments in the country."

Every one of us experiences conflict as a daily occurrence (Averill, 1982). In an example of the old maxim that "for every great truth, the opposite of that truth is also true," it is a fact that when people work together, there will be times when they do not get along. Clearly, when people work closely together, the tendency to bump up against one another is increased. It is also true that a group will squabble more about the implementation of a strategy than they will about principles and philosophy behind that strategy. For a group to work well together, there must be ways to deal with such ongoing conflict. If we follow the notion of *creative conflict*, the chances of open hostilities developing to such a level that they ravage the group are virtually nonexistent.

Creative conflict is that state where disagreements are open and public; where, while there is strong feeling that one way is better than another, both sides agree that they need to reach mutual commonality. The foci of creative conflict are ideas and things, not people or personalities. It is the responsibility of the team leader to develop a climate where creative conflict can thrive. Each of the Seven Cs, in it own way, does just that. The key to overall success is to be fully aware that these actions will not occur by themselves. The department head must actively pursue them.

The team leader should take heart that in actively addressing a conflict, there can be substantial benefits. Conflict will not disappear by ignoring or changing the focus to other areas. It will just be temporarily sublimated, only to rear its ugly head at another time and place. But when differences are brought into the open and a sincere effort is made to make the basis for disagreement clear to all, a surprising thing happens. People tend to come together. The act of disagreeing helps the group to focus on precisely what is most important to them.

The task for the group is to not let anger, which may be generated during the conflict, be confused for assertiveness. Ranting and raving get little accomplished and show a lack of confidence in oneself more than anything else. The ground rules for disagreement should be made clear: stick to the facts, no personal attacks allowed, everyone will have a chance to be heard, etc.

Above all, the problem at the heart of the conflict must be defined with clarity and confronted directly. In defining the problem, the team leader must ensure that everyone fully participates. When each person gets to say exactly what he or she wants in an atmosphere of candor and questioning, the pathway towards agreement will often be clear. It is essential that there be group definition of the problem, so that everyone understand the problem and be able to explain its nature to anyone who asks.

Yet precisely defining the problem is the hardest step in bringing a group to a common resolution. The initial tendency of most department heads, and even of people in the departmental group, is to "solve" the problem. This gut response must be resisted, because it will short-circuit the development of a full description of the problem. Immediately focusing your attention on the solution may be nothing more than a disguised avoidance strategy.

In physics problem solving, students are urged to make sure they understand all of the conditions before choosing a solution pathway. Novice students often want to use the first formula they see. This is invariably the wrong choice. Subtle messages in the problem point the astute student in a more refined direction. The same can be said for group conflict-resolution. The group must be trained to hold back from trying to solve the problem before they have actually described it fully.

In Helen's department, Carole probably has much to say. Helen cites this when she states that Carole often says "just the right thing." However, Carole is afraid to let her opinion be known in a meeting. It may be that other department members are also holding back their opinions. Helen is going to have to structure the discussion so that each member of the department can put the problem into his or her own words. Similarly, Helen might have to ask Bob to be more reserved and to listen to the others, before stating his point of view. In fact, in stating his point of view it would be wise to ask Bob to begin by stating directly the points of common agreement. Only after that has been done should he focus on the points of disagreement. If Helen can convince Bob, at a minimum, to remain open to being influenced by Diane's and Adam's methods for innovation, that would go a long way towards producing the kind of exciting and energizing atmosphere Helen desires for this department.

In following Bob's actions closely, it seems that he has the tendency to read sinister, or at least less than positive, motives into the actions of both Diane and Adam. As Argyris (1989) has discovered and we have previously read, many conflicts arise because one person ascribes a motive to another person's action, without checking to see if that ascribed motive is, in fact, accurate. In an open discussion, everyone can test his or her beliefs and understandings and have the opportunity to elaborate upon specific reasons for individual actions, methods, or beliefs. In the words of Samuel Taylor Coleridge, "Until you understand another man's ignorance, consider yourself ignorant of his understanding."

The leader of the team must have the will to work, continually, at bringing the two sides of an issue together. He or she must be willing to endure periods when it seems that a stalemate has been reached. It takes patience and careful listening, and then, restructuring of the discussions to foster an atmosphere of creative conflict. Tjosvold (1986) has noted that conflict can be considered beneficial when people (a) feel the underlying problem has been solved, (b) feel they understand one another better and can work effectively in the future and (c) believe that their time and resources have been well spent.

Ury (1991) stresses that the two sides in a conflict must be made aware of the positions and interests of all involved. The ideal in conflict resolution is to move away from positional bargaining and into joint problem solving. It's the leader's task to build the "golden bridge" between the two sides. Involving both sides in the construction of the bridge can ensure that the conflict will be resolved. Asking the question, "What would we have to do to satisfy both sides on this issue?" is often all that is needed for two sides to come to an agreement.

The "golden bridge" Helen needs to build is one where both sides see that, deep down, under the surface layer of methodological disagreement, there is a commonly held belief in the value of inspired teaching leading to effective learning. This nexus will serve all the department members well, if they are able to discern it clearly. If Helen can direct everyone's attention to the professed goal of effective education, she will have found the territory where each person can speak honestly and knowledgeably and where each can hear the other with unbiased ears. One sign of adult growth and development (Levine, 1989) is the ability to hear irritably, now, what, previously, couldn't be heard at all. Helen's department is on the threshold of a major adult growth spurt, if they can learn to conduct themselves in a spirit of creative conflict.

Experiencing such growth, when one member of the group is unyielding and uncompromising, is difficult. When this happens, the leader has little choice but to retreat for the time being and try again at a later time when all have had some time to think about the others' positions. When each side focuses on where they could modify their position to become more congruent, the leader has a better chance to help the group come to agreement. Those disagreeing with one another should not leave the discussion with their focus on strengthening their own argument in order to win. If this is done, the gap between the two sides will widen, and the likelihood is that misunderstanding will be the dominant strand in any future discussion. The goal is not to win, but to create.

Again, the department head simply cannot smooth over disagreements, because there will still be a lack of understanding between the two sides about what the other side wants. Avoidance will promote a false sense of group solidarity, which will be undermined at the first rough stretch of road. The leader needs to play an active role in bringing the conflict out into the open and to stress the need for interdependence in order to achieve success. When agreement, no matter how small, is reached, it is important for the leader to point out the success that has been achieved. The first step is to get the group talking to one another. Thus, spending time on communication processes will help when the inevitable conflict arises. See Exhibit 3.8 for an exchange of e-mail whereby the team leader does not avoid the conflict inherent in the sender's missive, but rather, takes the opportunity to focus on what a better response might have been and on the purpose of an upcoming meeting.

There will be times when stronger approaches to conflict resolution will be needed. Chapter 4, "Effective Communication," will illustrate some of those means.

Care

As the department head, you are responsible for the overall tone of the department. You must care for the professional development of each member of the group. One measure of the level of care a leader has for the department is the amount of time he or she is willing to invest in team building. It is normal for department heads to view themselves primarily as teachers. After all, most of the department head's workload is focused on teaching, especially since many department heads and team leaders do not receive release time from the normal job expectations. (By the way, this should be changed to allow every department head the time to perform this complex job effectively.) The importance of the job demands that time and attention be paid to the administrative and inspirational aspects of working with adults. No department will ever be outstanding without the leader's close attention to its workings.

There is an old New England aphorism that existed long before anyone thought of MBWA (Management By Walking Around), "The best fertilizer is the footsteps of the farmer." There is no one else to look after the details of teaching and learning in as intimate a way as the department head. The

---

**Exhibit 3.8 An E-mail Exchange between the Dean
of the Senior Class and the Academic Dean**

Date: May 26, 1994
To: Tom Smith, Academic Dean
From: Ed Gethy, Dean of the Senior Class
cc: Other Class Deans

Folks: The course selection forms and process have been virtually all-con-
suming for the past two or three weeks. Sally and I feel we have SERIOUSLY
NEGLECTED other responsibilities in order to do this work. I would estimate
that I still have 40–50 sheets on my desk and I will need—somehow—to see
the students about getting these straight. When Tom met with the deans
about three weeks ago and gave such a sanguine report on how well advisers
were doing, he was, at best, premature in his report . . . at worst, ducking his
head in the quicksand. The new system needs much thought and retooling. I
understand it is new, etc., etc., etc., but the fact remains, we have not been
able to do our job in its many other facets. In case you're missing my tone
here: I am angry. Whoever thought this through ahead of time has/had no
idea of the deans' roles in this. I hope we can make some time to discuss this
on Tuesday when the deans meet.

Date: May 27, 1994
To: Ed Gethy
From: Tom Smith
cc: Other Class Deans

First, I am sorry you're angry, but everyone is entitled to have the emotions he
or she feels. I was disappointed by the mild inference that somehow I
had/have my head in the sand—a polite way of saying incompetent. Whatever we may think personally, the helpful response must be "what can I do
to make this work better?" I assume we are all doing the very best we can to
make this school the best it can be and I know you, Ed, are especially devoted to the task.

Second, there will be some procedures and format issues that this office will
have to fix for next year. This would be expected whenever a fundamental
change such as this takes place. However, from what you say and from the
later forms we have received, there is a MAJOR problem with the understanding by many of our advisers about the school curriculum and the path-
ways to access that curriculum. To make your work easier, we are working
on a sheet showing each student's schedule for all terms and will get those to

you. We, in this office, are committed to serving and are willing to do whatever is necessary to make the process less problematic.

Finally, there is a greater good in all of this. We are seeing, perhaps for the first time, students choosing courses with a purpose in mind. The economics sequence is working as it was designed to work; there are students selecting history courses that will augment one another; there are students looking at arts courses in a sequential manner, etc. It is only a beginning, but it is a major step in opening up full access to and utilization of our curriculum.

So let's all hang in there and when we meet on Tuesday begin to analyze what the real problems are. Once we know those in detail, then we can begin to solve them.

Date: June 8, 1994
To: Tom Smith
From: Ed Gethy
cc: All other Class Deans

Thank You for your measured response to my shooting from the hip on one of the "lowest" days a few weeks ago. But the expression "sticking heads in the sand" doesn't mean incompetence; it means avoidance—the tendency of those who have created something, a new procedure, e.g., to see what they want to see re: results. However, the meeting was a success and I hope we can begin to forge ahead.

---

department head is the farmer, looking after the well-being of every plant in the field. Truly caring for a department demands an effort greater than you might expect and, though I am sad to note this, comes at the expense of time usually delegated to teaching preparation. This sacrifice of teaching time is more than worth the price, when it's understood that the level of effectiveness of all members of the staff increases in a well-run department. Increased effectiveness means more learning takes place, and that's the bottom line to which all department leaders should be paying attention.

Caring for members of the department demands a patient disposition. The motto of Wellesley College, *Non ministrari, sed ministrarae.* (Not to be served, but to serve), could well be the motto for the College of Department Heads. It takes patience and ability to serve and serve well. It means sacrificing the spotlight. To be caring, more often than not, means standing in the background, as the department members become the focus of attention. It may be difficult to do, but the well-being of each member of the department should come before your own.

While a caring attitude can be exhibited in departmental meetings or other public forums, a caring attitude, clearly displayed in little everyday actions, is much more meaningful and effective for creating a team than some splashy announcement or program. For example, when a member of the department comes to talk with you while you might be opening your mail, don't continue to open it. While most of us are smart enough to be able to carry on more than one action or to hold more than one thought in mind at a time, the message you convey through such inattention is not one that proclaims that you care about this person. Rather, the message to the person wanting to talk with you is "go away, my mail is more important than you are." Success, or the lack thereof, in relationships is all about the little things.

Breaking habits that lead to a non person-focused interaction, such as the aforementioned one, is not easy. We develop habits because they help us to save that most precious of all commodities . . . time. But saving time is not always in the best interests of team building. Looking directly into the eyes of the person with whom you are speaking and giving that person your full attention will more than make up for lost time by increasing that person's connectedness to you.

Hackman and Oldham (1976, 250–279) discovered three psychological states they believed to be critical in determining whether a person will be motivated to work. Those three states are

- *Experienced Meaningfulness*: The extent to which a person perceives work as being worthwhile or important given her or his system of values.
- *Experienced Responsibility*: The extent to which a person believes that he or she is personally responsible or accountable for the outcomes of efforts.
- *Knowledge of Results*: The extent to which a person is able to determine on a regular basis whether or not the outcomes of his or her efforts are satisfactory.

A department head conveys a caring attitude when he or she creates opportunities that ensure that these psychological states are reached.

As noted earlier in Exhibit 3.4, setting up an opportunity for discussion about teaching assignments can create an environment where people must work together in order for the department to be successful. If a department head assigns the teaching assignments based upon seniority or friendship, the full responsibility for staffing falls on his or her shoulders. In such a situation, none of the three psychological states necessary for motivation are likely to be satisfied except, perhaps, for the department head. Thus, it is crucial for the department head to bring everyone into the decision-making process and share real responsibility with the team.

It is a sign of care when Helen serves as a motivating source, operating unobtrusively in the background, pushing for a working partnership, a "hot group" if you will, between Adam and Diane. Helen would further the cause of departmental teamwork by asking the two of them to work together to determine how an interdisciplinary course could improve reading levels and broaden knowledge of the world. As innovators, they will attract attention of others in the department, and in the school, and can involve them in their efforts. Diane can function as the connective force drawing the group together. Both Adam and Diane will experience such an assignment as meaningful and laden with responsibility.

A side benefit to this approach will be the opportunity for new assignments to be developed. Often, a staff member would like to teach a particular subject, but hasn't given such a desire much serious thought. With a procedure of course assignment, as depicted in Exhibit 3.4, the possibilities are more varied. This system is not without its dangers, however. The department head might need to have discussions with faculty members who signed up for courses that are inappropriate for their teaching expertise.

But even this scenario can be used to further departmental well-being. By letting the teacher know why they presently do not fit the criteria for teaching this course and by laying out the kind of training they need in order to teach that course, the department head can put into place the ground work for purposeful professional development. The teachers, knowing what the expectations are to land such assignments, can develop themselves to accomplish the end they seek.

Understanding each person's needs is a crucial form of caring. This can be accomplished by setting up individual discussion time with each member of the staff at the beginning of the school year and again at the end. Together, discuss how you view their responsibilities and your expectations. Find out what each person would like to accomplish during the year. Then, make it your business to help reach those goals, in as concrete a manner possible.

Be aware, as you work with each teacher, of the whole picture he or she presents to you. You are in a position to create a work load that allows them to be successful. Be active in suggesting programs, seminars, and readings that would be of interest or benefit to them. Volunteer to cover teachers' classes, so they can attend professional development opportunities. This is one way of saying that you care about them as individuals and as members of the team.

Exhibit 3.9 Faculty Workload Questionnaire

NAME_____

CURRENT HOUSING_____

TEACHING RESPONSIBILITIES:

NAME OF COURSE   # OF SECTIONS   LEVEL   # OF STUDENTS

_____

_____

_____

_____

_____

_____

TOTAL NUMBER OF ASSIGNED TEACHING PERIODS PER WEEK_____

OF SUPERVISION PERIODS PER WEEK_____

WILL TEACHING ASSIGNMENT CHANGE DURING THE COURSE OF THE YEAR?_____ EXPLAIN_____

ADVISING: CLASS_____ NOT ADVISING_____

COACHING RESPONSIBILITIES: (Sports, Drama, Debate, Theater, etc.)
List Names/levels of teams.
FALL_____ WINTER_____
SPRING_____

SUPERVISORY RESPONSIBILITIES (Clubs, Open Labs, Study hall, etc.)
1._____
2._____
3._____

DORMITORY: CITE POSITION IN DORMITORY(HOUSE HEAD, ASSISTANT, FLOORHEAD, ETC.)

COMMITTEES AND ADMINISTRATIVE RESPONSIBILITIES:

_____

_____

_____

OTHER KNOWN RESPONSIBILITIES NOT COVERED ABOVE:

_____

OUTSIDE OF SCHOOL RESPONSIBILITIES:

_____

_____

Through careful listening, you will be able to determine which members are under stress, caused either by internal or external situations. Let them know you are willing to do anything you can to help them. Do not push your way into their problems, but don't shrink from talking about personal issues. There is no way a personal issue, if left unattended, will not effect the quality of a teacher's work with students. Sometimes, the offer of help is all that is needed to improve the situation. If the department member does ask for your help, you must be prepared to give it. Exhibit 3.9 gives a useful form to help structure such individual discussions.

Of all the Seven Cs, care is the most important. Nurturing the growth of each department member will result in a happier, more motivated and energized staff. This means that the real business that you, and the department, are about—improved quality of instruction—is more likely to occur. It is the responsibility of the department head to promote, invent, and participate in any and all actions that can create the climate for improved instruction. Team building is one important factor for the ongoing intellectual renewal of a school and for the improvement of teaching and learning.

Teamwork from Day One

Hiring the Best Team

In creating a great team, one of the most important activities in which you and your organization can engage is the hiring of the members of the team. Every organization engages in this practice, and each one of us, personally, had to go through the hiring process. However, the leader's role in this process is the personal care with which the hiring process is conducted.

There are several conditions under which a position may become available. A person may leave a job permanently, opening a slot for a new permanent employee. A person may leave a position temporarily due to illness or other such event, but will be returning eventually to the original position, which means the opening is considerably constrained. Finally, the position may be a new one, resulting in the widest set of possibilities for hiring. In all of these situations, the steps that must be followed are similar. Analyze the job, create an accurate job description, recruit applicants, select applicants to review, interview finalists, make the selection.

Analyze the Job

The first step in hiring is to make sure you know what qualities, attributes, and skills you wish the new hire to possess. But before you can know those things, you need to know exactly what you want the new hire to do. In order to know that, you must analyze the job.

Begin by imagining what you would ask this person to do on the first day of school. What assignment would he or she be given. What would you like this person to be able to handle—with minimum need for support from you. But this is only the beginning. Ideally, you need to look ahead for the next five years. What would the ideal hire be able to handle over this span of time? Will the job change measurably during that time, and what flexibility would the new person have to possess in order to still be an excellent employee after that five-year period?

It is not enough simply to list the duties of the job, without also describing what it means to carry out these duties successfully. A complete listing of behaviors and desired results should accompany a job description. Clearly, the job description cannot be completed in isolation. You must also think about the domains that must accompany the job. Some important domains to investigate, once the job has been defined adequately, might involve the following:

Education: What is the minimum formal education that will allow the job to be satisfactorily filled? What level of education would you prefer?

Training/Experience: What programs, apprenticeships, life experience, or job experience would provide the best background experiences for the candidate?

Skills/Abilities: This must correlate most closely with the job description. If the job description is adequate, then the skills necessary for success will be nearly self-evident. For example, if the job description calls for the use of technology in teaching the discipline, a candidate with experience with common software usage, webpage building, Internet and Intranet use, as well as the ability to absorb new software quickly, would be very attractive.

Physical Characteristics: Sometimes this category is very important. Does the job call for long periods of standing? Does the job entail speaking for extended periods of time? Does the job demand that the person begin work extremely early in the morning? Does the job call for some level of strength or size?

Knowledge: Is there specialized knowledge that the candidate needs to be able to employ in order to be successful?

Emotional Characteristics: Is there a need for the candidate to have a high threshold of frustration. A high "flash" point? The patience of a saint? In many teaching situations, emotional stability is nearly as important as knowledge of the discipline. Understanding age-appropriate behavior may be crucial to a successful teaching experience.

Recruiting Applicants

The methods for recruiting applicants vary from school to school. Some schools rely heavily upon unsolicited applications. Others rely upon commercial placement services. Still others use the word-of-mouth system. Advertisements for the job can be placed in the local newspaper, in papers with nationwide readership, in specialized educational publications, or in discipline-specific publications. Whatever the manner of solicitation, there will be many more applicants than positions.

I have found that it pays to keep track, over several year's time, of the very best prospects, so that when a position opens, you have a ready supply of teachers who might be interested in the position. Thus, if the budget allows for it, interviewing candidates, even when a position may not come open for two or more years, can be a judicious process.

Selecting Applicants

You will need to use a system for keeping track of your interactions with the applicants. Most applicants will not fit the qualifications you are seeking. A polite post card is usually enough, acknowledging the receipt of the application with the message that, if there is further interest from your point of view, you will be in touch. Lately, however, my experience has been that applicants follow up with a phone call to "check" to see if the resume≥ arrived. If these calls begin to overwhelm you, an added inscription to please not follow up with a phone call may be in order.

For those candidates who are active, a file, which labels the date the application was received and a reply sent, is all that is needed. Then, as you make your way through the most promising resumes, it will be easy to note those which will make it to the final review process.

In order to make the final review process, I look for an application that is grammatically correct, organized, includes complete job history information, along with referral sources. Additionally, I look for a cover letter or resume that conveys the candidate's career objectives and understanding of the appropriateness of his or her background for the job at hand. Too often, I must deal with applications for a specific discipline, such as physics, where the candidate has had only one college physics course.

I also want to see the college transcript of the applicant. Someone who earned Cs in his or her major is unlikely to understand the discipline well enough to be able to teach it. The teaching profession has been saddled over the last several years with many candidates who are clearly not qualified to fill the job. Hopefully, as the demographics slowly change and the high school population levels off, fewer teachers will have to be added to the teacher corp and selectivity can increase. Of course, countering school-age population decline is the graying of the profession and the likelihood of large numbers of retirees during the next ten to fifteen years.

Unfortunately, some applicants are less than honest in their paperwork. In their zeal to secure an interview, there may be exaggerations or ways of conveying information which can lead to incorrect conclusions. Be wary of the following:

1. *Omitted information.* What was that candidate doing from 1979–1986, which does not appear on the resume? What do the initials of the college mean? Did the candidate graduate from a school or simply attend?
2. *Fluff.* Does the candidate supply an overabundance of "fluff"? That is, does the candidate list membership in an overabundance of professional societies, including the National Geographic Association? While it may indeed be true, it could also point to a tendency to need to "embellish" when such is not needed.
3. *Hidden Work History.* Does the work history make sense? Did the candidate hold nine jobs in the last eight years? Is there an explanation as to why the candidate has left previous jobs? If it was for

advancement, did the following position actually show an advancement?

The Interview

This is the best part of hiring a new employee. It is also the most crucial. Not only is the candidate trying to "sell" him or herself, you must also be "selling" your department and institution. You should want to make all candidates leave the interview hoping they will be offered the job. To do this, you must first set the candidate at ease. The questions you ask must be structured to get the candidate talking. A good set of questions, based upon the STAR (Situation, Task, Action, and Result) procedure are available in a short article by Pawlas (1995). More importantly, you are building a team, and you must think about how all the individuals will work together and act synergistically. Hiring is one of the most important functions you can perform in teambuilding.

Using a written set of questions during the actual interview allows you to keep the interview heading in the direction you choose. You can also use the questions sheet for note taking during the interview. During the interview, look for some piece of the candidate's career that is important to know, but did not appear on the application or resume. It is best not to have the candidate speculate on how he or she would behave in the new institution. Rather, you want the candidate to be concrete about what he or she has done in the previous positions. How did they master situations that were difficult? To what do they aspire? Proceed from the formal to the informal in your question structure. For most people, the past is less threatening than the present, so begin with questions about the distant past before working your way to the present.

The following set of questions is adapted from a longer set produced by the National Association of Independent Schools.

Personal Questions designed to allow the candidates to talk about themselves:

1. What has meant the most to you in your previous job?
2. Who influenced your decision to teach? What was your teacher role-model like? Are there characteristics and qualities of that teacher that you now emulate?
3. Why is it important for you to teach what you do? What personal satisfaction do you gain from teaching?

4. What part of your subject do you like teaching the most? the least?
5. How do you characterize yourself as a thinker?
6. What kinds of things are important to you in choosing a job?
7. What has led you to wish to leave your present position?
8. What is the most important personal attribute of a good teacher?
9. What, in your background, makes you especially qualified for this job? Are there specific experiences that have prepared you for teaching?
10. What about you will help us improve the quality of life in our school?
11. How do you go about admitting that you made a mistake?
12. If, five years from now, you were able to look back, what would you be looking for that would define your success?
13. What would you like to be doing five years from now?
14. How do you renew and refresh yourself? What do you do to relax?
15. Tell me a "success" story from your last job.
16. What is your "hidden agenda" as a teacher?
17. What kinds of things make you frustrated?
18. What personality characteristics do you find annoying about others?
19. With what kind of student do you work best? What kind of adults?
20. What do you expect from your colleagues?
21. Tell me what you're reading presently? What's on the bookshelf next to your bed or beside your favorite reading chair?
22. Describe your ideal teaching position. Try to tell me everything you can about it, from students, to subject, to benefits. Anything that comes to mind, whether it be possible or not.

Classroom-Related Questions designed to clarify how the teacher functions as a teacher: These questions will uncover the tacit side of the teacher's understanding of his or her work. However, simply because candidates speak forcefully about his or her beliefs, there is always the possibility that their actions in the classroom will not match their theories of teaching. Thus, it is important that you sometimes ask follow-up questions which call for concrete examples. "What would I be looking for if I were to come into your classroom and see you . . . ?" This makes the candidate move from the realm of theory and into the realm of application and action.

1. Tell me about a project or assignment that went especially well for you in the last year or so.

2. What was a tough problem with which you had to deal recently and how did you resolve it?
3. How do you know your students are learning?
4. Describe your classroom style for me. What would I be looking for if I entered your classroom to verify this?
5. What is your ideal grading situation?
6. What does academic excellence mean to you in the classroom?
7. How do you select material for teaching?
8. What technology do you use in your teaching?
9. In your field, what do you expect students to know when they leave your classroom at the end of the year?
10. How do you deal with a department head or administrator who disagrees with your policies in the classroom?
11. Have you ever had to work with a learning disabled student? What did you do to help that student learn?
12. Do you teach content or skills?
13. How do you teach so that a student has some control over his or her learning?
14. Where would you say you are on the continuum of individual work versus collaboration in the classroom?
15. Are there times when you have designed a lesson so that you are just as much a learner as the students? Tell me what you did.
16. How have gender issues affected your teaching? How do you work to have a multicultural classroom?
17. What area of teaching do you feel you still need to work on or you wish to address?

Questions Dealing with Situations and Individuals External to the Classroom:

1. What means of parent communication do you use for the children in your classes?
2. Describe a difficult parent conference. How did you handle it? What, if anything, would you have done differently?
3. To what degree do you believe a classroom teacher should be involved in the school outside of the classroom?
4. What interests do you have outside of your professional life? What aspects of your professional life are also external to your immediate school? (Conferences, seminars, writing, painting, composing, serving community needs, etc.)

The following questions involve **short role play situations or dilemmas.**

1. I'm going to pretend to be a student who didn't do the assigned work last night. Work with me as you normally would as the classroom teacher.
2. Today is the day before the first major exam in the subject you teach. Show me how you would go about teaching that day.
3. Today is Thursday, and you are planning to give a major test tomorrow, Friday. As you begin class, three boys come to you and explain they won't be able to take the test tomorrow, because they have a soccer game that was rescheduled two days ago for Friday. What do you do?
4. You are in your end of the year review session with your Principal. What two or three things would he tell you about your work? What two or three things would he want you to work on?
5. You happen to be working within ear-shot of the payphone. You hear a student talking loudly with her mother about your class. What might you hear her say?

The following questions are useful once the candidate as had an opportunity to spend **time on site**.

1. What have you seen at our school today, or what do you know about it that makes you think the "fit" is right?
2. What are your general impressions about the students, people, facilities you have seen today?
3. Where else have you applied for this type of work, and do you have any current status there?
4. What is the most important thing for us to cover in your interview today? Have we done that? Is there anything you want to make sure I know before you leave today?
5. What are your plans for the future?

Ideally, the candidate should spend some time with each of the people who have to make the final decision. Obviously, the department head is one key person in the hiring of the candidate. But there also needs to be time spent with other senior administrators, such as the Principal, Head of School, Athletic Director, Head of Residential Life, if this is a boarding program, peer teachers, students, when possible. Also, candidates should teach a sample lesson for which they have had some time to prepare. (If this is not possible, the candidate can send a video tape of his or her work in the classroom at the present job.)

In finishing the interview, remember that the candidate may not be in a situation where he or she must have the job you offer. Job interviews are usually two-way streets. The candidate may be in just as much a "buying" mode as you are. So you must always be working to put the best side of the job forward and to make the candidate overwhelmingly desire the position you are offering.

Making the Selection

After all the appropriate people have had a chance to interview the candidate, immediate feedback about first impressions is best. Even a short e-mail or phone conversation while the candidate is on-site can be helpful to the person in charge of the interview. During the wind-up phase, it may be crucial to signal the candidate that he or she is strongly desired. If fact, you may wish to make the job offer at the end of the interview. But, just as likely, you may want to signal the candidate that, while he or she is certainly well-qualified, there are other candidates who are also finalists.

After conferring with each of those involved in the decision, the candidates should be rank ordered. First, contact only the top candidate. Make the offer, and give a reasonable time for decision making, usually a few days. If the candidate declines the offer, you should move to the second-highest ranked candidate. Once a candidate has accepted the offer and has returned a written contract, you should notify all the other candidates that you have made a selection and thank them for their time and interest. At this point, you may receive a phone call or a note from rejected candidates inquiring about why they did not measure up. It is helpful to be honest with these people, so that they might be able to work on those areas of weakness.

For example, if candidates have little or no interest in using technology for teaching, they probably will not be seriously considered in today's teaching market. Let them know that they should work on this area of weakness. However, letting a candidate know that the reason they were not selected was because they were humorless, unexciting in the classroom, boring, or worse, will be a much harder conversation and, perhaps, impossible to convey adequately. Such feedback is better left to those in more frequent contact with the candidate.

Bibliography and References

Argyris, Chris, and Schon, Donald (1989). *Theory in practice: Increasing professional effectiveness.* San Francisco: Jossey-Bass.

Ash, Mary Kay (1984). *On people management.* New York: Warner Books.

Averill, J. R. (1982). *Anger and aggression: An essay on emotion,* New York: Springer-Verlag.

Bennis, Warren, and Nanus, Burt (1985). *Leaders: The strategies for taking charge.* New York: Harper and Row.

Clark, Cynthia, et. al. (1996). Collaboration as dialogue: Teacher and researchers engaged in conversation and professional development. *American Educational Research Journal, 33.*

Clement, Mary C. (1997). How to interview and hire the best new teachers, Tips for Principals. *NASSP* (April).

Csikszentmihalyi M. (1990). *Flow: The psychology of optimal experience.* New York: Harper and Row.

Depree, Max (1997). *Leading without power: Finding hope in serving community.* San Francisco: Jossey-Bass.

Deutsch, Morton (1949). A theory of cooperation and competition. *Human Relations, 2,* 129–152.

———. (1990). Sixty years of conflict. *International Journal of Conflict Management, 1,* 237–263.

Dyer, William G. (1987). *Team building: Issues and alternatives.* Reading, MA: Addison-Wesley.

Grier, Terry (1996). "Chartering project teams: What to do and how to do it. *NASSP Bulletin, 80,* 96–102.

Guzzo, Richard A., Salas, E., et al. (1995). *Team effectiveness and decision making in organizations.* San Francisco: Jossey-Bass

Hackman, J. R. and Oldham, G. (1976). Motivation through design of work: A test of a theory. *Organizational Behavior and Human Performance, 16(2),* 250–279.

Katzenbach, John, and Smith, Douglas (1993). *The wisdom of teams.* Boston: Harvard Business School Press.

Kohn, A. (1992). *No contest: The case against competition.* Boston: Houghton Mifflin.

Larson, Carl E., and LaFasto, Frank M. J. (1989). *Teamwork: What must go right/what can go wrong.* Newbury Park, CA: Sage Pub.

Levesque, Joseph (1996). *Complete manual for recruiting, hiring, and retaining quality employees.* Englewood Cliffs, N.J.: Prentice-Hall.

Leavitt, H., and Lipman-Blumen, J. (1995). Hot Groups. *Harvard Business Review* (July–August), 109–116.

Levine, Sarah (1989). *Promoting adult growth and development in schools: The promise of professional development.* Boston: Allyn and Bacon.

Maeroff, Gene I. (1993). Building teams to rebuild schools. *Phi Delta Kappan.* (March), 512–519.

Mayo, Elton (1993). *The human problems of an industrial civilization.* Boston: Division of Research, Graduate School of Business Administration, Harvard University.

Parker, Glenn (1991). *Team players and teamwork.* San Francisco: Jossey-Bass.

Pawlas, George (1995). "The structured interview: Three dozen questions to ask prospective teachers. *NASSP Bulletin, 79,* No. 567, 62–65.

Richl, Carolyn, and Sipple, John (1996). Making the most of time and talent: Secondary school organizational climates, teaching task environments and teacher commitment. *American Educational Research Journal, 33.*

Senge, Peter (1990). *The fifth discipline: The art and practice of the learning organization.* New York: Doubleday Dell Publishing.

Sergiovanni, Thomas J. (1992). *Moral leadership: Getting to the heart of school improvement.* San Francisco: Jossey-Bass.

Tannen, Deborah (1990). *You just don't understand: Men and women in conversation.* New York: Ballantine Books.

Tannen, Deborah (1994). *Talking from 9 to 5: How women's and men's conversational styles affect who gets heard, who gets credit, and what gets done at work:* New York: William Morrow.

Tennant, Mark, and Pogson, Philip (1995). *Learning and change in the adult years: A developmental approach.* San Francisco: Jossey-Bass.

Tjosvold, Dean (1986). *Working together to get things done.* Lexington, MA: DC Heath.

Ury, William (1986). *Getting past no: Negotiating your way from confrontation to cooperation.* New York: Bantam.

Yates, Martin John (1987). *Hiring the best: A manager's guide to effective interviewing.* Boston: Bob Adams, Inc.

Chapter 4

Effective Communication

Person to Person Communication

The most important skill for any team leader is the ability to communicate. This seems self-evident, since all of us have been involved with teams and groups throughout our education and our work lives. However, the area of communication is probably the most problematic one for any group leader. As you will see in John's case, there are often times when we need to tell people something they don't want to hear and, probably, we don't want to tell them. When you must approach someone about an issue in any way related to "bad news," you will discover that you will be unable to say everything you'd like to say.

The reason is, no matter how well rehearsed your script may be, until you are in a face-to-face conversation, it is only a one-sided script. As soon as you speak your first sentence, there is no way to fully predict what the person to whom you are speaking is going to say next. And there is even smaller chance that you will be able to know what he or she is thinking, but not saying. In the light of this fact, it is important to have a model for how to conduct effective conversations in which participants truly communicate, that is, to engage in conversation where the participants hear, and understand, one another.

Before we go any further with communication theory and possible methods to improve your communication skills, try your hand at the following case. In attacking this case, try to answer spontaneously. Respond just as you would had the case been a real situation for you. Don't over-intellectualize or over-analyze the case. Shoot from the heart, so to speak.

Anyone who's been in a situation like this knows that the conversation with John is going to be quite difficult. The usual result is either misunderstanding or defensiveness. We ask ourselves why the other person is being

---

John's Case

John is a teacher of long standing in your department. He is a valued member of the department and is widely regarded as one of the most respected, and demanding, teachers in the school. Two weeks ago, the Principal asked you to spend some time in John's classroom, because parents have been complaining that John is too demanding and has "gone off the deep end" with some of his demands. You mentioned this to John, and his response was to ask you to see for yourself by visiting one of his classes.

This morning you took John up on his offer and you witnessed the following interaction. John, when handing back a test from the previous week, said to one of the girls, "Mary, I hope that you will do some serious studying during the next week. This test was pure drivel and I'm not going to waste my time on some blonde airhead. You'd better straighten up of you'll flunk this course, and I mean that. In my book, there is no reason why you shouldn't be working every day on this course. There is no excuse for being unprepared."

The girl tried to reply that during the last three weeks she had had to work extra hours at her job in the family store because of her mother's illness, but John would hear nothing of it. Later in the class, John made two references in a fairly negative tone of voice to "students who think work is more important than school." And later he asked all those who thought that there was any activity more important than studying to seriously reconsider why they were still in school. He speculated that anyone who thought this way needed to be honest with him or her self, leave school, and take a permanent paying job.

You are decided you had to speak to John about this outburst and when he knocks on your office door at 3:30 P.M., your first words to

---

so difficult. Why don't he recognize that he is doing something wrong and give it up? We tend to dismiss the other person as someone who is either obstinate, out to lunch, or consciously being a pain in the side.

The likelihood is very low that John will come into your office and say, "I was so wrong to be dogmatic about studying when you were visiting my class yesterday. And I know I must have embarrassed Mary terribly. She doesn't need my prodding and pricking to do the work. No, she is very self-motivated and, if I had it to do over again, I would simply ignore her lack of test preparation. In the long run, I probably did more harm than good by getting so worked up."

Rather, John is likely to deny doing anything harmful in that class. You can almost hear his logic. "I am the standard keeper here. So many teachers let students get away with murder when it comes to testing and deadlines. Why, there are teachers who regularly give retests. Such coddling is one sure reason why schools are so terrible and why the students today are a bunch of know-nothing, pleasure seekers. It is my duty, if need be, to be harsh with some of the students, because in the long run, I'm doing them a favor. The school and society have gotten soft on kids. It's only when students meet teachers like me that they can begin working again. Additionally, I like to consider that when something of a personal nature happens in my class between a child and me, you don't need get involved. It will blow over in a day or two."

The Johns of the world have all the answers and aren't about to listen to any department head about daily classroom operation when it comes to discipline and motivation. But that is exactly what they must do. Teachers who intimidate students or insult them or antagonize them, need to be confronted and made to think closely about what they are doing. I think the rest of this chapter will help those who are having a hard time helping themselves.

Specifically, you will have to decide where to focus, the test incident itself or the follow-up sarcasm of the teacher? You'll need a mechanism to get John's thinking out into the open. In John's head, you can imagine the following thoughts: "This new department head is trying hard, but she doesn't really understand us yet. Kids respect tough teachers. They may give you a hard time, at first, but what they all need is a teacher version of 'Tough Love.'

"Students have to be pushed in order to do any work. This pushing will motivate them to work even harder. There must be no lessening of the pressure we exert upon the students.

"My task is to motivate the students to learn. I am not behaving sternly to win popularity contests, as many of my colleagues here do. I am doing this for their own good."

What follows is a strategy to help you better to communicate, to understand the patterns that are created over and over again in miscommunication, and to appreciate that the view of the situation by the other person may be completely opposite to yours and yet no less valid.

You must also distinguish between a difficult situation and outright conflict (Kushner, 1996). Difficult situations are short in duration and usually involve single events. Conflicts, on the other hand, are long-term situations. To deal with a conflict takes much more time than any difficult situation.

You've Got to Listen to Be Heard

Whenever we work with another person we are entering into a "competition" for listening (Jentz, 1996). Think about the usual way in which a conversation that involves some tension occurs. Reflect back to the John case. Suppose the leader approached John in the following manner:

Leader: John, I'd like to talk to you for a minute or two. In today's class, I noticed you were awfully gruff with Mary. In fact, I think you were somewhat sarcastic in your approach. Do you think such behavior is OK?

John: I was not sarcastic.

Leader: Oh yes, you were. I saw it and heard it. I'm not trying to be judgmental here, but I think she was upset by the way she was treated.

John: Well, you are mistaken. I might have been stern with her, but I certainly was not sarcastic. If anything, I was being thoughtful, using language that the students themselves use, when I addressed her. This is how she can relate to my demands.

Leader: You mean calling her an airhead was OK?

You get the picture. This conversation is going nowhere. It is doubtful that John has heard anything that the group leader has tried to say. Instead, he is thinking—every minute the leader is talking—about how he will defend himself, since he feels attacked by the leader's first statement. Meanwhile, the leader is not understanding why John has acted as he has and, certainly, has not made any headway in getting him to change his behavior. In other words, both the initiator of the conversation and the receiver are giving information and requesting that the other person listen. Such conversations are all too common.

The competition for listening is observable. In the first statement, the leader has made a tacit request for John to listen. But John, predictably, does not. Instead, he responds by denying the accusation. Such denial is John's tacit request for the leader to listen to him. But, also predictably, the leader is not listening to John. Instead, the leader is thinking to himself that John is so obtuse that he doesn't even see his sarcasm when it is so blatant. John and the group leader are two trains passing in the night.

As the prime figure in this conversation and as the person who is holding the conversation for a particular purpose, the leader needs to create a structure for listening to occur. Suppose the initiator realized, at the outset, that John is unlikely to be listening. How could that realization help him or her to structure the conversation differently.

A simple way of viewing this is shown in Figure 4-1.

In this view, the initiator gives information and, as expected, the listener also gives information. It is at this point that the initiator breaks the competition for listening and tries to understand the situation as the listener understands it. The initiator tries to get inside the head and heart of the listener to see why their response makes sense.

Making sense is the goal of all effective communication. Communication that doesn't work, be it written or verbal, has at its core non-sense. You can hear non-sense in people's responses when they don't understand. "I don't understand what you mean?" "What is this saying?" "Where is she coming from?" "I just don't get it."

Figure 4.1 Parallel Conversations: No Understanding

1. Initiator:
Gives information and
requests to be heard

2. Receiver:
Gives information and
requests to be heard

3. Initiator:
Gives same information again
because the receiver hasn't "heard"
the message
etc.

4. Receiver:
Gives the same information
because the initiator
clearly hasn't heard.
etc.

In the typical interaction, both participants have, as their background thinking, the notion that there is something wrong with the thinking of the other person and that their task is to *correct* that thinking. Both actors in the conversational drama are thinking, "If only you could see things my way, you'd agree, in a New York minute, to do it my way." Your task, as the leader of the conversation, is to break that kind of confined thinking.

In giving negative information, the department head or team leader must understand the unspoken rules of conversation and why they must be broken. There are four major rules:

1. **Don't be concrete.**
2. **Don't express your feelings.**
3. **Don't give the impact on you.**
4. **Don't give quantities.**

1. Don't Be Concrete.

This may be due to the fact that we are educated and educated people tend to live in an abstract world. Figure 4.2 shows the typical abstraction ladder. Why would we want to break the culturally defined rule to be abstract? In this case, so that people knows what you saw. They don't have to agree with it, but they will be able to begin to understand what you are trying to tell

Figure 4.2 The Abstraction Ladder

	Wealth	Friendship
	Asset	Inference
↑	Team member	Professionalism
↑	Baseball	Your behavior
Increasing ↑	Outfielder	Your comments
abstraction ↑	Babe Ruth	Airhead

them, only when they can know what you saw . . . or what you *think* you saw.

2. Don't Express Your Feelings.

We live in a rational world. In such a world, feelings only get in the way of doing business. However, this rule should be broken, so the person knows the import to you of his or her offense. Are you miffed, irked, annoyed, very annoyed, angered, outraged? Knowing your level of concern is of great importance to the listener.

3. Don't Give the Impact on You.

Most often in a conversation the initiator gives the impact on the listener. "John, when you're sarcastic, you reduce your effectiveness as a teacher." Or " John, when you confront the students like that, you invariably lose their respect." But these are merely speculations. You cannot know the effect on John. You can only know the effect on you.

"John, when you called Mary an airhead, I was somewhat upset because it works against all that we have worked for as a department regarding teacher/student partnerships."

4. Don't Give Quantities.

You would have a difficult time saying: "John, when you called Mary an airhead and twice more referred to her poor test performance, I was somewhat upset because it works against all that we have worked for as a department regarding teacher/student partnerships."

As you can see in the last example statement above, the team leader has separated three different kinds of information: (1) what was seen, (2) what was felt, (3) what the impact was on him or her. We should supply all three kinds of information, so that we are not being judgmental. Faculty will know when you are not being honest with them. It is very difficult for them to believe that you trust them, if you are giving them the third degree and your hands are shaking. However, with practice you should be able to listen more effectively and think about both the conversation process and content while you are in the midst of it. This is an example of what Argyris calls reflection-in-action. There is more on Argyris's work in Chapter 9 on Evaluation.

In astronaut training, many conversations can become quite heated because of the importance decisions and practices may have upon the success of the mission. The training stresses that the astronauts should focus on the processes occurring during the conversation rather than on content (Gilbert, 1996). With practice you will be able to react instinctively to the process as it occurs and, at the same time, remain focused on what is being said.

The simplest way to make sure that all three types of information are being give is to use the following formula, first described by Robert Bolton (1979).

When_____.

> Be specific.
>
> Be concrete
>
> Be quantitative

I Feel_____.

> Give primary feelings.
>
> Reflect the intensity of the feelings.

Because_____.

> Give the tangible impact on yourself.

Now, having advised you to use a formula, let me caution you that this is not easy to accomplish. Instead, you should know how you would like to open the conversation with this format, and alter the format when circumstances call for it. However, since you are opening the conversation, there is every reason to believe that you will be able to get at least this far into the conversational model as presented above.

One of the great failings of most difficult conversations is that we do not test out our inferences. Both parties in the conversation make assumptions and inferences about what the other is saying (and has said), but neither party takes the time to check to see if their assumptions are valid.

For example, suppose you saw one of your teachers getting into his or her car in the parking lot twenty minutes before school was dismissed for the day and you knew that that teacher had a last-period class. You probably would make the assumption that the teacher dismissed the class early and was not meeting his or her obligations. However, it may be that the teacher had an emergency phone call from the hospital that his or her spouse had been injured and they needed his or her presence immediately. Usually, the department head does not want to ask the teacher why he or she was leaving early, because the answer *might actually be* that the teacher was shirking required duty. And then something would have to be done about it. So, instead, issues such as this go unmentioned, but not unrecorded. The knowledge of this incident is part of the department head's "lens" through which he or she views this teacher.

Yet, by behaving in this manner, the department head is actually depriving the teacher of the information he or she needs in order to alter his or her behavior and to grow as a teacher. Instead, there might be no growth and the leader will hold the teacher responsible for the lack of growth in this area of professionalism.

The Framework for Listening

In conducting a difficult discussion, there is no guarantee about what direction the conversation will take. Many times, a statement made during such conversations can be taken as an attack by the listener. In the following short dialogue, see if you can detect the two possible points of view which stem from the single event.

Department Head: Tom, I'm glad you were able to stop by. I'd like to talk with you about something I saw yesterday. I noticed that you were leaving the school building and getting in your car at 2:35 P.M. and I thought that was when you had a class. Was I mistaken?

Tom: Oh, I had to take care of some business and so I gave the class an assignment to be completed in the library.

Department Head: But our departmental rules say that you must meet every class every day.

Tom: Well, I did that. I just gave them an independent assignment to complete. I don't see the difference between what I did and my usual practice of using the last fifteen minutes of the large block for conference and small group work. I don't think I violated the spirit of our policies.

Department Head: But I think you did.

Tom: And I think I didn't, so I guess we'll have to agree to disagree. And I hate to tell you this, but I was making a run to the local ice-house to get the Dry-Ice, so I could practice before I give the laboratory demonstration tomorrow. You had said you would pick it up on your way to work this morning and, when I saw that you hadn't, I didn't want to confront you with your forgetfulness, especially in front of the rest of the department. I was trying to be helpful and cover for your inability to do some of the more essential tasks around here.

Department Head: Oh, no. I thought . . . well I guess I owe you an apology. Sorry . . . By the way, what do you mean my inability to do some of the essential tasks?

As you can see both people see the event in totally different light. Tom thinks he is being helpful, while the Department Head thinks Tom has been deceitful. The different data that each has at their disposal lead them to these conclusions. The department head sees

1. Tom leaving early;
2. that a class is not being covered;
3. hears the words "inability to do the essentials."

Meanwhile Tom sees

1. Going out of his way to arrange for a library time period
2. Being helpful by getting materials himself
3. Tone is low key and authentic
4. Tom is open in his interaction.

Figure 4.3 The Framework For Listening

Giving Information: Questions	Testing Information: Questions
What's the problem here?	What's the meaning to her/him?
What's wrong with her/him?	What's the implicit hope, intent, or fear?
What's wrong with this situation?	What's the central feeling? What's it connected to?
How will I fix this?	Where is s/he in sense making?

Here is a perfect case where the participants in a difficult conversation do not check on their inferences. As Barry Jentz explains it (Jentz, 1996), there is only one side of the framework for listening being used in this conversation. See Figure 4.3.

The left hand side is where almost all difficult discussions get lodged and remain, resulting in a lack of true meeting of the minds. However, when at least one of the participants works to use the components on the right hand side of the table, the conversation has a much higher probability of being effective, resulting in true understanding between the conversants.

The way to do this is to start by testing the information/data that you hear. The "Yes you did. No, I did not" routine is not useful because there is no testing of information and thus no true listening or understanding. A good listener, who is trying to break the competition for listening, will test the information he or she hears. In making such a test, the listener is not trying to solve the problem. Instead, he or she is trying to keep his or her remarks very close to the original statement which was made. Such a remark should be given in tentative terms phrased as a short inquiry with a definite end to it.

Here is how the conversation between Tom and the Department head might have gone, if the department head had been using the suggested framework for listening.

Department Head: Tom, I'm glad you were able to stop by. When I saw you get in your car and leave school at 2:35 P.M. yesterday I was mildly confused because I thought you had a class then and I'm supposed to make sure all classes are covered.

Tom. Oh, I had to take care of some business, so I gave the class an assignment to be completed in the library.

Department Head: Was this business personal?

Tom: Oh, no. It was school related.

Department Head: How so?

Tom: Well, I wanted to get the Dry-Ice so I could practice for the laboratory demonstration I'm giving tomorrow.

Department Head: That's right. I forgot to get that for you this morning on my way to work. I'm sorry.

Tom: So, I figured I'd just go and get it. I usually use the last fifteen minutes of the large block class for conferences and small group work so I didn't think this violated any of our policies.

Department Head: And on top of it you felt let down because I'd forgotten to get the materials.

Tom: Well, kind of. But I didn't want to say anything to embarrass you in front of the rest of the department.

Department Head: You know Tom, my feelings won't be hurt when you call me on something I said I would do. But, when you leave the class without my knowledge I'm concerned because I'm not doing what I have been entrusted to do . . . making sure all classes are met.

Tom: Are you saying I should not have gone to get the Dry-Ice?

Department Head: No, I'm saying you should not have left your class. You could have gone to get the dry ice after school had ended.

Tom: But, I was in a hurry to begin my practice as soon as school ended at 2:50.

Department Head: I understand that you were trying to be helpful, but I'd like you to meet your class for the entire period. And don't be timid in reminding me of what I've forgotten to do. I would then figure out some way to take care of it. Can you do that in the future?

Tom: Well, of course I can.

Department Head: Great. I meant it when I said that I appreciate being reminded about things I've forgotten to do.

You can see, in this second dialogue, that the department head has practiced good listening skills. He or she tests out the tacit assumptions. The testing is done without straying from the original statements and the responses are in the form of short, inquiry statements. In this way, Tom hears that the department head is still inquiring and is not accusatory. The department head also tests out how Tom might have been feeling. He or she is trying to put himself or herself into Tom's shoes. The desire to understand how Tom has seen the situation is the first concern of the department head. Once that has been understood, the department head makes a request for Tom to listen. But since the competition for listening has been broken, Tom is ready

Figure 4.4 Easy Versus Difficult Interactions

Easy	Difficult
You have power.	You have no power.
You are competent.	You are not competent.
You can easily define the task.	You cannot define the task easily.
The listener is passive.	The listener is an unwilling participant.
The listener avoids conflict.	The listener invites conflict, even causes conflict.
You do not fear rejection.	You have serious fear of rejection.

to hear. The department head has been effective in letting Tom know that classes need to be covered in their entirety, but has done so in a manner which leaves Tom his dignity and opens up some new avenues of insight for the department head about his or her personal behavior.

In all conversations there is a difference in the degree of difficulty that you either anticipate or know to be real. Figure 4.4 shows some factors that will make a conversation easy or difficult.

Group Communications

While it is essential to have good one-on-one communication skills, it is also important to be able to communicate to the entire department or team as well as to other groups with whom you might have contact. There are four main concepts to keep in mind when engaged in such communication.

1. *Keep it simple.* If it can be written down in a page, then try to reduce it to several bulleted highlights. Don't read anything to a group that they can read for themselves. In your memos, you should be clear and concise. The best way to make sure that your communications are clear is to try them out on someone who doesn't know the business of your group. A willing spouse or good friend might be available to read what you've written not so much for truth, but for clarity of message. Inevitably, because you will are much closer to the policy, event, or request you are making than most in your group, you might gloss over important details and give short shrift to important subtleties. An outsider's input can be useful in preventing this.

2. *Know the audience.* If you are speaking with your department and you know they are hostile to the topic you know you need to advance, then be prepared to handle the battle. If you know the meeting you are about to have will take at least an hour and everyone is chaffing at the bit to get home, know that you will have to condense what you're going to say, or else, create a plan where the discussion can take place over multiple meetings.

3. *Be prepared.* It is far better to have more than the needed data on a particular topic, than it is to be caught without the relevant documents. Whenever you stand at the front of a group, you can't know all the questions that might be asked. This does not mean you have to answer a particular question, if you aren't ready to do so, but the impact of being able to do so on the spot will bolster your image of understanding and knowledge in the department domain.

4. *Choose your words carefully.* Elgin (1987) gives a good example of what she calls "Trojan Horses " of conversation in the following three sentences.

1. I'm so glad you won that award.
2. I'm so glad you happened to win that award.
3. I'm so glad you managed to win that award.

Clearly, the first sentence is a true compliment, while the second and third have hidden implications. These statements begin with negative presuppositions. It may be true that once in awhile, the speaker doesn't recognize such an insult is buried in the words that are being using. However, a skillful leader makes sure that such hidden meanings are not part of his or her interaction with others.

Telephone communication

If you are like most group leaders, the telephone is both your biggest headache and your biggest ally. Here are ten tips to help you make better use of your telephone.

1. *When you must telephone, prepare in advance.* Get all of the pertinent documents together from your files *before* you make the call. Think about all the possible questions that might be asked, so that you will have some response ready. It may be that that response is "I don't really know," but at least by thinking about the issue in advance your "I don't know "can sound authoritative.

2. *Hold your tongue.* Try to let the person you are calling do most of the talking. Remember, they probably have been thinking about the issue for some time and need to get their thinking into the open. The competition for listening will be overwhelming in such a telephone call. This is reason to wait until the caller has finished.

3. *Concentrate.* Don't be reading your e-mail messages or correcting papers. Treat the conversation as if the person were physically in front of you. In fact, telephone conversations are good places to practice the framework for listening.

4. *Visualize the speaker.* Make a mental picture of what the person's face must look like when asking you a question or making a request. Does it seem hostile? docile? neutral? Is the person happy with the conversation so far?

5. *Don't interrupt.* Let the speaker continue until there is a natural pause in the flow of the dialogue on the speaker's part. Then, begin by using some verbal clue that will inform the listener that you have been listening to what was said.

6. *Take notes.* Record everything that was said and file it away so that later reference can be made to the conversation, if need be. Don't trust your memory. If a phone number is exchanged, make sure your write down the meaning of that number. Is it the home phone? the office? the fax? the car phone?

7. *Ask questions.* When it is your turn to speak, asking a question lets the listener know you've been listening. In addition, it allows you to find out more about the issue at hand. Without body language and facial expressions upon which to rely , you are working with only one-third of your sense-making systems.

8. *Don't jump to conclusions.* Test your assumptions. Do not attribute intention without verifying that intention. Employ the framework for listening suggestions.

9. *Listen between the lines.* Try to figure out what the speaker is really trying to say. Test out what you think this is. Don't guess. Respond when you hear the person's feelings by saying, "I can hear that your are irritated." "I can hear that you are frustrated." This kind of reading between the lines will also help the listener know that you are understanding his or her position. However, just because you understand the person's position, it does not mean that you have to agree or acquiesce.

10. *Practice.* Keep this list of ten rules taped to the cradle of your telephone. You will then be able to see it every time you are talking on the telephone. Make use of the skills that are at your disposal.

E-Mail

Given the tremendous expansion in the use of e-mail in our schools and work places, new rules of communication behavior are in order. Of course, everyone should use the same level of civility as in a person-to-person or telephone conversation. But people don't. It is simply too easy to quickly get onto the keyboard and rip off a quick riposte to counter an assumed attack. The effective leader holds this tendency in abeyance.

Take some time to think about what you wish to say. Thus, it is crucial to make sure that you wouldn't mind if your message were posted to everyone's e-mail box in the school. Any message you send can be saved, or printed out and distributed. If you do mind, then use the telephone or meet in person. Don't put anything into writing that you wish to remain confidential.

E-mail also gives an easy way to copy many people on a given message. While this is a great advantage, because it allows you to easily keep many people informed, it also generates a lot more mail to be read. If you follow these general rules, you will save yourself a tremendous amount of time.

E-Mail Rule 1

"I feel no obligation to respond to a message on which I am one of the copied. Though, if I feel like it, I may respond. I will always respond to message sent directly to me."

E-Mail Rule 2

"I will not copy all my team members when I have a bone to pick with my supervisor." Too often, the group leader sees the e-mail copy system as a way to let his or her group know that he or she is fighting the good fight. So, a mail message that should have been between the principal and the department head or team leader, now, is a public gauntlet thrown down in front of all the electronic eyes in the community.

E-Mail Rule 3

"I must always be aware of what the e-mail 'sounds' like, because tone is easily misunderstood." Calling your associates friendly nicknames or pulling their collective legs is usually not understood in writing. Unfortunately, people can misunderstand the tone of the e-mail. While you may have a smile on your face, as you write what you think is a tremendously witty message, the reader may have a frown on his or her face upon reading it. Keep the tone of your messages neutral. If you receive an e-mail, which you think has a negative tone to it, pick up the phone and call the sender to find out. Don't make assumptions.

Summary

True communication occurs when the listener hears what the sender intends. When you are the listener, as you will be on most occasions, the sender will feel much better about any further conversations with you if he or she has the impression that you are listening and actually hearing what is being communicated. This takes energy and focus on your part. It takes practice and fearlessness to try active listening. But there are no greater rewards in leading a group than when the individuals in the group communicate well with one another.

References and Bibliography

Bolton, Robert (1979). *People skills: How to assert yourself, listen to others and resolve conflicts.* Englewood Cliffs, NJ: Prentice-Hall.

Elgin, Suzette Haden (1987). *The last word on the gentle art of verbal self-defense.* New York: Prentice Hall.

Gilbert, Michael (1996). The Process Communication Model: Understanding Ourselves. *NASSP Bulletin, 80* (March).

Jentz, Barry, and Wofford, Joan (1979). *Leadership and learning: Personal change in a professional setting.* New York: McGraw-Hill Book.

Jentz, Barry. (1996) *It takes soft skills to succeed in a hard world: Communication as interpersonal learning.* Chestnut Hill MA: Leadership and Learning, Inc.

Kushner, Sister Remegia (1996). Some new ways of looking at conflict: Recognizing and dealing with it. *NASSP Bulletin, 80* (Jan.).

Nirenberg, Jesse (1988). *Getting through to people.* Englewood, NJ: Prentice-Hall.

Tannen, Deborah (1994). *Talking from 9 to 5: How women's and men's conversational styles affect who gets heard, who gets credit, and what gets done.* New York: William Morrow and Company.

Tannen, Deborah (1990). *You just don't understand: Women and men in conversation.* New York: Ballantine.

Chapter 5

Problem Solving:
Another Form of Communication

In the last chapter, you were introduced to some methods of interacting with another person or group to improve understanding. The reason we want to improve understanding is usually because there is a problem in which we are immersed. We are trying, desperately, to solve that problem. The quickest way to do this is to work directly with the people involved and to begin the discussions that will solve the problem. However, how do you know that you have adequately defined the problem that you are about to solve? What if you are completely off base in your approach? What if what you think is the problem is really not the problem. By rushing to judgment, you may have exacerbated the situation and now will have twice as difficult a task to right the wrong.

In this chapter, you will learn how to approach a problem in a manner least likely to cause future problems. By refusing to rush toward "Quick Fixes," you will be able to get to the heart of the problem and take effective action. You will be treating the cause and not the symptoms.

The first step in problem solving is to sit with the problem for awhile. Mull it over, analyze it, live with it for a few days. In doing so, you will have a much better understanding of the depth of the problem and its subtleties. Too often, department heads feel it is their job to solve problems. Many of you probably became department heads because you have a knack for solving problems, and that skill was recognized by an administrator who appointed you to the head position. Yet being a quick problem solver may not be the best skill to develop.

Just as the tale of the tortoise and the hare makes the point that speed does not always win the race, so too should a leader be wary of acting too quickly when faced with a problem. Think about the nervous parent who when asked by her nine-year-old, "Mommy where did I come from?" immediately runs for the sex-ed books and launches into the hows, whys, and whens of sexuality, when all the child wanted to know was if she came from Ohio. Precisely defining the problem will save you a tremendous amount of work and headache.

Sometimes solutions to problems come from actions that seem counterintuitive. That is, the obvious choice of action may not be the one that will solve the problem. When you are riding a bicycle and your wheels are close to slipping off the edge of the asphalt into the softer road shoulder, the tendency is to lean away from the edge. That is, you lean back out into the roadway. However, this action actually thrusts the bike further in the direction of the shoulder and will create exactly the undesired outcome, riding off the pavement. Instead, the rider needs to lean towards the shoulder of the road. This will cause the bike to move in the opposite direction or out towards the road surface, which is the desired outcome. Thus, the counterintuitive action wins the day. So don't be hesitant to live with the problem for a while and then proceed with an approach that may seem odd.

Solving problems also takes a very structured approach. Living with and analyzing a problem must be done in an orderly manner. The manner which works well follows the six steps listed in Exhibit 5.1

The following is a case study of a high school administrative group that did not function very well. By using the above six-step method, the principal was able to create a much more effective administrative team and, in so doing, substantially improve the academic life at the school. In this case, you will recognize the risk-taking behavior of the principal. Throughout the process, this principal felt the need to invoke the ideas of creative thinking and problem solving. The principal's plan was to loosen rigid patterns and provoke new patterns (de Bono, 1970) and to help the groups eventually generate meaningful policies. However, the first step the principal chose was to ask the groups to consider what matters in terms of individual events and activities (Fritz, 1991). The actors in the play need to move from the general to the specific. The principal uses these techniques very skillfully.

Exhibit 5.1 Six Steps for Problem Solving

1. Problem Recognition
2. Data Gathering
3. Data Analysis
4. Action Planning
5. Implementation
6. Evaluation and Problem Reformulation (If Needed)

Problem Solving Case Study: Solving A Problem That Cuts Across Multiple Groups

The principal of John F. Kennedy High School worked closely with a four-person administrative team, the Principal's Advisory Committee (PAC). It consisted of the Vice-Principal for Student Affairs (VPSA) and the Vice Principal for Academic Affairs (VPAA), the Director of Guidance and College Counseling, and the Director of School Safety. Each of the vice-principals led a group of faculty who were responsible for the operation of the school. The Vice-Principal for Academic Affairs chaired the committee of department heads, a group consisting of eight members heading each of the academic departments in the school along with the athletic department. Twenty percent of the department head's work load was devoted to serving as the head. The Vice-Principal for Student Affairs also led a group of eight faculty, one male and one female for each of the four grades, ninth through twelfth. These faculty spent half of their time serving as grade level advisers.

The problem that had arisen was complicated. The Vice-Principal for Academic Affairs had embarked on a curriculum study with the department heads and was now ready to make some recommendations to the principal. These recommendations, if implemented, would mean that the grade level advisers would have to monitor the new graduation requirements for their advisees. One of the recommendations was that the students take one term of economics and that the students take a term of art every year. Yet the VPAA felt that the academic program was the bailiwick of the department heads. They were the group that indirectly made academic policy by making recommendations to the principal, which the principal would usually endorse. However, the grade level advisers did not agree that the students should take a mandatory economics course. And while agreeing with the notion that students should take at least four terms of art, they did not want these courses mandated to one per year. This confused the department heads because they felt that the grade level advisers' job was to implement the curriculum that the department heads formulated and the principal recommended. Grade level advisers were not to question the development of curriculum.

However, the grade level advisers felt they were more than an advisory body. They felt they were the gatekeepers, so to speak. Their job was to make sure that the lives of their students did not spiral out of control. They felt the mandatory economics course would seriously affect many of the students, and they were solid in their opposition to any changes in the curriculum that would result in more student stress. Therefore, the principal called the following series of meetings over the next year to help all parties to the problem participate in its solution.

Meeting 1: Problem Recognition

The principal required that all of the members of the three groups set aside an entire week day to meet together to work on the issue of the specific curriculum changes. In addition, the principal wanted the groups to address the much larger problem of defining responsibility for school operation. All of the participants met in the library conference room and were expected to act as if they were off campus for the day. They were to give their entire attention to a set of five questions that the principal had designed. Each group spent the morning working alone on the principal's questions. Answering these questions was not an easy task for any of the groups and it took most of the day to complete the task. What follows are the questions and a summary of the answers to each question by group.

Question 1. What two or three things do you like about your group?

Principal's Advisory Committee

    a. We get things done and have a good time doing so.
    b. We feel we are capable, selfless, and hardworking in our commitment to the school and faculty.
    c. We have an investment in the success of all groups in the school.
    d. We feel we have a diversity of management styles that is healthy.

Department Heads

    a. We have good people serving as department heads.
    b. We trust each other's judgment.
    c. We have diverse talents, concerns, and experiences.

Grade Level Advisers

    a. We have a great deal of collegiality; we respect, support, trust one another. We know each other through shared experiences.
    b. We carry a healthy tension between subjectivity and objectivity.
    c. We care about all decisions that are made which affect students.

Question 2. What two or three items keeps your group from being as effective as you wish?

Principal's Advisory Committee

    a. Our different leadership styles often mean we give mixed messages.

b. Time pressures keep us in our own world and create tensions within our group.

c. We are not as deliberative as we should be.

d. Our visions are held hostage to fears of upsetting the faculty.

Department Heads

a. We have no common educational philosophy.

b. Each department might have different goals.

c. We are unclear about our influence.

d. Our agenda is not set by us. We are controlled by the VPAA.

e. Our decisions can be overturned, so we are always wary about going too far.

Grade Level Advisers

a. We are often too busy taking care of nonstudent tasks.

b. We talk too much in our meetings.

c. The nature of our job is rc-active rather than pro- active.

d. We let fear of legal action color our decisions.

Question 3. What actions do the other groups engage in that create problems for your group? Be as specific as possible.

Principal's Advisory Committee

a. The grade level advisers want to control the curriculum.

b. The grade level advisers and the department heads are too adversarial when working with us.

c. Other groups do not hold themselves accountable for the educational outcomes of the school at large. They have not developed standards against which to measure themselves.

Department Heads

a. Decisions arc made without our input by both other groups.

b. The principal's advisory committee is too isolated. Their meeting times make it impossible for us to attend, even if we were invited.

c. The faculty meetings that the PAC runs are neither very engaging nor creative.

Grade Level Advisers

a. Decisions are made without our consultation, and they affect our work.

b. We feel there is a lack of understanding about the younger students by the department heads. They concentrate only on the needs of the older students.

c. The principal's advisory committee employs a bureaucratic management style. This is wrong. We are a school, not a corporation.

Question 4. What actions does your group engage in that create problems for the other group? Again, be as specific as possible.

Principal's Advisory Committee

a. We do not consult all the relevant groups on topics of significance to them.

b. We have not made clear the lines of responsibility in our group.

c. We do not have a shared administrative identity.

d. We are seen as having a preconceived notion of outcome and then seeking affirmation of that notion.

Department Heads

a. Our vision is too limited.

b. We are way too territorial.

c. We question and undercut decisions by other groups.

d. We are not pro-active in identifying problems.

Grade Level Advisers

a. We engage in high-handed decision making and do not involve others.

b. We have not trained and supported the general faculty advisers.

c. We are entrenched advocates of the status quo.

Question 5. What are some concrete ways in which we can act to reduce problems we create and reduce problems others create?

Principal's Advisory Committee

a. We need to communicate with the other groups as often as possible. We should have group meetings.

b. We need to do more direct questioning of the other groups without ascribing motives to their actions.

c. We need to work with the other groups to develop a shared vision.

d. We suggest every group create multi-year goals and the methods for reaching those goals.

Department Heads

    a. We need to keep the entire school in mind when we make decisions.

    b. We need to listen to the other groups much better.

    c. We need to have more shared agenda-setting.

    d. We need to help make general faculty meetings better.

Grade Level Advisers

    a. We need to meet regularly with the other groups.

    b. We need to develop an openness to new ideas. We should be advocates for change, not blockers.

    c. We need to clarify our role in developing curriculum.

Meeting 2: Data Gathering and Analysis

After the groups met for the morning, the principal gathered them together for an afternoon of sharing. It was immediately clear to all the groups that there were several common problems. They used the afternoon as a data-gathering session. The groups each spent time talking about specific incidents, where one of the groups did not communicate or took unilateral action that affected the work of the other group. Each group told similar stories as the afternoon progressed. The principal then asked that the groups try to make sense of what these examples meant, so that a plan of action could be developed.

As the specific data were analyzed, each group realized that they had knowingly acted unilaterally to make decisions that impinged on the workings and responsibilities of the other groups. They did this because they felt that the other group would not want to go along with their plan and reaching compromise would take too long. The analysis showed that, in fact, this was not always true. But because the affected group was not consulted when the action became apparent, they were not very eager to support the action. For example, the grade level advisers, while they admired much in the curriculum plans of the department heads, did not support the department heads, because they felt ignored in the curriculum design process. Instead, they got their back up and tried to block any curriculum change recommended by that group. They agreed this was childish, but they also agreed that they felt as if they had been treated as children and so their action was justified.

By this time, the entire day had passed and the groups resolved to meet again in three weeks to consider plans of action.

Meeting 3: Action Planning and Implementation

When they met, they all agreed that the intervening time had allowed them to think about the problems they were experiencing in an entirely new light. In the past, they would have not seen any personal culpability in problem creation. But now they realized that the reason there were problems was due to actions by all parties and not simply by the actions of one of the groups.

The group created a set of behaviors in which they would engage over the next three months as a way to reduce problems and stress. They set a meeting time three months hence to spend the entire day reviewing the effectiveness of this action plan. The principal had these action plans printed on large sheets of newsprint and asked all administrators, grade level advisers and department heads to post them in their offices. That list appears below.

Plans of Action: John F. Kennedy High School

1. The department heads, grade level advisers, and principal's advisory committee will meet once per month to consult on the state of their groups and to share any actions or plans for action.

2. The department heads will meet every other week with the grade level advisers.

3. The three groups have committed to using e-mail to communicate and to copy the members of the other groups, whenever a topic for discussion seems to involve those other members.

4. Each group will create in the next three months a set of goals and plans for reaching those goals. These will be shared at the joint meeting of all three groups.

5. Two representatives of the department heads and the grade level advisers will meet with the principal's advisory committee to plan all faculty meetings.

Meeting 4: Evaluation and Problem Reformulation

At the end of the three-month period these groups met again for an all-day session. They agreed that things were working much better and that communication was the best it had ever been. They also agreed that they now understood that the department heads and the grade level advisers had vastly different ideas about the mission of the school. They agreed that that vision was not a shared vision and that these two groups needed to continue to meet to try and bring their visions of the school closer together and closer to the view of the principal and school system superintendent. They also agreed to rethink their communication by e-mail because the volume of interaction among twenty-one people was too much to handle and was creating a problem. The groups agreed that no one need respond to an e-mail message, unless that message was sent directly to them. Anything that was forwarded or where the recipient was simply copied could be read and discarded or even unread and discarded.

Thus, through the use of overt problem-solving strategies, the principal was able to bring three dysfunctional groups together. Their initial meeting, while somewhat tense, served to open the avenues of communication. By sharing in an open manner and planning together for new ways of interacting, the administrative team now has been able to devote its energy to more academic issues. The key factor in the success of this method was the attention and care that the leader, the principal, gave to the groups. He was very clear in stating that the purpose in meeting and engaging in these tough discussions was to make the school more effective. He gave the groups permission to criticize one another openly, to say what they had been saying anyway behind the closed department room door. By also giving the groups power to effect a plan of action and to self-monitor its implementation, the principal created the context for learning. And as we will see throughout the rest of this text, it is only through continual learning that a group can improve its effectiveness.

Another interesting way to define problems is to create a series of statements that define "cross-purposes" as seen by the members of the various groups involved in the organization. What follows in Exhibit 5.2 is a series of "cross purpose statements from a school that was trying to decide how to best spend its limited resources.

Exhibit 5.2 STATEMENTS OF POSSIBLE CROSS-PURPOSES
May 30, 1995

1. We desire to be a school of excellence competing with the very best in the nation, but we are hampered by a lack of fiscal resources.
2. If students carried six courses they would show increased academic distinction, but there isn't enough compensation to staff all the sections we'd need to accomplish this goal.
3. Colleges are looking for specialists and "impact" students, but our graduation requirements and philosophy are aimed toward generalization.

4. The study-abroad program was designed for juniors, but this is the least ideal time to be off campus, as far as producing a demanding academic profile for college application.
5. We are expected to be experts in multiple areas (teaching, dorming, coaching), but do not have the time to become experts in all these areas.
6. We are encouraged to take time for reflection, but our schedule is created to keep us busy at all times.
7. We seek more ways for students to distinguish themselves, but limit the number of AP and Honors courses we offer, or create gateways that ensure a small number of students in such courses.
8. We say we are committed to the arts, but we are informed that colleges do not value arts courses as much as the five traditional academic areas of English, history, math, science, and language.
9. We encourage students to work together, but create structures that make this hard to accomplish.
10. We have policies on record to govern our behavior, but do not have means to ensure they are adhered to.
11. We say we value a multicultural curriculum, but do not take action to ensure such a curriculum.
12. We are encouraged to have as many year-long courses as possible, but much of our curriculum is based upon term-long electives.
13. We are rushing into technology, but haven't had a discussion about the moral, educational, or disciplinary issues in doing this.
14. Our faculty governance system is based upon representation, but almost all issues have to be debated on the floor of full faculty meetings.
15. We are told that budgets are tight and we must find ways of economizing, but there is skepticism about the priorities of dollar decisions.
16. We want every minute of teaching time we can get, but have a system whereby school meetings, athletics, and free days can cut into class time.

References and Bibliography

Adams, James L. (1986). *The care and feeding of ideas: A guide to encouraging creativity.* Reading, MA: Addison-Wesley.

Conner, Daryl R. (1993). *Managing at the speed of change: How resilient managers succeed and prosper where others fail.* New York: Villard Books.

de Bono, Edward (1970). *Lateral thinking: Creativity step by step.* New York: Harper & Row.

Fritz, Robert (1991). *Creating.* New York: Fawcett Columbine.

Schein, Edgar H. (1988). *Process consultation, Volume I: Its role in organizational development.* Reading, MA: Addison-Wesley.

Senge, Peter M. (1990). *The fifth discipline: The art and practice of the learning organization.* New York: Doubleday Currency.

———— et. al. (1994). *The fifth discipline fieldbook: Strategies and tools for building a learning organization.* New York: Doubleday Currency.

Siskin, Leslie Santee (1994). *Realms of knowledge: Academic departments in secondary schools.* Washington, D.C.: Falmer Press.

Chapter 6

Using Time to Work Smarter, Not Harder

I. Theoretical Time

Time always seems to be in short supply. When was the last time you heard someone say, "I have time to kill? I have no idea what I'm going to do with all the extra time I have next week"? But unlike the weather, which no one can do anything about, time use is something you can alter. You may not be able to stop time in the absolute sense of the word, but there are ways to change your approach to time. For the most part, faculty cannot work more hours in the day. However, they and you, as the department head, can work differently. This chapter contains activities, approaches, and ideas that will help you and your staff be more effective teachers while, at the same time, improving the quality of the work experience while at school.

Relative Time

To realize that many notions of time do not fit those we traditionally hold to be true, look at time from a physicist's point of view. We all have heard of the special theory of relativity of Einstein. In this theory, Einstein makes the point that time is not an absolute for everyone. Rather, time is a relative idea dependent upon your physical location. The book, *Einstein's Dreams* by Alan Lightman, a series of fables purporting to be from the dreams of Albert Einstein, gives the reader a sense of what it would be like if time moved backward everyday, or if there were no future, only the present, or if there were no past, and many other time related scenarios. Each of these fables is designed to cause you to rethink your ideas about time.

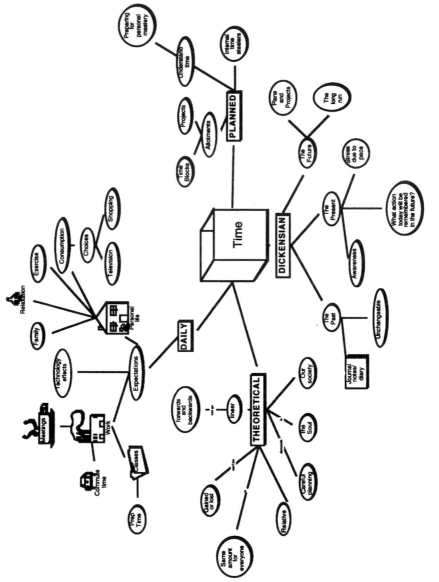

FIGURE 6.1. The Aspects of Personal Time

20 May 1905

When it is time to return home at the end of the day, each person consults his address book to learn where he lives. The butcher, who has made some unattractive cuts in his one day of butchery, discovers that his home in no. 29 Nageligasse. The stockbroker, whose short term memory of the market produced some excellent investements, reads that he now lives at no. 89 Bundesgasse. Arriving home, each man finds a woman and children waiting at the door, introduces himself, helps with the evening meal, reads stories to the children. Likewise, each woman returning from her job meets a husband, children, sofas, lamps, wallpaper, china patterns. Late at night, the husband and wife do not linger at the table to discuss the day's activities, their children's school, the bank account. Instead they smile at each other, feel the warming blood, the ache between the legs as when they met the first time fifteen years ago. They find their bedroom, stumble past family photographs they do not recognize, and pass the night in lust. For it is only habit and memory that dulls the physical passion. Without memory, each night is the first night, each morning the first morning, each kiss and touch the first.

A world without memory is a world of the present.

Alan Lightman, Einstein's Dreams, pgs 80–84

Unconventional Time

Another uncommon idea about time was put forth many years ago by the physicist Richard Feynman. In Feynman's view of the universe, the difference between matter and anti-matter is that time moves from the past to the present for matter and from the future to the past for anti-matter.

For example, physicists have studied a process known as pair production. See Figure 6.2.

In this often observed and well-known phenomena, electromagnetic energy is suddenly transformed into two particles, one a positron, a positively charged electron, and the other an electron. If you look at Figure 6.3 you will see that this can be interpreted as a positron moving backward in time, which suddenly, for some reason, begins to move forward in time. During this reversal, energy is the product. It exists in the past while the process of turning around is occurring in the future. In the Feynman time

Figure 6.2 Electromagnetic Radiation

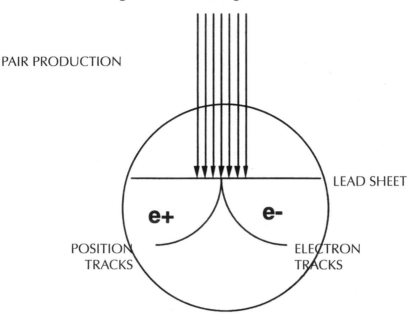

PAIR PRODUCTION

e+   e-

LEAD SHEET

POSITION
TRACKS

ELECTRON
TRACKS

CLOUD CHAMBER

world, there is no reason why the future can't already exist. What we take as two particles, the electron and the proton, existing simultaneously and independently, are really one and the same particle. A single particle first is moving forward in time and then later is moving backward in time. Both particles, therefore, can be observed at a single moment in time.

This same logic can explain the phenomena of annihilation. See Figure 6.4. When matter and anti-matter bump into one another, they annihilate one another, giving off pure energy according the Einsteinian formula of $E=mc^2$. But in the Feynman world, one can see that what is happening is that an electron moving forward in time suddenly turns around and begins moving backward in time. What appears to be annihilation is just the moment of "turn around." Turning around in time causes energy to be given off. None of these ideas violate any of the physics laws which govern the world and so, while they are definitely extraordinary, they are not forbidden.

Figure 6.3 Pair Production through Time Reversal

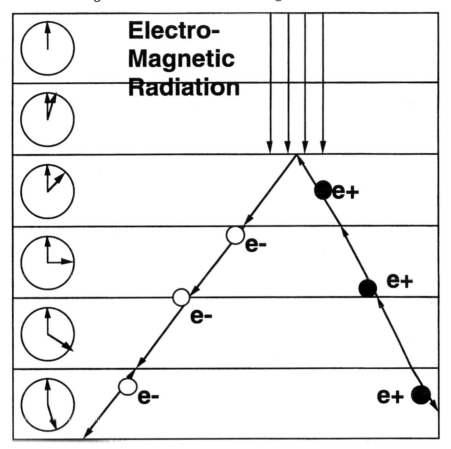

But what relevance can this concept of time have to the concrete, modern world, where the use of time is one of our greatest preoccupations? The point of using this example is not to turn department heads into physicists, but rather to challenge everyday conceptions about the way time works. In order to be successful as a department head, you must alter the way you, and your staff, think about time.

The Facts About Time

Everyone knows that a second is not a very long period of time, at least for a human being. After all, what can be done in a second? Maybe you can blink a few times. Maybe your heart beats once or once and a half. It takes about

Figure 6.4 Annihilation through Time Reversal

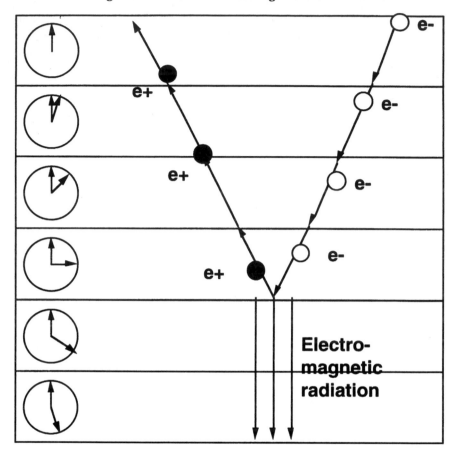

one second to write down a letter of your name. So not much can be accomplished in that one second. But what if we start stringing those seconds together. In a day there would be 86,400 of them and in a twenty-five year career 788,400,000 of them. Suppose one devoted 10 percent of this time to writing. Allow for wasting at least half of this time thinking about writing and procrastinating, etc., and there would still be 39,420,000 seconds devoted to actual writing. In a typical novel of 400 pages length and 60 characters per line, this amount of time could be translated into the production of nearly 50 full length novels. If you've ever wondered how the authors Steven King or James Michener can be so prolific, I think these numbers and the premise behind them give you a hint. See Exhibit 6.1 for another example of what can be accomplished by making use of every second available.

Exhibit 6.1 MAKING EVERY SECOND COUNT

1 Minute	60 seconds
1 Hour	3600 seconds
1 Day	86,400 seconds
1 Year	31,536,000 seconds
a 25 year career	788,400,000 seconds

A 400-page book contains approximately 150,000 words. A typical reader can read 300 words per minute or five words per second. If you spent 1 percent of your career time reading novels, you could read nearly three hundred novels of this length.

What are you waiting for?

All projects are completed bit by bit. It is the continual application of small increments of performance that result in the finished product. Even small amounts of force, continually applied, can move the largest object in the universe. If the largest object in the universe can be made to alter its direction by a series of small pushes and pulls, isn't it logical to think about applying small forces to create change in your staff's perception of time.

This small force you have to exert is the one in the back of your mind that keeps nagging at you to get the project done. The tiny voice that reminds you that you didn't get done what you wanted to and that you need to start now. By acting upon your dreams, goals, projects, and tasks in an incremental manner, the amount you can accomplish is astounding. The key is to understand how to build the structure that allows for incremental progress.

Time and Our Soul

The concept of time is very closely related to who we are as individuals. There are many clichés that point this out. Jeremy Rifkin of Harvard has pointed out that changes in civilized societies have often come from changes in the conception of time in those societies. For example, the literal competition between the bell in the medieval cathedral tower and the clock tower of the guild hall signaled a significant change from a religious to a secularly centered work society.

On a grand scale, we feel the changing of the seasons and the different declinations of the sun in a very deep manner. On a smaller scale, we have internalized the 40–45 minute period so effectively that every teacher and student knows when a class is over, even when there is no bell system to signal the end of the class. In fact, some students have internalized this time period to the nearest minute.

And yet, we do not make use of time in a way that recognizes it as a limited and valuable resource. Suppose we replaced the word "time" in some of the more familiar clichés with the word "life." Would that help to illuminate the valuable treasure that time really is. "There is never enough 'life' around here." "There's no 'life' like the present." " 'Life' is of the essence." "Next 'life,' do it right."

In running a great department, you will be faced over and over again with the lament that as a faculty member, there isn't enough time to do all the things expected and desired. Your task is to help everyone understand that while this may be true, there is much that can be done—as long as something is actually done. H. L. Mencken said it best when he said "When all is said and done, more will be said than done." Only you can help your team garner and protect time, so that the things they wish to do can be done.

TIME SAVINGS TIPS

1. Do your thinking on paper. Actually write the Pros and Cons.
2. Use a "slush" file. Unimportant papers aren't trashed, only stored.
3. Answer routine letters on the original. Copy your response and send original back.
4. Arrange your work space so you can work standing up OR sitting down.
5. Get up or come in early to get quiet time for work. It will save time in the long run.

II. Daily Time

Expectations

Work and Play

Every day, your time must be divided into segments devoted to the many facets of ongoing life. Everyone has the same total time to allot to work and personal life. The question that many ask is what amount should I allot to each of these? But this is the wrong question to ask. Everyone knows that "all work and no play, makes Jack a dull boy." But underlying this aphorism is the assumption that work and play are somehow fundamentally different. One way in which your staff will feel better about time use is if there is a blurring of the distinction between work and play. The more playlike work becomes, the more engaging it is. For kindergarteners, play is certainly the work that they do, and there is little doubt that when they "work," they are also having fun.

One department head, with whom I've worked, has commented that she had come to love working thirty-five hours a week so much, that she now does it twice a week. This may not be the approach you wish to take, but the message is clear in the sentiment. When work becomes more enjoyable, time does not become an issue. Your task is to figure out a way to structure their work so that "fun" is an integral part of the day or week. See Exhibit 6.2 for one way to gather information about what your staff might consider fun.

Mihaly Csikszentmihaly, in his work on the psychology of optimal experience, has stated that students and learners enter a state of "flow" when the interface of challenge and skill is just right. See Figure 6.5. "Flow" is a state where the learner loses a sense of time. We've all had this happen to us. We set about a task and then look at our watches to discover that two hours have transpired though it felt as if only ten minutes had gone by. To produce a state of "flow," the task must be hard enough that it is challenging, but not too difficult relative to the person's skills. In other words, it would be enjoyable to play tennis or golf against a peer, but probably would not be fun if you had to play against Martina Navratilova or Greg Norman.

Figure 6.5 The State of "Flow"

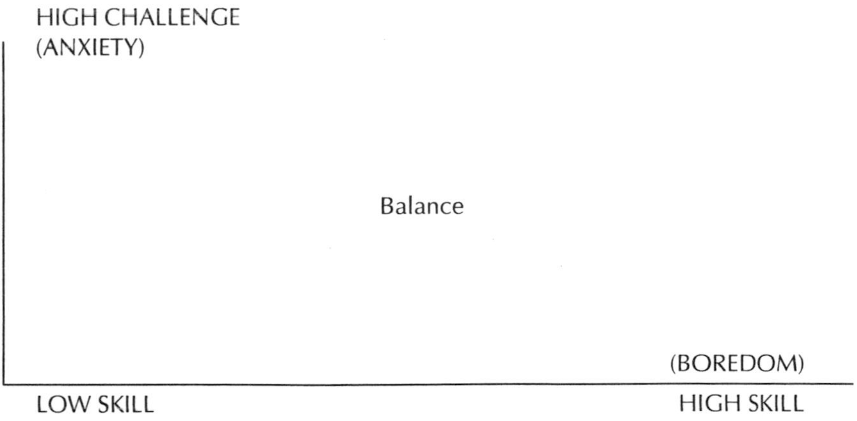

HIGH CHALLENGE
(ANXIETY)

Balance

(BOREDOM)

LOW SKILL   HIGH SKILL

For a department person to enter the state of "flow," a state most people say is enjoyable, there has to be the right mix of challenge and skill. One challenge that faces every department head right now is how to integrate the use of computer technology into the classroom. Exploring the possibilities new technology offers for improving learning is one way that a faculty member can be rejuvenated and feel better about the use of time. Teaching with new technologies will most certainly be challenging, but as long as there is careful training to develop the teacher's skills, there can be the enjoyable feeling that "this is fun." It will take skill on the department head's part to structure the training so that it is fun. To that end, you must make time available for this training. Additionally, it must be time that the faculty member is willing to give up. Clearly, a Friday afternoon training session won't do. Perhaps, by using a professional day with some knowledgable teachers leading others in the exercises, you can create the ideal state of flow.

Work and Teaching

In our schools, for the last twenty-five years, there has not been a significant increase in the total amount of time that a student must be in class. It has remained somewhat constant with a 180-day school year and 5.5–6.0 hour day. However, the expectations for productivity have increased. Students are expected to perform at higher levels than in the past. National testing allows schools and districts to make comparisons not only to what they accomplished in the past, but also to what neighboring districts are doing. This added pressure can lead to dissatisfaction with the way time is used.

When faculty are concerned about test scores and levels of learning, they are much less likely to feel good about wasting time in any day. A meeting where such a faculty member is not engaged or which does not directly affect that faculty member will quickly be characterized as a waste of time. Thus, it is essential for the department head to make sure every commitment of the teachers be important, useful, and related to their work. In studying productivity and time use, research has shown that workers with greater responsibility are much more concerned about wasting time than workers with less responsibility. So you can expect your faculty to be critical whenever they feel their time is being wasted. This criticism is less likely to be lodged when time is used for class-related activities.

In our society, everyone is expected to work upon reaching adulthood (and sometimes before) and to become a productive member of society. One of the stigmas attached to the homeless is not so much that they don't have a home, but that they don't have jobs. But even when one has a job, the expectations about performance and productivity are never far from the surface. Every school principal and parent is concerned about the bottom line of performance.

In American society, work is paramount. Contrary to popular belief, the typical Japanese worker does not work longer than his or her American counterpart. In fact, American workers spend about 1904 hours per year working compared to 1888 hours per year for Japanese workers or 1639 hours per year for the typical German worker.

Juliet Schor, Lecturer in Economics at Harvard University and Director of Studies in the Harvard University's Women's Studies Program has noted that since the end of the 1960s, the average working American has added 160 hours of work to his or her annual schedule. Downsizing has led to increased workloads for people because the same amount of work has to be accomplished, only now with a smaller work force.

In fact, she has discovered that for the year 1960 the sum of all the time that the typical husband spent at work and at home and the work time that the wife and full-time homemaker did was 5400 hours. A typical 40 hour per week job with two weeks of vacation is a 2000 hour commitment. Thus, the 1960s family held two and one half full time jobs. In 1989, this same typical family was working 6500 hours per year. This is the addition of a half-time job. Not surprisingly, during this extra 1000 hours of work, the children in the family are usually relegated to unsupervised time. How many of these 1000 hours of work translated into "fun"? If the answer is "not many," then there is a serious problem.

How Can the Department Head Help?

Preparing for and teaching classes is the major time absorber for most teachers and department heads. Altering the amount of time devoted to this area implies change in classic assumptions. There are two specific areas regarding class preparation, where teachers could save time. First, teachers often prepare for classes they never actually give. The amount of prep time devoted to becoming knowledgeable about the next lesson may be completely in excess of the lesson needs. In some ways, to suggest that a teacher could spend less time preparing might sound like heresy, but that is what I am suggesting.

Why might a teacher be loathe to do this? I think, again, this is connected with the idea of how work and play overlap. For many teachers, one driving force behind the decision to become a teacher was love for a particular discipline. Preparing for lessons allows the teacher to continue to delve into that discipline. This results in pleasure. Learning more about one's discipline is a conditioned reflex. Thus, preparing for class is an excuse to use time to follow one's own interests and to pursue what is enjoyable. This is nothing more than the old Freudian drive to seek pleasure and avoid pain. If the faculty members see that too much preparation is one reason why they might be feeling somewhat negative and pressed for time, then there is the possibility for change. However, if they find such preparation truly enjoyable, there is little you can do or say that will alter their behavior.

Another time absorber directly related to teaching and fully under the teacher's control is the amount of time devoted to daily correcting. In some subjects, there is the widely held belief that homework must be collected, corrected, and graded every day. Yet, in the literature about instructional effectiveness, there is not any such recommendation. It is true that homework may be very effective for learning, but it doesn't necessarily follow that every assignment must be collected and graded. Instead, a teacher can assign homework and then visually check to see that the students have done the assignment that night. By reducing correctable assignments by one per week, a teacher might recover 20 percent of correcting time to attack some other areas of interest and need.

The department head can also lead by example in both of these areas. I have discovered that, commonly, when a department head gets release time to perform the myriad duties of department leading, that time gets taken up with teaching tasks. There is great temptation to let the primary time-focus be the classes that you teach. Yet, as the department head, the faculty need you to be leading them to greater effectiveness. Such leadership will be time demanding. In fact, it may call for more time than your job description calls for or allows. Thus, you too, need to guard against classroom-preparation time creep.

The judicious use of technology can release many hours of time. If you commute to work, listening to tapes and books relating to teaching and learning can save you many hours of reading. The Association for Supervision and Curriculum Development has an extensive audio department and is a good resource. As a side comment related to commuting, the average commute to work has remained unchanged over the last fifteen years at 29 minutes each way. What has happened is that highways have gotten better, allowing workers to live father away from the work site, but keeping the commute time the same. At present, the number of new highways that are being constructed has reached a static point, and we can expect that commute times will begin to increase as highways become more congested.

With the advent of electronic mail, many department heads and administrators can now maintain closer communications than ever before. However, reading and responding to the many e-mail messages that which you receive every day can be quite a time waster. If you adopt a policy whereby you only respond to those messages that are sent directly to you and not those for which you are one of the parties copied, you will still remain informed but won't have to spend time writing to every person who decides to put you into the loop of communication.

Personal Life

It is all too easy to think about work and personal life as two separate entities. However, I think that if we were to merge the two more closely, everyone would be much happier. When Americans are asked to reflect upon professions and work they consider to be rewarding and stress free, they often point to farming as the ideal. There might be a kernel of something important in that sentiment. If teachers could view their work simply as if they were working on a farm, they would see that farming, like teaching, is not a nine-to-five job. Instead, it is a job with which you learn to live. On a farm, there is always work to be done, and yet no farmer works all the time. Instead, farm work has been merged into personal life in such an intimate manner that it is hard to see where one begins and the other leaves off.

How might this metaphor work for a teacher. Take the writing of end of semester or year reports. If the teacher is at all interested in becoming a better writer, then the chore of writing the end of year reports can be viewed as an opportunity to experiment with new metaphors, analogies and sentence structure. In other words, it is a chance to use work time to do something that, in fact, is personally rewarding and interesting. Many coaches of teams coach, not only because they enjoy students and athletes, but also because coaching allows them to stay connected with the sport they love or to stay in shape. They exercise with the students. I chose to coach the school's men's cycling team precisely because I could ride every day as part of my job. I would have taken time later to ride anyway, so this was a very judicious use of work load.

When I listen to experienced teachers talk about time, I find that they are more frustrated than younger faculty. This may be due to the fact that as faculty get older, the number of activities that call for their attention increase. Older adults tend to do more and more or get involved in many more organizations, especially in leadership roles. In addition, the responsibilities for taking care of elderly parents and also bringing up their own children, create a drain upon their time. There is little a department head can do other than help the teacher see that each part of the job and life are related.

By holding a yearly discussion with each team member about all aspects of job and external influences, the department head can be aware of the pressure points. If, for example, you know that the swimming coach, who is also your chemistry teacher, will be completely overwhelmed during the last week of the term, when the state swim meet is held, you can volunteer to step in and help out with a class or two. Again, leading by example is the best way to gather respect and help your teachers deal with time issues.

It will come as no surprise that the two most common evening activities for the typical American are shopping and watching television. Yet, when people are asked what activities give them the most pleasure, both of these activities are rated low. What makes this so? I think it's because no one is likely to make a conscious decision about the need to do either one. I would suggest that one simple recommendation for a teacher who wants to manage his or her time better is to use the local television guide. Do not watch any program that you have not searched out beforehand and written down as a must see. Turning the television set on to "see what's on" will surely result in the waste of a substantial amount of time at the expense of some other activity that may be more enjoyable. And with the explosion of merchandise catalogues allowing you to shop for just about anything at home, cutting down on trips to the mall should be a cinch.

Finally, each of us has made purchases of devices that call for the use of time—time that we have never factored into our daily schedule. Every device probably should have a sticker on it similar to the stickers that come with kitchen appliances to give the consumer some inkling of what the energy costs for typical use of the appliance will be. Imagine how we might change our purchasing habits if the items we bought had a sticker on them giving us an estimate of what the typical time use might be. The VCR, which allows us to tape programs we hardly ever watch, might say ten hours per week. The books that pile up next to our bed might say eight hours or five hours. The stair stepper, easy rider, ab-roller or what have you, all take time to use. Even decisions about which meals we will prepare is a decision about how we will use our time. As a department head, it might be interesting for the department members to look around the department and school and give time values to the various activities or items

---

Exhibit 6.2

In the following exercise, the goal is to develop an overlap between activities and interests of the teacher and activities in the workplace. This can be done as part of a department meeting or one on one with a teacher.

1. To what activities and interests are you continually drawn?
2. To what activities do you ascribe the word "fun"?
3. How do the above ideas relate to my work at school?
4. Which of the above do I make time for?

---

that exist there. Having a personal understanding of hidden time demands can go a long way toward improving morale and making the job more enjoyable.

TIME SAVING TIPS

1. Get at least twenty minutes of exercise each day. Use walk and talk for a meeting.
2. Avoid clutter. Tidy your desk before leaving.
3. Make sure you have a tickler file for routine year-to-year tasks.
4. Never do errands on impulse. Plan carefully.
5. Use catalogs for shopping whenever possible.

III. Dickensian Time

Past, Present, and Future

In Dickens' *A Christmas Carol,* Scrooge is visited by the ghosts of Christmas Past, Christmas Present, and Christmas Yet-To-Come. Just as Scrooge cannot change the past or even the present, he does have the opportunity to change the future by acting in the here and now. The question that needs to be answered is "What do I do now to take charge of the future?" Before spending time on how to make the future more rewarding, it is important to use the past and the present in a way that informs, and even satisfies, your faculty's need for time responsibility.

The Past

It is simple to recognize that the present soon becomes the past. In fact, the present instantaneously becomes the past. Some philosophers debate whether the present actually exists, since there can be no such thing as having an understanding in an instantaneous way. We are always mentally experiencing something that happened in the past. A readily understandable example of this is our interpretation of the sunlight we receive from the sun. Since it takes over eight minutes for the light, which has been created on the sun, to travel to us, we experience the sun as eight minutes in its past. Even though that is true, this reality has no real effect upon everyday life. The sun's past is not necessarily our past.

The point is that we should figure out ways to make the past important to us and something upon which we can look back with fond memories. To call attention to this you might want to place this saying in a prominent place for all to contemplate.

What will you do today that you will want to remember tomorrow?

If thinking about tomorrow informs your actions today, then surely the past will be a rich source of pleasure. And as such, you will not be so likely to think of time as having been squandered. By thinking about the future meaning of present action, you will be making choices congruent with your tacit goals and dreams.

Sometimes what we think we will want to remember may not be easy to put into words and exists only as a generalized and vague thought. For example, a teacher may want to reflect upon his or her work with a difficult student and express pleasure knowing that student had an epiphany of sorts. Such reflection follows the Romantic tradition of Ralph Waldo Emerson that "education begins by respecting the pupil." Now, epiphanies are not going to be the reality for every student, but if the teacher doesn't act as if it were possible with each and every student, then, surely, opportunities for such turnabouts are going to be missed. So by acting in a manner that helps to define the supportive environment for the student, the probabilities for viewing time as having been used well are improved.

Keeping journals and summaries of readings are other ways to work towards making the past an important factor in the present. Journal use is a great professional development device. The journal should contain items upon which the teacher can reflect and react. It is not so much a detail of *what* is happening, but instead, a place where the teacher tries to make sense of *why* certain things have happened and *why* he or she acted in a particular manner. Toby Fulwiler, one of the experts on journal use, has written that the best journals are those that are long. It is through writing that we recognize what it is we want to say and what it is we truly think.

For the department head, keeping a detailed journal of your actions and encounters is essential. In so doing, you can analyze your methods and strategies reacting to complicated interactions. Only through reflection can you learn from both success and failures so that future actions can be made from an informed position. The key to such a useful journal is to be as detailed as possible. You must record not only the specifics, but also your feelings. It is the feelings that will trigger an emotional response and help you make sense of the situation. Psychologists have discovered that the senses and emotions make for powerful memory devices. Just about everyone reacts with strong feelings when thinking back to a particularly pleasant day or a welcoming food smell from childhood. Thus, recording emotional detail, as well as factual detail, will bring the moment of the past alive. Bringing the past alive helps us to extend the sense of time, because it is a way to relive that moment, and thus, recover what somehow seems to be "lost."

Professionally, it is good to keep summaries and notes of your readings. In this notebook, you can rip out articles or portions of books and paste them into the journal. I suggest using a small three-ring binder, so that material can be added and subtracted. In addition, while taking notes you only need the filler paper in front of you and not the bulk of the binder. Such a binder allows you to go back over past readings and pull out thoughts and points as needed. The front section can be set up to be the table of contents and by numbering the pages as you add them, you'll have a ready-made reference book.

Finally, it does not serve much purpose to think on the "what might have beens." Since you cannot alter the past, it is best to not dwell upon the regrets of the past. If you have handled a situation poorly and wish you could turn back the hands of time, you must give up that notion. Instead, think about how that failure helped you to move forward. Every great scientist is both driven and haunted by the notion that to make a great discovery one must also be at the edge of great failure. You should not view your department headship as one of trial and error, but one of trial and learning.

The Present

It is clear from the preceding section about the past, that the present is the time when you work out what will be meaningful for both the past and the future. But the present is also the place where we must confront our perceptions about time. Often, we cannot think either in the past or the future.

Exhibit 6.3

What are our attitudes and perceptions about time?

1. Where do you get your attitudes about time?
Make a list of what your parents said about the following:
Being on time

Being late

Not finishing what you started

Doing your duty

Being prompt

Being early

Being the first to arrive

Being the last to leave

Wasting time

Keeping busy

2. List as many metaphors for the passage of time as you can. Example: Time passed in a heartbeat.

3. Close your eyes and raise your hand when you think one minute has passed. Does this tell you something about your patience with the passage of time? (In the classroom the classic research on this was that dealing with the time interval between the teacher's question and the students answer. Surprising to many teachers, was the fact that only three seconds separated the time between the teacher question and either the student response or another statement by the teacher. Waiting for ten seconds or more felt like an eternity to the teacher.)

4. Stop Action:
Describe some activity you've done today in as much detail as possible. Be as descriptive as you can and include any emotions that you can recall. Force yourself to be as over detailed as possible for this exercise.

We can only be in the present. Thus, it might be interesting to lead the department in the following exercises:

In Exercise #3 in Exhibit 6.3, most people raise their hands after less than thirty seconds, which implies that people really don't have a good feeling for time passage. Since this is true, you should guard against the impulse to compress time. If people are already predisposed to judging time as shorter than it really is, and if you try to compress this time, you will be creating stress rather than relaxation.

As a way to create some personal relaxation time, you should make a daily appointment with time. By using a portion of the day to plan quietly how you will use your day, you will find that you'll be less stressed. For just about everyone, having a plan is comforting, even if the plan is only somewhat defined. Even very general plans will help to focus a person's energies.

Solitude

One of the things that is missing in most people's lives is the chance to be alone. Solitude has been defeated. The every day world of face to face interaction in school and society is augmented by the ubiquitous world of electronic communication. The most shocking example of this was probably the cellular phone call from the husband about to die at the top of Mount Everest to his wife in her living room in California. So while true solitude is unattainable for most of us, one can create the semblance of solitude by consciously taking a lone walk or closing the door and sitting in the quiet. You will be surprised how ten minutes per day of such solitary activity will allow you to think clearly and purposefully.

One of the most important activities of a department head is leadership in all facets of the program. Such leadership often calls for careful thought about direction and action. In the frantic pace of day to day living, there is simply not any natural time where this thinking can take place. Getting away, alone with your thoughts is essential for becoming a good leader. You must know what you think if you are going to lead others in that direction.

I have found that riding my bicycle for an hour a day helps me to think in a very relaxed manner. The combination of the routine, repeated physical activity of pedaling, and the fresh air and solitude brings me into a contemplative state. I can think about what has happened during the day and what I need to do, either later that day or the next day.

The Future

The future is the most elusive of all concepts with which we have to wrestle when dealing with time. But in dealing with the future, time is not necessarily the problem. Choices are the problem. I will deal with how to make good choices in the last portion of the chapter called Planned Time. But, before you can address your plans for time, you need to think about the future.

Plans and Projects

Plans allow the future to be enjoyed in the present. All of us have felt a sense of enjoyment as we planned a vacation or trip. In such planning, we were priming our mental pump to bring forth a full experience once we arrived at our destination. Having to plan a home or building is an exercise in imagining space and our relationship to it. Mentally spending a day working in the, as yet, imaginary facility can yield a great sense of satisfaction. Working on a complex project can set individuals into motion and mobilize even the most inactive department.

One way to make careful plans is to use the storyboard technique. Determine on what date you would like to have a particular outcome and work backwards from that point to the present. For example, on January you must have all course descriptions camera ready for the central office publications department. It is on that date that the next year's course catalogue will be sent to the printer. This means that you must work backwards with the tasks that have to be completed. You should end at the day upon which you are making the storyboard. This means that every day you have a plan for action to perform some task that brings you and the department closer to the goal of producing the catalogue.

You can bring the larger group into the activity if you invoke group participation, not only with the tasks at hand, but also with general calendar deadlines. Make available a large calendar for all members of the department to see. Use stick-it type paper to detail the tasks and post them on the calendar. Then ask the group to think about the tasks for a few days and to move the pieces of paper around into what everyone feels will be a doable time frame. Each person can volunteer for one of the tasks or to work with someone else in the department upon the task. The result will be that there will be less procrastination because the task has been divided into smaller activities, and the dates for those activities have been set and made public.

The publishers of *Newsday* on Long Island were able to increase subscription by nearly 30 percent because they were able to guarantee a newspaper at the reader's door by 5:30 A.M. To do this meant changing the total time from the news desk to final print job by 45 minutes. However, the publishers also wanted to be able to respond, at the last minute, to breaking stories as they always had. This meant not going to press until midnight. In other words, they could not just roll back the entire process by forty-five minutes. Every group who had some hand in the process had to cut its work time by five minutes. This five-minute cut didn't seem like much, but it caused the groups to completely rethink what they were doing. The net result was that new relationships between departments were forged. Using the storyboard technique to map out how the five minutes per group would affect each group along the line, resulted in something everyone could take some pride in having participated in producing.

There is no holding back the arrow of time. Next year, you will be a year older whether you want to be or not. However, you can be a different person only if you want to be. You can use the year to learn a new language, become a better cook, understand a new computer application, or any other goal that you choose. But whatever you do, it is important to remember what John Maynard Keynes, the great economist said when he was asked what he thought the future might hold. His reply was:

"In the long run, we're all dead."

This sobering thought should help to keep in perspective the balance between work and play, past and future, success and failure, public and personal life. All of us have a short time here, and to make the most of it we must plan and act with care. Sometimes, we may be lucky in our actions. George Burns upon his ninety-fifth birthday was asked about his longevity, and he, in his own ironic manner, replied "If I had known I was going to live this long, I'd have taken better care of myself." We might use this thought as we think about the future. Will you, ten years from today, be saying that you wished you had planned more carefully? Will the members of your department look back and say they are glad they had a goal and a mission, whether it was realized or not. In the next section, you will be introduced to some techniques for developing both personal and group goals.

TIME SAVING TIPS

11. Use the phone to find out information and to order ahead.
12. Plan each night exactly what you will wear the next day, and lay it out ahead of time.

13. Don't get hung up on the "do it myself" syndrome. It may be cheaper in the long run to hire an expert.
14. Plan your TV viewing a week ahead. Never turn on the set to "see what's on."
15. Write a memo to yourself for future reference whenever you have completed a difficult task that is going to recur. Describe your successes and omissions.

IV. Planned Time

"The most powerful Time Management tool is YOU."

Your beliefs create your reality. Your dreams help you to determine your actions. If you think you'll never be able to have time for some activity, then chances are you probably won't. However, if you let your dreams guide you in setting your goals, the chances are that you will accomplish what you would like to—and much more.

In his classic book, *The Time Trap*, Alec MacKenzie pointed out that the most important time wasters do not originate from external sources.

Exhibit 6.4 What Time Type Are You?

adapted from *It's About Time* by Linda Sapadin with Jack Maguire, Viking Penguin: New York, 1996.

Below are 36 statements. Thinking about how you are at work, not how you would like to be, give a number value to each sentence using the scale below.

SCALE

1, 2, 3   LEAST LIKE YOU AT WORK
4, 5, 6, 7   SOMEWHAT LIKE YOU AT WORK
8, 9, 10   MOST LIKE YOU AT WORK.

GROUP I

A. I have difficulty starting or completing projects because I'm afraid I won't meet my own standards.
B. I think a lot about what I'd like to do but rarely get projects off the ground.
C. I have difficulty making decisions.

D. I get irritated when I have to do something I don't want to do.
E. I often ignore important tasks, then work frantically at the last minute to get them done.
F. I run around doing things but don't feel I'm accomplishing very much.

GROUP II

A. I get preoccupied with details other people don't seem to care about.
B. I wait for opportunities to find me.
C. I seek assurances from others before I take action.
D. I tend to work inefficiently when doing a task I don't like.
E. I feel that life is chaotic and I can never be sure what tomorrow will bring.
F. I have difficulty saying no.

GROUP III

A. I'm reluctant to delegate tasks unless other people do things my way.
B. I still wonder what I'm going to do when I "grow up."
C. I avoid unfamiliar situations that might cause me anxiety.
D. I often feel others make unreasonable demands on me.
E. My moods change rapidly.
F. I give priority to what I should do and put off what I want to do.

GROUP IV

A. People say I'm rigid, stubborn, and finicky.
B. I spend more time imagining a finished product than thinking about how to get it done.
C. I get flustered when something disrupts my normal routine.
D. I frequently forget about or ignore unpleasant obligations.
E. I react to circumstances and respond to the needs of the moment.
F. I often complain that I have no time.

GROUP V

A. I'm critical of what I do or how long I take to do it.
B. I wish someone else would handle the bothersome details of my life so I could just be creative.
C. I paralyze myself before starting a project, wondering about the "what ifs."
D. I feel resentful when people ask why I didn't do something.
E. I pride myself on living on the edge.
F. When I do have free time, I fill it with work.

GROUP VI

A. I'm satisfied with my work only if it is as good as it can possibly be.
B. I do what I feel like doing at the moment, forgetting or ignoring previous plans.
C. I think I could perform better if someone would show me how.
D. I get defensive when people suggest how I could be more productive.
E. My life is so dramatic that it could be made into a soap opera.
F. I enjoy being busy but think maybe I don't know how to be any other way.

Score Sheet

Group		Value				
I	A	B	C	D	E	F
II	A	B	C	D	E	F
III	A	B	C	D	E	F
IV	A	B	C	D	E	F
V	A	B	C	D	E	F
VI	A	B	C	D	E	F
TOTALS	—	—	—	—	—	—

The greatest time wasters are creations of our own actions. We work under no self-imposed deadlines. We seek perfection. We do not have a work plan. We are interested and involved in too many things, which waters down our ability to concentrate and act on the matter at hand. We do not know how to say NO strongly and positively. We are indecisive. We lack order in our actions.

If these are all true, then we need to understand ourselves and our relationship to time much better. Exhibit 6.4 is designed to help you and your department understand how they approach time.

After you have the totals, you will see that you probably have a dominant strength as well as weakness as noted by the totals. For example, if you were a perfect A type, you would have a maximum score of 60 in column A. More likely you will discover that you have a mixture of strong types within a single personality. The type labels below will help you and

Time Types

A. The Perfectionist

You believe other's standards are too low. You feel that if the job isn't perfect, then somehow you've failed, and when this happens, you criticize yourself mercilessly. What you don't recognize is that there might be several correct ways to do a task, all of them different from the way you might have chosen. You can feel better if you change your internal "shoulds" to "coulds."

The department head should never ask the perfectionist to head a time-sensitive committee or task force.

B. The Dreamer

You have a hard time distinguishing between feeling good and feeling good about yourself. This can lead to false images of yourself and your ability. Dreams and goals are the same for you. This can be a big problem because your dream depicts an end result, but has no steps on how to arrive there. Goals that are measurable and testable are missing from your use of time. You tend to use generalities such as "someday I hope to . . ." instead of a concrete statement such as "By Saturday I will be finished with. . . ."

The department head should make use of the dreamer in brainstorming sessions but should not rely on the dreamer to implement a plan.

C. The Worrier

You tend to dwell on the negatives. You're a "what if . . ." kind of person, but you take the negative side of the view. You probably should break your decision making into two parts. (1) Decide *if* you want to do it. (2) Decide *how* you will do it. By doing one thing you've been putting off each day, you'll be able to break away from the worrier time mode.

The department head should ask the worrier to review any plan for change. The worrier will discover many of the scenarios that would sabotage the plan.

D. The Defier

You immediately think of all the reasons why you can't do such and such when asked. In fact, you get somewhat hot under the collar when someone asks you to use your time to help them. You tend to view requests as demands. Sometimes you find it hard to be a team player because you want to protect your time; You're just not sure why you're protecting it. Sometimes, you'll say what you know someone wants to hear, even though you don't mean it.

The department head should approach the defier with the knowledge that there will be some sparks. However, it is essential to have the defier on your side whenever you plan to make changes.

E. The Crisis Maker

You deal with feelings so much that the facts can get lost. Your emotions can carry you to a decision and a state of panic even when it is not warranted. You tend to use dramatic language somewhat out of proportion to the task at hand. "This is the most important letter I've ever written. If I don't get it right, I'll probably be fired." You need to satisfy your need for excitement in other ways besides creating a crisis. Keep a record of causes and effects, so that in the next case, you will have some direction upon which you can rely as a plan of action.

The department head should be proactive to help the crisis maker stay calm and focused during changes. Giving the crisis maker as much information and personal support as possible will keep the crises minimal.

F. The Overdoer

You want to do it all, but you really can't. You don't distinguish between priorities and demands. All requests, especially the latest ones, get your attention. You try to please everyone. You need to be able to say NO without feeling guilty. By paying attention to what you did during the last week that was of importance to others versus importance to you, you can see how you should begin acting. You need to delegate or get help.

You, the department head, are probably an overdoer. Be aware that you are and act with caution as new ideas come to you or you will be overwhelmed trying to do it all immediately.

---

your department understand how you interact with time and why some folks may get on the nerves of others in the department. Understanding what your time type is may be nothing more than an interesting departmental activity, but you could also use it as a starting point for a more meaningful discussion of departmental goals and team work.

Exhibit 6.5 allows you to work with individuals in the department to help them bring their dreams into concrete description. But further, it allows you to know more clearly what motivates each and every person. This will enable you to structure your actions to help these individuals reach their goals. Serving others is one strong tenet of the model of servant leadership. To be a servant leader calls for you to know exactly how you might serve. Department members can use this exercise in a generalized way to bring life goals into focus, but as it is presented here, the emphasis is upon school-related goals.

Exhibit 6.5 BRINGING DREAMS INTO FOCUS

(adapted from Senge et al., *The Fifth Discipline Fieldbook*, New York: Doubleday, 1994).

STEP ONE

Begin by bringing yourself into a reflective frame of mind. Take a few deep breaths, and let go of any tension, as you exhale so that you are relaxed, comfortable, and centered. You can recall an image that is particularly meaningful to you. It could be an animal or pet, a favorite spot or feeling. Shut your eyes for a moment and stay with that feeling.

Now open you eyes and begin answering the following questions:

Imagine achieving a result in your school that you deeply desire. For example, imagine the school has the physical plant you most desire or you have close relationships with others that you most want to have. IGNORE how possible or impossible this vision seems. Imagine yourself accepting, into your life, the full manifestation of this result.

Describe in writing the experience you have imagined using the present tense, as if it is happening now.

What does it look like?

What does it feel like?

What would you use to describe it?

STEP TWO

In your response to Step One, did you articulate a vision that is close to what you actually want? Did you find this hard to do? Can you give an explanation why? Where does the need for time or the constraints of time fit into your vision?

STEP THREE

Most people, in doing this exercise, have a mixture of selfless and self-centered elements. Part of the value of this exercise is to suspend your judgment about what is worth desiring and to ask instead: Which aspect of these visions is closest to your deepest desires? To find out you need to expand and clarify each dimension of your vision.

Ask yourself the following questions about each element of your vision.

1. If I could have it now, would I take it?

Sometimes what you wish for might be more trouble than it is worth. Let's say, as a varsity coach, you wished that the school had unlimited resources for athletic pursuits. However, this might mean that the expectations for winning would be unusually high. Would you want that pressure?

2. If I could have it now, what does it bring me?

This question catapults you into a richer image of your vision, so you can see its underlying implications more clearly. For example, maybe you wrote that you wanted each student to have a computer. Why do you want that? What would it allow you to create? You might say you want it because it would allow the students to have wider access to information. But why would you want that? The point is to not denigrate the vision, but to expand it. If wider access to information is important, what else could that produce? A more learned student, one more open to various ideas, even if controversial? And a more open student would allow for greater exploration of ideas from multiple perspectives which, in turn, might make for a better educated citizen, which, in turn, would bring an enlightened approach toward learning in general. But would the students then question the values you hold? Could you support those values if they were challenged? Could you alter those values? Would creating such a freethinking student body change your thinking about any part of the faculty evaluation process? Would you think about hiring in a different way? Etc., etc.

3. Ask the set of questions several times.

What you will discover is that your vision leads you to three or four primary goals. Asking the question over and over, "What would it bring me?" immerses you in a gently insistent structure that forces you to take the time to see what you deeply want.

Exhibit 6.6 is another interesting exercise for the department to engage. Knowing where one's "to do" list is generated can help faculty take more control of their own destiny. Sometimes work is generated from external sources. Such work may be routine and necessary, but not always crucial. However, work that is self-generated is the most motivating. Your task, as the department head, is to help the department create work in which they

Exhibit 6.6 Where Does the Work Come From?

Place each element of your work under one of the categories below.

1. Those "above" you on the institutional structure.

2. The system: Routine activities that must be fulfilled.

3. Those "below" you on the institutional structure.

4. Self-imposed goals and activities

To Do List Format

Description	Urgent/important priority	Pure time estimate

Exhibit 6.7 Time Log

Few time management tools are as useful—or as surprising—as the time log. We think we know where our time goes, but we don't. We remember the important things but soon forget time spent on nonproductive activities—yet those are the things we must identify if we are to plug the leaks.

A time log is not intended as a permanent routine. It is merely a diagnostic tool to be filled out daily for one or two weeks. This system is a double entry system. The first category deals with **WHAT** you are doing, and the second deals with **WHY** you are doing it. In other words, which goal you are trying to achieve by doing what you are doing.

There are four rules to using this time log.

1. Try to be as accurate as possible using fifteen-minutes blocks.
2. Do this for ten consecutive work days
3. Realize this log is for your eyes only. You won't be honest if it is for other than diagnostic purposes.
4. Do go back and fill in times that you might miss.

Department Head/Team Leader Time Log

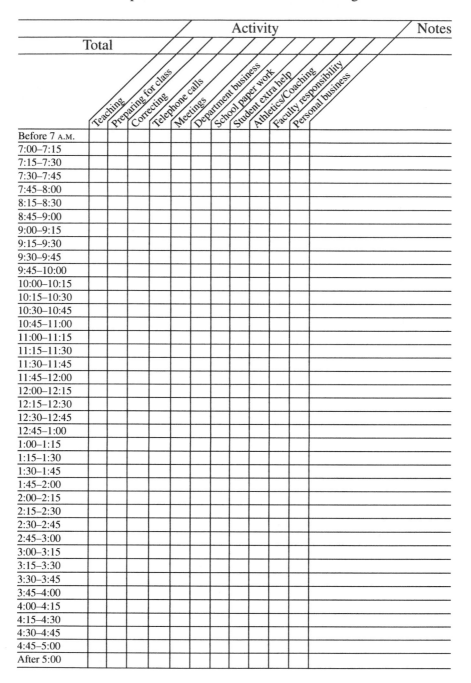

	Total			Activity										Notes
		Teaching	Preparing for class	Correcting	Telephone calls	Meetings	Department business	School paper work	Student extra help	Athletics/Coaching	Faculty responsibility	Personal business		
Before 7 A.M.														
7:00–7:15														
7:15–7:30														
7:30–7:45														
7:45–8:00														
8:15–8:30														
8:45–9:00														
9:00–9:15														
9:15–9:30														
9:30–9:45														
9:45–10:00														
10:00–10:15														
10:15–10:30														
10:30–10:45														
10:45–11:00														
11:00–11:15														
11:15–11:30														
11:30–11:45														
11:45–12:00														
12:00–12:15														
12:15–12:30														
12:30–12:45														
12:45–1:00														
1:00–1:15														
1:15–1:30														
1:30–1:45														
1:45–2:00														
2:00–2:15														
2:15–2:30														
2:30–2:45														
2:45–3:00														
3:00–3:15														
3:15–3:30														
3:30–3:45														
3:45–4:00														
4:00–4:15														
4:15–4:30														
4:30–4:45														
4:45–5:00														
After 5:00														

are interested before external sources demand work from them and their time.

One final common exercise as a way to understand where time is spent is to develop a time log. When people are asked where they spend most of their time, researchers have discovered that these people don't have a good grasp of where they spend their time. By keeping a detailed time log for a week, the places where time is spent become quite clear. What most often occurs when keeping such a time log, is that it becomes clear that time is not being spent on major goals and initiatives.

For example, every school has a mission or vision statement. Teacher time and effort should always be referenced to this statement. If the teacher is not spending the majority of his or her time fulfilling this mission statement, then there is a discongruity that needs to be reconciled. For most department heads, the vast portion of time available to them is not spent in meeting the overall mission of the institution.

Summary

Steven Covey in his book *First Things First* uses the following story to illustrate the principles behind judicious time use. Suppose you have a jar and you fill that jar with rocks. Can you say that the jar is filled? Of course not. And if you add some sand to the jar, would you say that jar is filled? Again, the answer is no. But if you now added water to the jar, would you say all the space in the jar is filled? Yes, you could say so.

It is clear that the space in the jar represents the time we have allotted to us. The rocks, sand, and water represent the things we do every day. The point is not to infer that every scintilla of space should be filled. Rather, the point is that the large rocks could never be placed in the jar unless they were placed there at the beginning. Thus, you need to place those items that are most important to you into your time-jar before you go filling the space with other things.

Time must be reserved for many reasons. We need time for the body, for leisure, for sensuality, for consumption, for travel, for rest, for love, for others, for family, for reading, for development, for creating, for meditating, for regression, for solitude. There are other needs too numerous to mention. However, in all of these needs, it is clear that the governing factor is you. When you first fall in love, there is always time for nourishing the relationship, no matter how busy you are. No phone call is too long, no lack of sleep is too tiring. The fact that you are in charge of your time may not be so clear where matters of the heart are concerned.

But, in matters of the head, you would think that logic would be the dominant factor and we would all be using time in a very efficient and helpful way. Looking around you'll see that isn't true. Time use isn't necessarily logical. Time use is much more a matter of the heart. The task for the department head and the teachers he or she supervises is to make time use less a matter of the heart and more a matter of the head.

TIME SAVING TIPS

1. Ask yourself the following:
   "Is what I am doing, or about to do, moving me toward my objectives?"
2. Listen to time management cassettes from the library whenever you can.
3. Work on only one item at a time.
4. Always carry a paperback book with you. If it is too fat, cut out the chapters and only carry part of it with you to read.
5. Rewrite your goals and activities every three years and reprioritize them.

References and Bibliography

Calano, James, and Salzman, Jeff (1982). *Real world 101.* New York: Warner Communications.

Covey, Stephen R. et al. (1994). *First things first.* New York: Simon and Schuster.

Drawbaugh, Charles (1984). *Time and its use: A self-management guide for teachers.* New York: Teachers College Press. How to arrange your life as a teacher to do more with less time.

Grudin, Robert (1982). *Time and the art of living.* Cambridge, MA: Harper and Row. A series of short ruminations about time from philosophy, science, literature, history, and personal experience. Very engaging.

Johnson, Philip (1992). *Time out: Restoring your passion for life, love and work.* Toronto: Stoddart Publishing, 1992. A good self-help book. Good suggestions on how to step back from life's pace.

Lakein, Alan (1973). *How to get control of your time and your life.* New York: Signet. Another hint-filled short work on time-management techniques.

Lightman, Alan (1993). *Einstein's dreams: A novel.* New York: Warner Books. A series of fictional stories about the dreams of Einstein dealing with time during the year 1905, the year Einstein explains his theory of relativity. Lots to ponder here especially if you know some relativity theory.

Linder, S. B. (1970). *The harried leisure class.* New York: Columbia University Press. Another classic. General information on complexities of modern living. An interesting read when comparing 1970 to 1995!

Mackenzie, Alec (1990). *The time trap.* New York: American Management Association. A re-publication and expansion on the original 1957 classic time management book.

Rifkin, Jeremy (1987). *Time wars: The primary conflict in human history.* New York: Holt and Company. If "small is beautiful" challenges "bigger is better," then Rifkin's view that "slow is humane" challenges speed and efficiency arguments. A survey of western culture concluding that changes in civilization take place only when there is a corresponding change in the conception of time.

Rutherford, Robert D. (1981). *Just in time,* New York: John Wiley and Sons.

Rybczynski, Witold (1991). *Waiting for the weekend.* New York: Penguin Books. A history of leisure time from ancient Rome to today. Insightful comments on the nature of the structure that dominates our weeks . . . the weekend.

Servan-Schreiber, Jean Louis (1988). *The art of time.* Reading MA: Addison Wesley. A philosophical treatment of time.

Winston, Stephanie (1983). *The organized executive: New ways to manage time, paper, and people.* New York: Warner Books. A classic on how to do more in less time; some very good hints.

Chapter 7

Evolution Without Revolution:
Making and Living with Change

Change: It Will Always Be with Us

Change and innovation in schools are, paradoxically, a constant fact of life. In fact, change is a constant fact of all human interaction. There has never been a process or device about which someone at sometime hasn't said, "We could improve that." And yet, for something that is ubiquitous to our existence, there is no harder goal to achieve than changing what has come to be seen as "comfortable practice." Machiavelli said it best in *The Prince*," There is nothing more difficult to take in hand, more perilous to conduct, or more uncertain in its success, than to take the lead in the introduction of a new order of things." As the department head and team leader, all change will present significant challenges to you. Your ability to lead will be sorely tested, depending upon the level of change to be accomplished. However, there will be nothing more rewarding than looking back at a successful change and knowing that without your leadership and direction, the change would never have occurred.

In today's world, the motto that every department head should have on the wall is the following:

> CHANGE IS A PROCESS, NOT AN EVENT.

The process of making change happen is sometimes a direct function of the drive and vision of a single person, or a few people in an organization, of how the status quo can, and should, be altered. But also, it is just as likely that change will be driven by external forces.

Case Study: The New Daily Schedule:
The Trail of Tears or the Stairway to Heaven?

The superintendent of schools and the board of education for the eastern school district announced last week that beginning next fall, Eastern High School would move to a block schedule. The schedule will consist of two long daily blocks of two hours duration followed by three shorter blocks of forty-five minutes duration. Every student will take two courses during the long blocks during a ten-week trimester. This means that, throughout the course of one year, a student will take the equivalent of six year-long courses. During the shorter blocks, the student will be scheduled for lunch, physical education, health, music, study hall, etc.

This innovation had been expected by the faculty, as there were some discussions about alternative schedules and effective learning at two faculty meetings earlier during the year. However, it still came as a surprise that the board of education and the superintendent moved so quickly. Most teachers figured it would take three years of talk before any changes actually occurred.

Now you are at the weekly meeting of the committee of department heads and are trying to decide how to handle this somewhat expected, but nevertheless, surprising change. The head of the language department speaks first, "This will be the ruination of our program. Students just can't learn enough vocabulary every day to carry on for a two-hour class. My teachers will have no idea what to do." The math department head agrees, "We might be able to do math for two hours a day, but what's going to happen to the students' retention of material if they then don't take the next math course until two trimesters later. They'll forget everything they learned. This is a great step backward." This reminds you of some of the conversations you had just last week in your department meeting. You had devoted the whole hour to how a new daily schedule would make teaching different and, in fact, better. You vividly remember some of the dialog that ensued.

"I'm concerned about the time it's going to take me to develop materials for this new class format. When am I going to do that? Can I sustain interest with a two-hour class. I've never had to do that before, and I worry that the students will be completely bored after the first hour."

"I'm not really concerned about the new schedule. I'll just do what I usually do, only it'll be for a longer period of time."

"Well, I'd like to know more about the whole thing. Where could we get some help? Are there other schools nearby that have tried similar schedules?"

"If we're going to have to move to this schedule, won't we have to coordinate our program in new ways. Right now, we know exactly what the previous course brings to us, but in the new system we'll have to improve that coordination. I think we need to get to work right away on a plan to develop new priorities and make clear what we expect each teacher to cover before handing the students on to the next level."

"Well, since I'm only a first-year teacher, I'll follow the leads of you veterans. But I've got to tell you, I'm excited about the new possibilities of this schedule. My only worry is that I'm going to be much more isolated in my class. Right now, I only have to be in class for forty-five minutes and, if I'm having a problem, I can see one of you right after that class. Now, I'll only be able to discuss any problems at the end of the day, since we'll all be in front of the students for four hours."

"Don't worry about the new schedule. I've had some experience with this kind of thing during summer school. In fact, I have some ideas that will allow us to actually improve on the schedule as it was explained to us. I'll bring in some of my notes tomorrow."

"I'm concerned that there will be unintended consequences of this schedule. I think that we don't even know right now what those will be, and I have the feeling that they aren't going to be for the better."

"I'm not very excited about this change. Isn't it just another one of those fads that come along, like teaching the "New Math," and ruin us for a couple of years and then we go right back to what we were always doing? I don't see what has been so bad with the schedule we have always had. Our students are learning perfectly fine with our present schedule, and I'm afraid that we're heading down the wrong path. Don't fix what ain't broke! Could we appeal this decision in some way?"

"No, I'm afraid we can't. This is a done deal, and we need to pitch in and make the best of it. If we monitor our work and the student work closely, I'm sure we'll be able to manage this change without much difficulty. Why don't we spend some time thinking about what a typical class might look like. In that way, we could anticipate some of the problems we'll encounter and be ready for them come the fall."

"That's easy for you to say, but I don't have the time right now to do any of that. I can barely keep up with my corrections now. When am I supposed to take time out of my present schedule to map out something that's not happening until next fall. If the school board is so intent on making this change, then they can pay me to come in during the summer to get ready for the new schedule. If they don't want to do that and the schedule fails, it'll be their own fault. Those people have no idea about what we have to do to teach well."

From that point on the meeting dissolved into a discussion of past initiatives that did not work, and you had a sinking feeling in the pit of your stomach as you began to think about leading this department into a successful experience with the New Daily Schedule. It's late April, and the spring is always the busiest time of year for your teachers. You adjourned the meeting and went straight to your office, closed the door and began the following list of questions. If only you could think of the answers to them!

1. What are the primary emotions surfacing in the statements of the department members?
2. If there are three months left to the year before summer break, how will I structure the weekly staff meetings to address this innovation?
3. What do I anticipate will be the greatest hurdle the staff will have to overcome in making the new daily schedule a successful reality?
4. No one even mentioned the students and their feelings about the change. How will I help the staff deal with those issues? Do I have the time to plan for that?
5. What are the risks inherent in this innovation? Are they worth taking? If they are not, do I have any options? What am I going to do if the innovation *must* be implemented.
6. What will happen if some members of the staff fail to perform in the new format? What do I do when that happens?
7. What will the department feel like in three years time, after the new daily schedule becomes a somewhat entrenched reality? What do I want it to feel like?
8. I know the teachers who will absolutely resist the new schedule. How will I work with those resisters? Should I ignore them (there

In our modern society there are several major forces driving change in our schools. The globalization of society and subsequent demographic changes in the student body have necessitated new approaches to education. Bilingual education, renewed focus on world history and events, investigating, understanding and evaluating other cultures all are making schools different places from what they were forty years ago. The burgeoning development and use of information technology has caused schools to create new departments, alter their work force, and spend vast sums of money to wire campuses. None of this existed fifteen years ago. These major issues force us to create change on a structural level, as well as on personal and political levels, with a pace and relentlessness unique to our modern times. Such change calls for skillful leaders to help transform educational institutions without chaos.

The important issue to manage when major changes face a school or department is to ensure that the change takes place in a planned and controlled manner. This is the goal of every change agent, whether that person be the superintendent, the principal, or the department head. But planning and control can be difficult when the change must be viewed from multiple perspectives. If conscious effort is not devoted to developing multiple perspectives, unintended consequences will, most likely, be the order of the day.

Figure 7.1 shows a matrix of how change and discomfort are inextricably intertwined. The goal is not to eliminate discomfort, but, rather, to address it. Getting to Quadrant I is no easy task, and yet, it is in effect the only worthwhile task. Beginning in Quadrant III and moving to Quadrants II and then to Quadrant I is the ideal transition, which the remainder of this chapter addresses. Being stuck in Quadrant III, or worse, finding your department or school mired in Quadrant IV, is common—and lamentable. However, it doesn't have to be the final resting place.

In schools, as well as other institutions, change is a natural part of the landscape. Every year, new students fill classes and present new challenges to the ingenuity and resourcefulness of the teacher. The spaces where the teachers teach may change from year to year. Colleagues change as new teachers arrive and veteran teachers retire or transfer to other schools and

Figure 7.1 Discomfort and Change

II We could be a better school, but it'll be hard work to get there.	I We are a better school and the hard work has been worth it.
III We're as good a school as we're ever going to be. We should stay the course.	IV We used to be a better school, we just weren't willing to change when we had the opprotunity.
NOW	FUTURE

districts. The principal may be new. The courses or grade that teachers teach may change. The books that are used may change.

Teachers accept these changes, blithely, because they do not fundamentally alter basic aspects of individual life. The main subject the teachers teach doesn't change. The way the teacher interacts with the students doesn't change. The names of the students may change each year, but the faces remain the same. The basics remain static. And while chalk dust may not settle on the clothes and hands of teachers as it has for the last hundred years, white board marker ink and copier toner dirty hands and fingers as effectively.

The changes that cause personal upheaval and turmoil are those that alter the basics. Working with a new daily schedule, using computers and other technology to teach, moving toward interdisciplinary teaching, addressing the fact that the subject one teaches no longer attracts students, running classes that have collaboration and cooperation as the basic method of instruction, using portfolio assessment techniques, or facing increasing parental involvement in the daily operation of the class, all cause strong personal and collective response.

This list doesn't include the inevitable kinds of personal change that occur outside of the workplace. Aging brings about new life stages and phases. New interests arise, and former interests wane. As families grow and mature, new concerns call for increased teacher attention and energy, which formerly could be devoted to teaching. Whether it be attending to the care of children or aging parents, life events have a way of forcing teachers to think about life's meaning and the legacy they will leave behind. These kinds of changes affect the teachers' lives in the classroom as well as out of the classroom. The experienced and savvy leader must take all of this into account when leading the group through changes.

Above all, the size of any change will have the most profound affect upon teachers. Adding five minutes to every class does not have the same disruptive affect as creating a two-hour block for the same class every day. Even the former will generate some amount of resistance, as the sum of the five-minute additions will probably mean thirty-five–forty minutes total during the day, and those summed minutes have to alter some other functional portion of the day. But the latter is such a profound change that the feelings of fear and loss can be overwhelming to the teachers, and resistance can be very strong.

In order to make fundamental changes like those previously mentioned, it is essential that change be seen as an ongoing process, a continuum of events that lead to a new goal. Communication and preparation for such changes are essential. One model for addressing change that has been used extensively and successfully is the **Concerns-Based Adoption Model (CBAM)** described by Hord et al. Exhibit 7.1 shows one version of this model. These stages of concern represent a teacher's movement from a level of unawareness to a level of not only acceptance, but complete engagement. This is a stage beyond mere compliance with the change. It represents true adoption and personal integration of change.

In similar change models, for example that of Conner (1993, 148), the degree of support for a change over time follows clearly defined stages. Beginning with unawareness and moving through awareness, understanding, positive perception, installation, adoption, institutionalization and, finally, internalization, all change is subject to many pitfalls. In moving from the preparation phase to the acceptance phase and, eventually, the commitment phase, the leadership skills of the department head will be tested. All along the way, confusion, negative perceptions of the change, decisions to depart from the original plan and decisions even to abort the plan, sometimes after considerable time and resources have been devoted to the

---

Exhibit 7-1 Stages of Concern

Stage of Concern	What it sounds like
6. Refocusing	"I have some ideas about the new daily schedule that would make it work even better."
5. Collaboration	"How can this new daily schedule allow us to work together any longer? We'll be so tied up in our class that we won't be able to talk to one another."
4. Consequence	"I'm worried about how the new daily schedule will affect student learning."
3. Management	"I don't have time to keep up with my corrections now. How will I manage to do them with this kind of schedule?"
2. Personal	"How can I keep student interest if the class is two hours long?"
1. Informational	"We should find out more about what other schools did when they moved to block scheduling."
0. Awareness	"I'm not concerned about the new daily schedule."

Adapted from G. E. Hall, R. C. Wallace, and W. A. Dossett, *A Developmental Conceptualization of the Adoption Process within Educational Institutions.* Austin: Research and Development Center for Teacher Education, The University of Texas, 1973.

change, constitute a black hole of behavior into which the department head must ensure the faculty do not fall.

In all change models, it is clear that change is going to take time. People need to work through their various stages of concern. As will be mentioned later, change forces people to move through the classic stages of grief, similar to those that occur when a person is confronted with the loss of a family member (Marshak, 1996). Some research points to the need for three to five years before teachers move from the stage of personal concern to one of concern for the students. In the case study that opened the chapter, you can hear those kinds of concerns in the departmental dialogue.

The department head or team leader needs to approach change with an understanding that these concerns are normal and, more importantly, that the teachers will need help in resolving their ambivalence or resistance to the changes. Knowing that transition between these stages will take time allows the leader to create many professional development activities to focus teacher energy and outlook in the right direction.

Oftentimes you will hear that some change is "way ahead of it's time." Think about the Dymaxion car of R. Buckminster Fuller. The car that Fuller designed in the 1930s was a radical departure from cars of the time. It had many safety features, including what could be considered an early version of an airbag safety cushion, that are standard on today's cars. The problem was that the car did not look familiar. It had three wheels, so that turning was much easier. It was bulbous, rather than boxy, in order to be more aerodynamic. In short, it was so different that no one wanted any part of it. Educational changes that are ahead of their times may, ultimately, be the ones that would have improved learning sooner had they been implemented.

When Thomas Edison first began to press for electrification of towns and cities, he knew that the electric light bulb had to be seen as only slightly different from the gas lights of the time. If his lighting system appeared too radical, it would be rejected by the masses. Thus, he designed the light poles and the globes that contained the bulbs to look just like the gas lamps that already existed. When introducing the light bulb in the home, he did not place them on the ceiling, where the effect of the light would be maximal, because gas lamps were obviously never found on the ceiling. Since the people were unfamiliar with the properties of the electric light bulb, to place them on the ceiling would be to cause fear of fire. By placing the fixture on the wall, just as gas sconces had been placed for years, the light bulb would appear familiar and be accepted more readily.

Often, it is the perception of what change means that is more important than the change itself. And once the change becomes familiar, people look back and wonder how they ever survived without it. This is one of the more interesting facets of change. Perseverance can transform the alien into the familiar from the experimental to the tried and true. To accomplish that feat, the department head must anticipate and plan for the various stages of concern that will develop in his or her staff.

Personal Dimensions of Change

Stage 0: Awareness

Not surprisingly, the first stage of concern is one of nonconcern. The symbolism of this stage being numbered at the zero level, I hope, is not lost on the reader. Before changing anything, the teacher must be aware that there is a change being suggested. Termed the **stage of awareness**, this is nevertheless a key stage for a teacher to move through, when implementing a successful innovation. In the case study, you can hear this stage clearly when one of the department members says, "I'm not really concerned with the new schedule, I'll just do what I usually do, only, it'll be for a longer period of time." This person is not only unaware of the goal behind the change, but is also somewhat resistant to the change. In his or her eyes, the change calls for no new behavior or alteration in practice.

With the proper focus, the leader can and must help the staff understand what the change is and what the proposed change will do, not only for the teachers, but also for the students. Making the case for an innovation is hard work. It is difficult for the staff to see the positive side of the change when they have no experience with the new situation. And in any new situation, there will be unforeseen events and effects. These will become apparent only once the change is actually implemented. Evans (1996) makes a salient point when he avers that most people would rather live with the devil they know than with the one that is unknown. It shouldn't be surprising that doing things differently is usually resisted. Even our Declaration of Independence makes the case that it is easier to live with the status quo than to change. "All experience hath shown, that mankind are more disposed to suffer while evils are sufferable, than to right themselves by abolishing the form to which they are accustomed."

Awareness leads to many possible outcomes, but the two most common ones are confusion and understanding. Confusion, of course, will not further the cause of change or acceptance of change. Thus, it is important for the department head or team leader to be clear and concise in any explanation of the possible change. It is better to respond that you don't know the answer to a particular question than it is to try and answer in a manner that results in further confusion. Confusion will develop into a predominantly negative perception of the change and thwart the change before it gets off the ground.

Yet, even understanding the goal and projected positive outcome of change is not an end in itself. "Understanding" falls well short of compliance and is a world away from commitment. While some of your faculty will never be able to reach a level of commitment, all should be able to reach a level of compliance that does not thwart commitment by others in the department. Compliance is a universe away from resistance, and it is resistance that you must overcome.

Stages 1 and 2: Informational and Personal Stages

Once the case for change has been made, the department head must continue to give clear and direct data, information, and feedback on the change. It is through such communication, that the staff will be able to understand what the change encompasses or demands, and to see themselves in the changed situation. This awareness of the change will drive them into two further stages of concern, the **informational stage** and the **personal stage**. These stages, while theoretically separate, will sound very similar. Listen to the statements from the case study that characterize these two stages. ""Well, I'd like to know more about the whole thing. Where could we get some help? Are there other schools nearby who have tried similar schedules?" And, "I'm not very excited about this change. Isn't it just one of those fads which come along, like teaching the "New Math" and ruin us for a couple of years? . . . I don't see what has been so bad with the schedule we have always had."

The general sentiment behind such staff questions and concerns is one of wanting to know more about the change, but also wanting to know how it will personally affect them. There may be other such questions, which surface in conversations with the teachers. These questions can range from specific concerns about small details to concerns about general philosophical principles. See Exhibit 7.2, Typical Stage 1 and 2 Questions, for further examples of typical questions.

Change causes people to feel incompetent, needy, and powerless (Bolman and Deal 1991, 377). This means that the department head will have to help staff develop new skills. Retraining and reframing roles may be es-

Exhibit 7.2 Stage 1 and 2 Questions

Detail Questions

Will my salary change?
Will I have to do more work?
Will my relationship with co-workers change?
Who will keep track of the new processes?
Will I be able to arrive and leave at the same times every day?
Will I have to keep track of more students?
Will I have the same room as before?
Can I take a coffee break under the new system?
Will I be able to advance in the same way as before?
Will my department head still be my immediate supervisor?

"Big" Questions

How might my educational values change?
Will the work be as challenging or more challenging than previously?
Will my prestige be enhanced or lessened?
What will my workers think of me?
What will my family think of me?
Will I be as interested in my work now?
How will the skill demands upon me change?

---

sential, depending upon the nature of the change. Creating opportunities for involvement by everyone affected by the change, while also attending to the psychological and social adjustments necessary for commitment, will consume much of the leader's time.

At the outset, change is rarely a simple choice between the good and the bad, between the black and the white. The shades of gray will conspire to create some level of reluctance to dive headlong into the change. And those shades will be different for each individual in your team. Robert Frost in his poem "Mending Wall," describes a situation where change, represented by the elimination and destruction of the wall, is not possible. "He is all pine and I am all orchard. My apple trees will never get across and eat the cones under his pines, I tell him." But the wall remains, in large part, because the neighbor who is being invited to change "will not go behind his father's saying, 'good fences make good neighbors.'" Psychological and social adjustments will be necessary to give permission to release attachments to unexamined beliefs.

Along with any positive benefits of change, there will always be the possibility of a negative impact. The negative impact may be one that applies only to a portion of the staff, or it may be universal, but less strong than a universal positive effect. Whatever the change is, the team leader must be prepared to do battle with the emotional tide that will surge once the change is underway. It is important to recognize that initial confusion and even negative comments do not signal, necessarily, resistance. When a certain amount of negativism arises, it is an opportunity for the department head to spring into action and reclarify the situation. In fact, it may be an opportunity to use the negative side of an argument to push forward the change agenda.

As the leader, it may not be enough to make the case for an innovation or change. Having a positive explanation for why the change is a good and right thing to do is only half of the necessary communication. You must also make clear to everyone, the negative consequences of *NOT* changing. Negative consequences always accompany remaining with the status quo, though sometimes these consequences will not seem unpalatable to the staff. You must clearly describe the downside of remaining unchanged.

When focusing on the negative side of not changing, it will be important to emphasize that you will support and help each person throughout the change process. Admit that while there will be, no doubt, some mistakes, no one is going to be blamed for trying hard and failing. You may have to say at the outset that while it is important to try one's best to make the change work, there will be setbacks. Let them know you are determined to help everyone become successful with the new initiative. Failure will be viewed as a kind of learning stage and a step toward progress. Emphasize that the school is willing to move beyond initial failure in order to realize the greater good that will result from such "learning." Making the staff feel secure about the effects of trying new behaviors is essential.

In his classic work *Leadership*, James MacGregor Burns defined transforming leadership. It is easy to make the direct association between transforming leadership to leadership for change. He said that transforming leadership "occurs when one or more persons engage with others in such a way that leaders and followers raise one another to higher levels of motivation and morality." Change must be about raising people up to new levels of what is right and good. It is these two underlying tenets that motivate people to change more than any other reason, especially in schools.

Bolman and Deal (1991, 401) recognized that "Change usually benefits some people more than others: it creates winners and losers, which is bound to produce conflict. Change agents often underestimate the opposition or drive conflict underground." This means that the team leader is going to have to pay close attention to the atmosphere surrounding change and be vigilant in discovering and airing differences.

In leading your staff in any major change, the more trust and confidence they have in you, the easier it will be for you to bring about a successful change. According to P. Morris (1986), the best metaphor for change is LOSS. Your staff will undergo an emotional response to change in every way similar to the stages of grief experienced when a loved one or someone close dies. This is one reason why it is so difficult to effect long-lasting change or to have a culture, in an institution like a school, which values continual change. There are strong benefits for an organization to maintain the status quo. In fact, almost as soon as a change becomes successful, it embeds itself into the culture and becomes almost as entrenched as the original process or behavior that it replaced.

In the 1970s the former speaker of the United States House of Representatives, the late Tip O'Neil said that "All politics is local." It is also true that in change, all change is personal. Commitment to change is built one person at a time. It will be your task to spend time talking about the change, not just in group meetings, but with every person on your staff whom you can buttonhole.

Stage 3: Management Stage

"I don't have the time to do any of what the change is asking right now. I can barely keep ahead of my class, never mind creating new exercises to supplement what I already do." Such statements almost always accompany curricular changes. In the management stage the teacher spends a good deal of attention focusing on the processes and tasks necessary to use an innovation. Finding the right resources and information uses up a very large segment of the teacher's planning periods and even beyond. The teacher often feels as if he or she is merely reacting to daily events, rather than being in charge of the innovation. He or she will spend time organizing, managing, scheduling, and generally coping with the demands of the change. The larger the change that is expected, the harder it will be for that teacher to manage the change event.

Robert Evans recognizes this stage as one in which the faculty member is trying to persist with patterns that had always held meaning before. In feeling that a change is a substitution for a previous behavior or standard, holding onto meaning or making new meaning is unsettling, takes time, and creates confusion. Just as students must construct new knowledge out of context, specific relationships and environments, so also must your staff. Only this is much harder for the adults. Because their knowledge structure is larger and more complex, with more interconnected meanings, it is harder to change than the adolescent knowledge structure. This means that you are going to have to help your faculty manage the change by being patient and supportive. You are going to have to listen to them rant and rave a bit about why the change will never work. It is crucial that you empathize as much as possible, but without giving into the idea that the change need not be accomplished. Your understanding and empathy are needed to identify with the emotions the staff member feels, but strong emotion is not an excuse to derail the change train.

"The way we do it here . . ." or better yet, "the way we've always done it here . . ." will spill effortlessly from the mouth of the staff member who is asked to give up or alter some valued event or operating procedure. However, if you can show that person that the new way has definite advantages over the old, that the new way will soon become just as comfortable, yet more effective, then you will have made major progress on the road to a successful change.

Your challenge is to frame the change as nothing more than meeting old goals and traditional values in a new way. "New wine in old skins," if you will. Following a new daily schedule is nothing more than a way to emphasize that short blocks of time are too small and keep children (and adults) from thinking well. New blocks of time help all faculty and students reach the time-honored goal of increased learning. Of course, it may be that there is no demonstrated proof that such changes actually make a difference. In such cases, the only defense is to claim that there is some dissatisfaction with the old way of doing things and that an experiment to determine if A is actually better than B, is more beneficial than attempting nothing at all.

One idea that may help a department head in the quest for creating a culture that allows for change, or better yet, embraces change, is to be a manager who understands the need for a departmental mission statement where change is viewed as a valuable asset. In crafting the mission statement, it would do the department (and school) well to include a statement that the department welcomes, seeks out, values, and supports change.

Stage 4: Consequences

Once the personal impact of change is overcome, or at least understood, both intellectually and emotionally, the teacher will suddenly think about the effect the change will have on the students. The change may have profound and complex effects upon a faculty member, but it will certainly have similar effects upon the students.

The consequences of any change are also very personal. What is merely a tiny pebble to one person is an insurmountable boulder to another. As the leader, your staff will look to you to set the standard and to shoulder the responsibility for making the change both desirable and feasible. Desirability is clearly something that the department head can manage by communicating and interacting with each person on the staff. Developing a strategy to make sure that the teachers know the impact of the change upon his or her immediate sphere of influence, the students, is essential.

Every change must have a relevance to the faculty member that can be translated into student improvement in terms of competencies and performances. If the faculty member can see no benefit accruing to the students, you can expect a very difficult time in trying to effect change. When all is said and done, no teacher ever changes his or her approach unless he or she believes that the new way will increase student learning. For example, this is why changing the daily schedule to a block schedule has not caught fire around the country. There is not enough information and research at this time to give teachers undisputable evidence that the block schedule improves learning beyond that in present traditional schedules.

That being said, there is the inevitable worry that change will disrupt the teacher's life. But that stage is prior to this one, and if the department head has been able to manage that stage, it will not be a drawback at this time. What is more likely to happen is a lack of resolve. Just as making change takes time, seeing results from change also takes time. The consequences may not be readily visible nor readily measurable. However, if the faculty can maintain their commitment to the change, the likelihood of success is much more probable.

Leo Tolstoy once wrote that "everyone wants to change the world, but no one wants to change himself." Changing one's own behavior is a consequence that strikes fear into many teacher's hearts. In fact, it is precisely such fundamental alteration, in personal belief or practice, that makes change so difficult. When the consequence of a change is somewhat unclear, the faculty member's degree of loyalty to the standards of the department and to the other members of the team, can serve as an important motivator for sticking with the innovation. Thus, the department head should work to develop situations whereby loyalty can be increased and demonstrated. This kind of attention to the personal side of making change happen will pay back enormous dividends.

It is incumbent upon the department head to keep the focus of each teacher on the long-term positive benefits of the change. It is certainly wise to be honest in addressing the outcome. Telling the staff that the change may not result in immediate and unqualified success is an honest way to gather trust and to use realism to further the chance that change will be successful. Being too optimistic is not necessarily the best way to handle complex change.

Conner refers to this stage of change as the time for installation. "The installation stage is not only a pilot period in which change is tested for the first time; it is where the first opportunity for true, committed action arises. And this action requires constancy of purpose, an investment of resources, and the subordination of short-term objectives to long-range goals" (Conner, 152). The main impediment to commitment will be how the department head and the faculty deal with the problems that will inevitably arise. If the problems are allowed to overwhelm the people involved in the change, the pessimism that will result will doom any chance for success.

By nature, the teaching act is one where criticism is essential. Teachers are only too quick to make criticisms of their environment. If problems arise that evoke a storm of criticism from the faculty, the department head must act swiftly to bring back the sense of positive optimism about the change and the reasons why the change is necessary. Again, understanding and acting to keep the cycle of the change process unbroken (see Figure 7.2) is an essential element for the committed team leader.

Stage 5: Collaboration

In this stage of the acceptance of change, the faculty member is well on the way toward internalization of the change. His or her focus is on coordination and cooperation with others. Each faculty member is concerned with relating what he or she is doing with what other instructors are doing. This level of change was expressed in the case study in the statement, "If we're going to move to this new schedule, won't we have to coordinate our program in new ways? Right now, we know exactly what the previous course brings to us, but in the new system we'll have to improve that coordination." Such an atmosphere is often denoted as a collegial one.

However, Evans cautions department heads and team leaders not to confuse collegiality with congeniality. When there is resistance, efforts to increase collaboration and collegiality can often result more in apathy than resistance. Evans feels that the complexity of the task of teaching prohibits serious collaboration in many faculty groups. He cites two possible reasons for this.

Figure 7.2 The Change Process Cycle

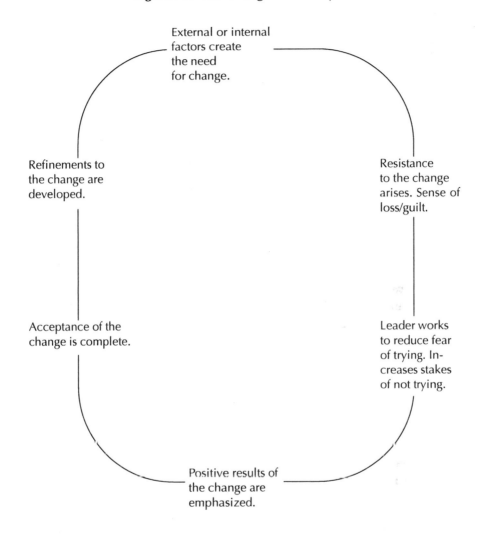

External or internal
factors create
the need
for change.

Refinements to
the change are
developed.

Resistance
to the change
arises. Sense of
loss/guilt.

Acceptance of the
change is complete.

Leader works
to reduce fear
of trying. In-
creases stakes
of not trying.

Positive results of
the change are
emphasized.

First, teachers work primarily with children and adolescents, not adults. But changes and innovations often force teachers into new interactions. They have to work more closely with adults. This is not the norm that has been the hallmark of what brought them into the profession. Teachers are energized and get their motivation from working with the students.

Second, teaching is idiosyncratic and fosters a high degree of autonomy, not to mention isolation. To expect that collaboration and coordination will be the order of the day, will take a fair amount of time to effect.

This is not to say it is not a worthy goal. It is only realistic to be aware that teachers' primary tendency is to work alone. Institutional change alters that basic tenet, because most changes call for self-monitoring and then feedback to the group.

This means that the team leader must create opportunities for adults to work together in substantive ways. Using a day to focus on the changes at hand would be one good way to bring adults together around the change process. Of course, there will probably be the chance that there will be some griping. The leader shouldn't let that deter him or her from holding such a day of discussion. It is highly unlikely that the complaints, if there are any, haven't been heard by most of the group in informal settings, such as the lunch room or the faculty room. By allowing the open airing of concerns in an atmosphere where collaboration is valued and the goals are clear, can only be a healthy activity.

But remember to think Teflon. Some of the criticism that inevitably will arise might get under your skin, if you let it. So don't. Think of your self covered in Teflon and anything that tries to stick to you cannot. It simply slides to the ground and can be discarded. After all, any negative feelings of faculty, most likely, will be with the system and not with you.

It is important to acknowledge the pain that the person might be feeling relative to the new innovation or change. "I can understand that this has not been easy for you as you have worked long and hard to get your course to fit perfectly into the old schedule. However, the reality is that we are going to have a new schedule, and you'll have to modify those old syllabi. I'm willing to give you some time to reorganize your course, and I would imagine that students are going to need as much time to readjust to the new assignment blocks as teachers are going to need to readjust to the new teaching blocks."

Evans gives a good generalizable statement on how the leader can structure his or her comments to link old and new thinking and action. "We've always been good at Z here and have pursued it with vigor and zeal using A and B. Now because of changes around us, the way students learn, the way our parents want to be part of the school, (etc.), we need to pursue Z in different ways. We need to expand our goals and methods of teaching to include X and Y. We must change to C from A and B and also add D to our strengths. these changes will be challenging, but if we concentrate on our commitments and draw on our skills, we can do it."

Linking thinking and then linking people is one good way to help everyone cope with the change. Helping your staff get outside of themselves will be beneficial not only for the immediate change, but also for future innovations. Collaboration inevitably leads to a higher degree of purposefulness. People who understand each other are more likely to want to link arms and move ahead together.

As the department head, you should be seeking optimal participation by each person. This doesn't mean identical participation or equal participation. Optimal must be judged on an individual basis and is a relative term. But relative participation is a step beyond neutral compliance. It is not what John Kenneth Galbraith called "the bland leading the bland." Participation is active. And participation means the person has a stake in making change succeed.

Stage 6: Refocusing

At this point in the change stages, the faculty member has adopted the change and the change is on its way toward internalization and then institutionalization. The teacher's focus is on the exploration of more universal benefits from the innovation, including the possibility of major changes or replacement with a more powerful alternative. The individual teachers have definite ideas about alternatives to the proposed or existing form of the innovation.

In the case study, there is only one statement that exhibits a teacher who is at this stage. "Don't worry about the new schedule. I've had some experience with this kind of thing when I worked at East Side High. In fact, I have some ideas that will allow us to improve on the schedule as it was explained to us. I'll bring in some of my notes tomorrow."

The only reason such a statement can be made is that this teacher has already had the opportunity to pass through the various stages of concern and arrive at the point of internalization and refocusing. Without this previous experience, no such statement could be made, nor should the department head think that reaching this stage will happen early on. However, having someone in the group who has experienced a similar change and apparently felt positive about it will make the process of change much easier for the team leader. It would be just the opposite if this teacher had had a negative reaction and experience to the change. If that were true, the leader would have to spend much more time keeping the group focused on the change in its present form and context, and not the change that had been experienced by this one person. Additionally, the leader will need to spend a good deal of time working one on one with this person to help dispel the understandable negative reaction that will be attached to the change at hand.

It is during this stage of change that two possible outcomes can occur. First, the change could be discarded or canceled. Second, the change becomes institutionalized. Both of these phases have long-term focus. Both of them have long-term implications for the team leader as well as for the institution.

If the change is canceled, after being installed and tested, there can be a backlash that may prevent future change. After all, getting everyone ready to adopt a major change has taken substantial emotional commitment by the faculty and, perhaps, the expenditure of some scarce resources, such as personal time. For example, in making a substantial change in the daily schedule, faculty may have had to alter their day care plans, rewrite all their syllabi and lesson plans, reorganize or refurnish their classroom, while the school may have invested money to reprogram the bell system, hired consultants to work with the faculty, spent money to send teachers to summer professional development conferences, etc.

Yet, even with all that, if the change is not doing what it was designed to do, improve learning, then it must be discarded. Again, this creates an opportunity for the leader to exhibit skillful management of the group. As every scientist knows, there cannot be great breakthroughs in understanding without high risk. You cannot create new knowledge by remaining with status quo thinking. Even if the change is not ultimately adopted, the process and experience with new models of behavior and thinking are growth-producing. The faculty will be the better for having gone through the process. Helping them make sense of why the change was not adopted takes further communication.

The reasons for cancellation could be many, but among the usual reasons for change being halted are the following:

- Economic problems arose, which showed that the change was not viable for the long term.
- It became clear over time that there was a major logistical problem with the change that could not be overcome.
- The initial conditions that sparked the change no longer exist.
- The people who spearheaded the change have left the organization.

All of these reasons make sense if the leader chooses the right method of focusing the group's attention. Debriefing meetings about what positive portions of the change might remain as part of the group's behavior is one way to bring closure and to help the faculty look ahead to future change. It is at this point that the group can engage in "what if . . ." discussions. "What if . . ." discussions can be very productive, especially when led by faculty who have invested substantive time and energy on the change.

The alternative pathway is for the change to have been determined to be effective and, thus, be institutionalized. By institutionalized, I mean that if you were to leave the school for a few years and then return, no one would remember much about the turmoil that surrounded the change when it was initially proposed. Instead, it will feel as if the "change" had been around for as long as could be remembered.

A real life example of such an institutionalized change is the use of ATMs, Automatic Teller Machines. In the early 1980s, such machines were first being introduced. Prior to their introduction, people had to make sure they took care of withdrawing money from the bank by Friday, if they wanted to have cash on the weekend. This meant that Friday trips to the bank were essential and banks stayed open on Friday night, partly to accommodate their customers. Now, while banks still remain open on Friday nights, it is unlikely that anyone feels the need to withdraw cash for the weekend. ATMs are everywhere, making cash readily available. In fact, very few people truly remember the time when such machines were not available.

In education, there have been similar changes that have made their way into the teaching culture in such a manner as to become institutions in themselves. Use of the hand-held graphing calculator, or even calculators in general, has fundamentally changed the nature of mathematics teaching. At the same time, the use of these low-cost machines has destroyed the slide-rule manufacturing business. No math or science teacher can imagine going back to the days of the slide-rule. In fact, it seems as if calculators have always been here. When you realize that for present high school students, the calculator has existed all their lives, it makes sense that the use of calculators has been institutionalized.

Once a change has been institutionalized, faculty no longer see the change as tentative or pending. It becomes the norm, not the unusual or experimental. This does not mean that there still are not problems that may occur. Institutionalization remains a step away from internalization. Compliance, after all, is not the same as commitment. However, as with many changes, it is not essential that everyone like the change. Personal belief may not be a factor in a successful change.

For example, changing the daily schedule does not alter the fundamental reasons for teaching. Love of students, personal contact with students, pride in their accomplishments, and support for their growth will not change because the length of classes has changed. But in general, it is better if change is internalized. It is easier to work with faculty who not only understand the reasons for change and the mechanics of the change, but who also accept and welcome the change, making it a fundamental part of who they are.

Summary

The key to successful change is the degree to which the leader has been able to serve as a "transformational leader" (Bass, 1985). Transformational leaders, in Bass's view, fundamentally change followers by elevating their expectations of success, increasing their confidence in the leader, and moving to higher levels of need relative to Maslow's hierarchy. In such an environment, the department head's staff will move beyond the original expectation and be transformed into more motivated followers who provide effort that exceeds the minimal needed for change.

Becoming such a transformational leader takes hard work and understanding and acting upon the concepts below:

- Change is a process and not an event.
- There are distinct stages that people and institutions go through during change.
- The leader is the key person in the adoption of a successful change.
- Change evokes an emotional response similar to grief.
- People react to change in individual and unique ways.
- Communication on change must involve many one-on-one conversations.
- There needs to be continual feedback on how the change is going.
- Change takes time. Taking time can make the change happen sooner.
- Forcing can increase the cost for the long-term.
- Change can, and in certain instances should, be canceled or altered.
- Change is inevitable in education as education becomes more valued and necessary for "the pursuit of happiness."

References and Bibliography

Bass, Bernard M. (1985). *Leadership and performance beyond expectations.* New York: The Free Press.

Bolman, Lee G., and Deal, Terrance E. (1991). *Reframing organizations, artistry, choice, and leadership.* San Francisco: Jossey-Bass.

Burns, James MacGregor. (1978). *Leadership.* New York: Harper and Row.

Conner, Daryl (1993). *Managing at the speed of change.* New York: Villard.

Evans, Robert (1975). *The human side of school change.* San Francisco: Jossey-Bass.

Kubler-Ross, Elizabeth (1975). *Death in the final stage.* New York: Simon and Schuster.

Marshak, David (1990). The emotional experience of school change: Resistance, loss, and grief." *NASSP Bulletin, 80.*

Morris, P. (1986). *Loss and Change.* London: Routledge and Kegan Paul.

Wren, J. Thomas ed., (1995). *The leader's companion: Insight on leadership through the ages.* New York: The Free Press.

Chapter 8

Don't Waste Their Time:
How to Run Effective Meetings

In the case it is clear that Stephen has spent a long time thinking about what needs to be done to make a meeting effective. He, as many of us, has sat through too many meetings which he felt were a waste of his time. Upon becoming the department head, he swore that his meetings would be different and that he would devote the time and effort to making them work, not only from a leadership perspective, but also from a participant perspective. You can see that from the very beginning, running a good meeting takes not only time and effort but also skill and practice. In many respects, running a good meeting is similar to running a good class. Preparation, knowledge of the content, having a goal and a plan to reach that goal are the same essential components needed for a meeting to work well.

Stephen also has trained the department to work together and feel responsible for making the meeting work. This is no different from training students in the classroom to realize they need to work together and contribute if the class is going to work well. When students do not know what they are expected to do and are not educated in how to accomplish such expectations, the class works poorly. Running a good department or team meeting depends on much the same spirit of participation. It takes education and responsibility by the participants to make the meeting work.

Mark and Mary serve as timekeeper and recorder. Both of these tasks may not be part of the repertoire of behaviors of most groups. It is only through Stephen's strong desire to make the meeting function that these jobs are attended to. Stephen also has paid attention to informing the group about the purposes of the meeting and has helped them come prepared for the meeting. Again, this is not any different from what a good teacher would do to help students prepare for a class.

In addition to stating clearly the reason for meeting, the methods that will be used for decision making are clear. In this case, the purpose of the meeting is pure discussion. Stephen states in the agenda that there will be

---

Case Study: Stephen's Meeting

Stephen held twice monthly department meetings of his Mathematics and Computer Science department. These meetings were always held when everyone in the department was free on Monday during the second period of the day. He began preparing for this department meeting about five days before it was scheduled. First, he began by creating the agenda(s) (See Exhibit 8.1a and Exhibit 8.1b.)

Exhibit 8.1a Agenda

Time: 8:45 A.M.–9:30 A.M.
Date: Monday January 23, 1996
Place: Room 244, Mathematics Wing of Schoolhouse
1.   Book order forms for spring term courses. I will bring the materials for each teacher. Due back to me in one week (January 30) (5 minutes).
2.   Computer Literacy Requirement (35 Minutes).
        It is crucial that you read the attached memo before coming to the meeting. We will be discussing the proposals I have set forth and will be open to additional proposals you may wish to present. We will not be making any decisions at this meeting.
3.   Summary (5 minutes).

Exhibit 8.1b Expanded Personal Agenda

1. Book order forms:
   Sally (book store director) needs to know who will be using new editions, so she can return those that are not being used this year. Remind everyone of our desire to have students spend as little as possible on new books. Use what is needed, but make sure that any book ordered is used extensively. Don't go beyond what the kids can realistically handle in a ten-week term.
2. Computer Literacy requirement
   a. Of the seven peer schools, only three still have such a requirement.
   b. Proficiency is one of the main assessment alternatives that we learned about during the opening of school professional development workshop.
   c. We need to use staff to teach core courses in each discipline. Now they are siphoned away because of the requirement aspect of the course.
   d. Kids don't seem to like the course very much in its present form.

He sent the short agenda to every member of the department three days before the scheduled meeting. While the bulk of the agenda was the usual mix of old and new items, there was one item in particular that he needed to discuss with the department. Since the meeting time was only a single forty-five minute class-period long, he decided to also include some informational material. (See Exhibit 8.2.)

Exhibit 8.2 Informational Material

MEMO

TO: Math Guys and Gals
FROM: Old Reliable
DATE: January 18, 1996
RE: Department Meeting Monday January 23, 1996 8:45 A.M. Meeting Room/Schoolhouse
TOPIC: Possible elimination of the Computer Literacy Required Course for 11th and 12th grade students.

Presently the GRADUATION REQUIREMENT is as follows: "Use of the computer is integrated throughout the ninth and tenth grade curriculum, thus insuring all students are exposed to a variety of applications. Eleventh and twelfth grade students who have not been through the ninth and tenth grade must take a one-term course on computer applications including word processing, spreadsheet analysis, data base access, network communication, electronic mail, and simple programming."

PROBLEM ONE:

Students are exiting the ninth and tenth grade with only word processing instruction and use. They may be exposed to other uses of the computer but not in any organized and universal manner. In addition, a fair number of students, who have been through the ninth and tenth grades, still come to the computer center without floppy discs and without the ability to use the server. In addition, they have no knowledge of spreadsheet analysis, network communications, Internet use, or multimedia use. If we believe that such computer training should be integrated into our curricula, we must have a system of accountability where each department agrees to take on a portion of the training.

Solutions:

1. Institute a **required** course for all students. There is great reluctance on the part of the administration to do this. It will cost a great deal in terms of teacher power to offer all the needed sections and will limit a student's ability to access core courses.

2. Agree to **integrate** some computer use into every course that is required for graduation. I favor this approach. The educational research shows that learning at the point of application is extremely effective. While this approach would insure exposure, it would not necessarily guarantee expertise.

3. Create a **competency** exercise that a student must pass to graduate. This would be the boldest approach. Combined with #2 we would insure competency in computer usage. The format and content of the test would be provided to all students and faculty. The students could plan to learn what is required by taking particular courses where the skills would be integrated into the fabric of the course.

PROBLEM TWO: (Not to be discussed at the Monday meeting, but needs to be addressed at some point soon.)

The computer programming courses are drying up. Each year there seem to be fewer and fewer students interested in actual programming. In addition, those that do take the course are overwhelmingly males. Since there is no programming graduation requirement, the question we need to address is: Can any department survive when there is no graduation requirement? If so, how?

In this way, everyone would be up to speed on the issues at hand. In addition, Stephen was careful to inform the department of the communication mode in which he was approaching this issues. (See Exhibit 8.3.) He also asked the computer center coordinator to attend the meeting.

Exhibit 8.3 Decision Modes

As an administration, we seek to maintain an active role for faculty in decision making. However, we also understand that there are matters, not necessarily those that might be considered major school policy, where too much time is devoted to the decision making process, distracting us from our primary purpose in the school, educating students. So, it is with this in mind that we offer the following clarification as to the different ways we, or any of the secondary administrators (Department Heads, Deans, etc.), can elect to broaden participation in the consideration of policy. These guidelines are not meant to stifle discussion or disagreement, as we all favor a certain amount of healthy interchange. Rather, they are offered so that we may move forward with clear understanding of how decisions are going to be made.

Informative Mode: The administrator has already decided what course of action is to be taken and is presenting the decision as a fait accompli. This mode is not meant to be used with major school or departmental policies. For example, it would be inappropriate for a department head to decide that all teachers must be available for two hours of extra help after classes. It is appropriate, for example, for the department head to inform the department that everyone must attend the end-of-term student seminar program.

Consultative Mode: The administrator thinks he or she knows what should be done, but is not sure how to do it. Thus, groups are consulted to give advice and to help shape the thinking of the administrator. For example, the school calendar must have 175 days, but determining when the year begins and when it ends can be a faculty discussion.

Deliberative Mode: The administrator does not have a strong feeling about an issue and seeks faculty consensus about the matter. Whatever the faculty decide on the issue will be implemented by the administrator. For example, the faculty might wish to raise or lower the bar for the Academic Honor Roll. This can be a totally faculty controlled issue.

On the day of the meeting, Stephen made sure there were enough comfortable chairs in the room for everyone to sit at the table and that the overhead projector and screen were in place. In addition, he made sure the meeting supply kit was full. (See Exhibit 8.4 for contents.) Before the meeting took place, Stephen asked Mark to take the minutes and Mary to be the time keeper.

Exhibit 8.4 Meeting Supply Kit

Pencils and paper for 7 members of the department
Five overhead transparency sheets
Five different colored transparency markers
Academic Year Calendar, including dates for all future faculty meetings and committee meetings
Regular calendar for the next two years
Tin of candy/fudge
Summary notebook of all previous meetings
School Adviser handbook
School Student handbook
Course catalog
Extra copies of the meeting agenda

Stephen made sure he was the first person at the meeting room and brought out the tin of fudge for members to snack on before the meeting began. Crazy as it seemed, Stephen had learned that one way to get everyone to arrive on time was to have the fudge available before the meeting began, but that it had to be put away once the time to meet arrived. Those who were late did not get any fudge.

Stephen began by stating that in today's meeting there would be no final decision made on the main issue of eliminating the mandatory computer literacy course. He outlined in one sentence the key questions to be discussed and stressed his desire that every one of the department's members should be prepared to state his or her feelings about the proposal. The meeting ran smoothly as Mary made sure no one spoke for more than five minutes about any single point, while Mark used the overhead to record all the varied suggestions that were made by each member.

At one point during the meeting, the group began to discuss the kinds of computers that were available in the computer center. Stephen interrupted and reminded everyone that the discussion was to focus on the elimination of the computer literacy requirement and that the group was veering off-track. At another point, Donna began to get very agitated about the fact that eliminating this course might lead to her losing her position, since her main assignment in the school was to teach the computer lit classes. Stephen could see that she was getting near the point of uncontrolled anger, and he made it a point to inform the group that the head of school had promised that no one would lose his or her job if the course were eliminated. This seemed to bring Donna back to a level of comfort, which, in turn, made everyone else breathe easier.

Near the end of the meeting, Mary spoke up to say that there were only five minutes left and that a summary was in order. Stephen used his personal notes, as well as those on the overhead transparency, to summarize the main points that had been made. He asked Donna to determine how many students would be affected by simply introducing a competency exam. He asked Mark to find out how the Registrar's Office would keep track of students who passed a competency exam. Stephen also asked for two volunteers to do some background work on programs at peer schools. Both Mary and Donna volunteered. Stephen noted that the group had done good work and had made substantial progress toward clarifying the departmental position on the course issue. He assigned Donna the task of recorder for the next meeting. He adjourned the meeting at one minute after the scheduled ending time.

Upon returning to his office, Stephen created a short e-mail document summarizing the highlights of the meeting, clearly stating who was responsible for completing which tasks before the next meeting. He attached a special note on Faith's message, noting that she was missed at the meeting and that he hoped that nothing serious had happened to keep her from attending.

Stephen was then able to begin his classroom preparation for the interesting day that lay ahead.

---

no decision made. While this makes the purpose of the meeting clear, it should also be noted that discussion alone will bring about a certain amount of decision making.

A guaranteed responsibility for any department head or team leader will be to run meetings. What is less guaranteed is the success of those meetings. If you follow the information, hints, and techniques presented in the following chapter, it is more likely that your meetings will run smoothly, be effective, and bring praise to your leadership. Remember no one wants to have time wasted by an ineffective meeting.

Before the Meeting Occurs

Your First Concern: Meet for a Purpose

A meeting is nothing more than teamwork in action. The "Seven C's"— common goal, cooperation, collaboration, consensus, camaraderie, conflict, and care—are essential themes to foster in all meetings. The reason you have called the meeting is for a group of people to get work done. There is no other reason to meet for business except that overarching purpose. And the nature of the work to be done needs to be important to the people who are being asked to meet. One would not call a mathematics department meeting to compose a group letter to be sent to the United Nations protesting the refusal of Libya to turn over the terrorists accused of bombing TWA Flight 103. While this may be an important task, in a political sense, it is not the primary work of a department.

As the team leader and the leader of the meeting, you should make sure that you are meeting for a purpose. If there is no purpose, then do not call the meeting or cancel a standing meeting. However, such an occurrence should be rare. A good meeting leader always has a working agenda that is both short- and long-term, and there should always be some business that can be accomplished.

Having a backlog of agenda items is one way to keep everyone involved in making the meeting work. When agenda items come from the meeting participants, there will be a spirit of cooperation when you ask the person who suggested the agenda item to be prepared to lead the rest of the group through the concern or issue. This means that the group is not always single-leader-centered. But as the leader, it is your responsibility to decide how the group is going to act.

Ask yourself the questions: "Do I need to have a meeting to get accomplished what I want to? Do I need to have everyone present? Do I need to bring others besides the team together?" If the answers point towards a meeting, then also ask yourself if others need to assist you in planning the meeting or can this be done by you alone? Remember that you are asking for a complex event to take place. I say complex because any time more than a few people meet, the chance for surprisingly unpredictable outcomes is highly probable.

There are certain kinds of meetings where the purpose is to begin a process or to define an area that is going to be studied. A common meeting you will have to run is the opening or closing session of the group's year. To set the stage for those meetings, it is useful to give the participants time to think about the exercise you have chosen to launch the meeting. Exhibit 8.5 is an example of how you can set the stage for an opening meeting where goals for the year can be discussed and expectations shared.

In some respects, calling a meeting is an act of power, since those who are asked to attend usually cannot say no. In most meetings, the person who benefits most is the person who called the meeting. Thus, to insure that everyone feels that the meeting was useful, it is essential that all participants, not just the leader, get something out of the meeting.

There are basically three ways in which a group will act when they are meeting. The group can be leader centered and not be able to function without your presence. This is true when you are acting as the decision-making or policy-setting official. One would not want a department deciding that the graduation requirement be reduced, without having the department head present for the discussion.

A group can work much as a discussion class. The leader is the person most prepared, or assigned to be prepared, to lead the discussion. This type of meeting can be held successfully without the official leadership of the department head. However, there does have to be someone to lead the meeting. No meeting can be successful without a leader of some type. There always has to be someone who is responsible for making the overall flow and tone be one that facilitates forward movement.

Finally, a group can work at cross-purposes. The leader wants the group to discuss one particular item, while the group decides that it wants another topic discussed. This can result in a power struggle. Such dysfunctional meetings often occur when the team leader has not been keeping an ear to the ground to know if there are any hot, but somewhat silent, issues. When such issues arise, the leader is taken by surprise.

In order to make sure that your meeting works, the first place to focus is the agenda. After making the decision that there is a need to meet, developing a flexible, realistic agenda is the first task.

The Agenda

Meeting experts all agree—never hold a meeting without an agenda. The agenda should be distributed well in advance of the meeting because not only do *you* want to prepare for the meeting, you also want *the participants* to prepare for the meeting.

The form of the agenda can vary, but usually, the following items are standard:

- Date,
- Location,
- Starting and ending times,
- What will be covered in order of priority (along with the person presenting if possible),
- The time allowed for each item,
- Any pre-meeting information that must be gathered or read by the participants. See Exhibit 8-1a.

Simply producing a well-structured agenda is not a guarantee that the meeting will be successful. However, it does act as the foundation for building a good meeting. The agenda needs to be well thought out. It is the blueprint for how you and the group will act. Therefore, it is essential that the agenda have realistic times associated with each item, and you must adhere to these times. The items on the agenda might be generated by you, by the group at an agenda-setting meeting, or from an ongoing agenda item pool. You can set up a continuous agenda item pool by placing a black or white board in a convenient place for all members to see and asking that anyone with a concern place that on the agenda board. The agenda board should be divided between short-term items and long-term items. That is to say, short-term items are those that need to be discussed almost immediately, while long-term items are less time sensitive, though no less important, and can be placed on the agenda when there is time.

If a meeting is going to have a complicated or sensitive issue presented or discussed, it is advisable to prepare a second, personal agenda. See Exhibit 8.1B. This is an expanded version of the short agenda, which was sent to everyone. The personal version has the techniques you will use to run the meeting, as well as extra information about possible pitfalls. While this is certainly more work than the usual one, it can pay off when your meetings are much more effective and the people attending feel that the meeting was worthwhile because something was actually accomplished. The personal agenda is your script for meeting success.

The Location and Seating

Both the room and the chairs should be comfortable. A well-lit space, especially with natural light, is preferable to meeting in a closed room. The setup of chairs or tables should be conducive to discussion. It is best to hold the meeting in a space where everyone can be seated at the same table or in a single circle. When people are forced to sit outside the main body of the meeting, they become nonparticipants—observers—and thus will not feel part of the team. They will also be forced to look at the back of a speaker and will not be able to read facial expression.

Making sure that the seating is appropriate might be one of the more difficult tasks in setting up a meeting. There is nothing that will cause a meeting to lose energy quicker than uncomfortable seating. But paradoxically, if the seating is too comfortable, you can expect the meeting to lack energy. Holding a meeting where several people sit on a couch or in soft chairs can bring heavy eyelids quickly into play, rather than heavy ideas. When people are seated at a table, they tend to want to do business. Try to work a balance between comfort and the need to be alert and thoughtful.

It has been discovered that the person who both gets and gives the most eye contact, often emerges as the leader of a meeting. You should position yourself accordingly, if you want to make sure you do not relinquish this advantage.

In addition, a lack of eye contact can be used to diminish negative interactions. If you know two people are going to disagree or even attack one another, try to seat them together, to lessen eye contact. Seating them directly opposite one another is the first step towards losing control of a meeting.

The Food

If the meeting is going to be short, there is no physical need for food or drink. But providing refreshments can convey a feeling of camaraderie and informality that may be very important to the goal you have set concerning teamwork. If the meeting is to be longer than two hours, you should plan on something light, such as fruit or muffins, along with the appropriate beverages. Sugary food can give a short burst of energy, but in the long run depletes the energy of the participants. Note: the fudge Stephen used in his pre-meeting time coincided with a short meeting of less than an hour's duration and should not have a detrimental effect upon the participants.

The Meeting

The Beginning Phase

Introduction

Make sure you *begin with energy*. Don't slide into the beginning of a meeting. Get everyone's attention. It's not too farfetched to consider using a dinner bell to signal the beginning of the meeting. You have to be "in charge" here. The group expects you to do this and will not be even the slightest insulted if you ask them to end their conversations and focus on the topic to be discussed. In Stephen's Case, Stephen uses the first few minutes of the meeting for somewhat low-key business. This allows any latecomers to still participate in the main item of business on the agenda.

You should never wait for anyone in particular to appear. You should start the meeting on time. As people come to realize that this is what will happen, they will also be there on time. If you have people who are continually late, you must speak to them outside of the meeting, and determine why this is happening and fix it. If the entire group begins to habitually assemble a few minutes late, remind them that you wish to begin the meeting at the stated time because every minute counts. Of course, you must make sure that every minute does count.

Sometimes you will have a special guest at a meeting. Make sure to introduce him or her and explain why he or she is in attendance. In **Stephen's Case,** Stephen invited the director of the computer center, since the topic of discussion would be the computer literacy course. It may have been important to hear from this person or for that person to hear the discussion.

In addition to introducing people, you need to get the meeting started. You should have the expanded agenda at your fingertips with either an opening statement or a clarifying statement prepared. This will allow you to outline what everyone will be doing during the meeting. The opening does not have to be elaborate. It is enough to restate what was given in the agenda.

You may have prearranged with one of the members of the group to be the opening speaker. In doing this, you help the group get launched and you are assured that there is not the commonly encountered dead zone where, after you ask for the first comment, there is nothing but the sinking sound of shuffling papers.

Another technique to make sure that the meeting begins with an active atmosphere is to ask for one person to give the pro-argument and another the con-argument. You can also do this in a pre-meeting informational memo with the instruction that you are going to ask someone to support the pro-side and someone else to support the con-side.

Another surefire method to start meetings with thoughtful activity, rather than silence, is to ask each member of the meeting to write out his or her answer, thoughts, feelings, opinions on the matter at hand. Then call on one or two people to read what they wrote. This technique also has the effect of getting everyone focused on the same issue. In many situations, the participants in a meeting have just come from some other mentally taxing activity and will still be processing those past events. Writing clears the mind and sets the stage for thinking about what is at hand, instead of what is in the past.

Exhibit 8.5 shows a possible opening exercise that can get a group started at the very beginning of a series of meetings.

In **Stephen's Case,** Stephen could have asked a particular member of the department any of the following to get the discussion started.

- Is the outline of the problem and its possible solutions clear and complete?
- Are there any other solutions that should be considered?
- Are there disagreements with the statement of the problem?
- Would anyone like to rephrase the statement of the problem?

Procedural Understanding

Exhibit 8.5 Opening Meeting Exercise

August 3, 1997

Dear Science Colleagues,

While it may still be the dog days of summer, the winter constellations of Taurus and Orion are beginning to become visible in the early morning (about 4 A.M.). To somewhat mangle Churchill, this certainly does not mean the end of summer. And it clearly isn't the end of the beginning of summer. Rather, this signals the beginning of the end of summer and the inevitable opening of school.

In preparation for that event I'm taking the liberty of sending you the enclosed book, *The Art of Time*. This is not a "how to" book, describing how to fit fifty minutes of work into thirty minutes of time. No, it is a philosophical treatment of time. The frustrations we all have with the "lack" of time that we have are of concern to me, and I'm hoping we will use some of the ideas contained in this book to address how we can deal with our frustrations.

The real purpose of this letter is to describe what I would like us to do at our opening meeting on September 7th. We will meet at 1 P.M. and adjourn at 4 P.M. To prepare for that meeting, I would like each of you to come to the meeting with responses to these three questions.

1. What are three behaviors, actions, or expectations you have of yourself in your role as science teacher for the coming year?
2. What are three behaviors, actions, or expectations you think your students have for you in your role as teacher for the coming year?
3. What are three behaviors, actions, or expectations you have for me in my role as department head for the coming year?

I want us to share these answers by putting them on large sheets of newsprint to be displayed for all to read. After we have a chance to read what everyone has written, I'd like to have an open discussion to help us make sense of what we share and help us make concrete suggestions as to how we can ensure that these expectations will be fulfilled. In sharing this way, it is my hope that we will become aware of the needs of colleagues, both from an individual and a collective basis. We will be better able to support one another in creating the best possible educational environment for our students as well as an energizing and satisfying working environment for ourselves.

So enjoy the last few weeks of your summer break and I look forward to our meeting in September.

George Sartenwolf

Everyone in a meeting must know what the procedures are going to be. Will there be voting? If so, what form will that vote take. What will the vote mean? Who will act on the vote? If there is no vote, then what will occur with the results of the meeting?

If you wish to have everyone pulling their oars together, voting should be discouraged. Rather, trying to reach consensus is more useful. While it will take longer to reach consensus, it will result in more positive change in the long run. Do not force consensus beyond the stage of "I can live with it." You will never get everyone to fall in love with every proposal and policy. You only need positive support, not necessarily complete embrace.

When voting, one positive approach is to use approval voting. In approval voting, all participants get to vote as many times as they'd like to. If there are three options on the floor and a person likes all three, he or she can vote for each one, rather than having to vote for only one of the three. The proposal with the most votes will carry. This will ensure that the largest number of sympathizers have carried the day. If there is a tie, then the two options that are tied now undergo the approval voting process.

Exhibit 8.6 shows a detailed procedural document and agenda for a week-long meeting dealing with substantial curricular change. In this case, it was essential that all parties understood how decisions were to be made. In order to develop these procedures, everyone who was to be involved in the meeting/workshop was invited to participate in setting the procedures. In this particular case, four of the eleven members of the group came forward. The entire group had also agreed that they would abide by the meeting procedures developed by this subcommittee.

The Middle Phase

The Discussion

It is important for you, the leader, to know if you are discussing policy, problem solving, explaining, predicting, or debriefing. Each of these involves a different kind of question to be asked.

Discussion Type	Question to be answered
Policy	Should we . . . ?
Problem solving	How will we . . . ?
Explaining	Why do we . . . ?
Predicting	What if . . . ?

Debriefing   What can we conclude now that . . . ?

With controversial issues, you may want to present a set of opinions. These don't have to be your opinions, but rather those that you have heard. By stating them up front, you save time and do not have to identify those members who hold strongly to one side or the other. Whatever the discussion, it is essential that the participants remain close to the facts. This is where you, as the leader, play a crucial role in making a meeting work.

Your Role

Ensure Participation

You must bring everyone into the discussion. There are always silent people at every meeting, but these participants often have good ideas that should be heard by the group. They just need encouragement to get them into the swing of things. You can ask a silent type pointedly, but gently, "What do you think about this, Bob?" This usually allows Bob to say what he's thinking without feeling traitorous to his inner self. Do not go about involving people in a manner that threatens their inner image of themselves. For example, you would not say to the quiet Bob, "Well Bob you've been awfully quiet over there. You must be thinking about something? What is it?" Bob is likely to say he is thinking, "What a waste of time this meeting is." That will certainly not help you meet your goal of running a successful meeting.

As the leader, it is all right to do some probing with participants. You might ask the respondent to "go into a little more detail" on a topic. When probing, it is better to use the interrogative "How?" rather than "Why?" It is less threatening to be asked how did you come to that conclusion than it is to be asked, "Why did you come to that conclusion?" One is related to the speaker's process of decision making while the other tends to call out for justification.

When any kind of interpersonal dispute erupts, as is often likely to happen, quickly ask another person in the group to comment on the issue at hand. This will serve to defuse some of the tension that may be developing as two people square off.

You must be alert to the facts of every issue. When the facts are not correct you must either correct them or ask another in the group to correct them. Holding a discussion where the facts are in dispute will not lead to any useful decision making or productive discussion. Remember, you don't have to be the person who has all the facts in mind. You only have to be alert for the nonfactual statement. Use the other meeting participants to help set the record straight.

Check for Understanding

The former Mayor of New York City, Ed Koch, would always ask his constituency as he toured about the city "How am I doin'?" You should use a version of this to make sure that everyone not only feels that the meeting is accomplishing something, but also has the same understanding of the areas of agreement and disagreement.

You can ask the recorder to restate certain portions of what has been said, or you can paraphrase and ask if everyone is in agreement with this point. If the group is not in agreement, you can focus the discussion on the areas of disagreement.

You can also check to see if there is agreement that the meeting should continue in the direction it is headed. Often, a meeting will come upon a tangential issue that may be very important in the scheme of overall resolution of the problem. You should ask the group their preference at that point. "We seem to be at a point where we either need to table this discussion and move back to the main point or postpone the main topic of discussion and finish this first. What do you think we should do?" Asking the group to decide the direction of forward movement will generate positive feelings about the meeting and keep everyone involved. Remember, people support that which they create.

In **Stephen's Case,** Stephen does not have to check with the group when he moves them back to the main topic, because the discussion does not play a significant role in the main question about the necessity of a computer literacy course. The discussion about types of computers is definitely a tangential diversion for the group.

Assign Roles

As mentioned earlier, it may be necessary to have people preassigned to particular roles. Possible roles include those of timekeeper, first presenter, periodic summarizer, recorder, resource person. In **Stephen's Case,** Stephen has used three of these roles. He has a timekeeper, a recorder and a resource person. Notice that this assignment is done well before the actual meeting time. No one likes to be surprised with a role to play.

The most common role is that of recorder. Many groups are quite used to keeping minutes. However, the person assigned to take the minutes often doesn't know that will be his or her role until showing up at the meeting. It is quite common for the leader to say, "Let's see, I think Bob took minutes last week and Mary is next on the alphabet, so Mary would you take the minutes?" If Mary had known last week that she would be taking minutes, she might have brought her laptop computer, so that she could take the minutes directly into the machine, rather than having to transcribe them at a later date from handwritten notes into a computer processed document. Thus, one of the tasks that Stephen does is to keep the list of minute takers and assign them well in advance and in the order that is agreed to. Lastly, if the person knows he or she will be taking minutes, he or she will make an extra effort to be at the meeting.

Control the Emotional Climate

There are times when strongly held opinions will lead to an emotional setting. This, if not handled well, will result in a negative impression of the meeting. Conflict in itself can be useful as long as it is "creative." As the leader, you have to make sure that you protect those who may be too weak to protect themselves. You should feel free to interrupt a speaker who is going too far. You should acknowledge the level of strong feeling you observe and let the group know that it is fine to disagree, but it must be done with less heat and more light. You don't want to deny the emotions of the speakers, you just want them to be a bit more neutral in their support of an idea. You must never let one person attack another by demeaning their position. If you see this happening, it is your duty to step in and state clearly that such an attack is not appropriate and will not be allowed to continue.

It is particularly crucial to control your own emotions. Oftentimes, when a question is asked of you, it may feel like an attack. This need not necessarily be so, but some people have a tone that sounds particularly threatening. If you can remain open in your return, approach, and speech, the potential emotional powder keg can be kept from exploding. Ronald Reagan used to be referred to in the national press as the "Teflon man." If you can hold the image in your head of letting what feels like an attack just hit your Teflon barrier and slide harmlessly to the floor, you will be able to run a better meeting.

To maintain a positive climate, one technique is to make sure you build upon the participants' ideas. Pointing out that what Bob has said is quite useful or asking Mary to expand upon what she said because there seems to be a very productive path that can be followed will go a long way toward supplying the positive tone that you want to foster in all your meetings.

Provide Resources

You must have the right materials and the right people at every meeting. Even in a small meeting of three or four people, using overhead transparencies and visual aids can do wonders for the meeting. The research shows that people remember 10 percent more with visuals, are more persuaded 43 percent of the time, and meetings run 27 percent faster with visuals. It is in your best interests to have visuals that will help the group make good decisions. In addition, a visual can remain displayed while the discussion occurs and serve as a constant reminder of what is being discussed or of a point that is particularly important.

If you decide to use an overhead projector or play video tapes, you must make sure that these devices are working before the meeting begins. If they fail at the outset or during the meeting, much time will be wasted, and the outcome will be an ineffective meeting.

The End Of the Meeting

Closure

A good meeting has a definite objective to be reached. And this objective should be reached before time has run out for the meeting. With five–seven minutes to go, the time keeper should note that there is this small amount of time remaining. As the meeting leader, you should ask that the final thoughts be finished and the summary be produced by the recorder.

Ron Hyman in *Improving Discussion Leadership,* makes the distinction between ending and closing. All meetings end at sometime or other, but they do not all reach closure. He says, "When you close a discussion, you recapitulate the key points of the discussion and then you launch the group into what it has decided to do next. If the group hasn't decided what it wants to do next, then you, as the group leader, have the obligation to make suggestions for the future in terms of further group activities or further individual follow-up."

It is the task at hand to see what needs to be done next and then make sure everyone knows who will do what. In **Stephen's case,** Stephen has been thinking about what had been said during the meeting and felt that Donna needed to do some work to alleviate her fears about the impact of the loss of the course. She could do that by investigating what other schools do.

In addition, ending with a word about how well the meeting went is a good technique to help people leave feeling that their time had not been wasted. You should not say this if the meeting has been an obvious flop, but complimenting the group on their interaction should be a regular part of your behavior.

In coming to a close, it is important that you not go over the allotted time for the meeting. This tends to aggravate more people than any other meeting faux pas. If you choose to start on time, you must also choose to end on time.

Follow-up

As soon as possible after the meeting, you should write up a summary. This is different from the minutes of the meeting. Minutes are more detailed and are carefully worded with respect to exact decisions and votes. A follow-up summary is more a listing of the highlights of the meeting. You are trying to make sure that everyone is on the same wavelength with respect to the major focus of the discussion. You also want to have a document that you can send to any members who were not present or to admin-

---

Exhibit 8.6A Follow-Up Memo

TO: All math teachers
From: George
Re: This Morning's Meeting

I want to thank everyone for helping us have such a productive meeting this morning. I think the following summarizes the major points that were made and/or to which we agreed.

1. We need to reexamine our policy on winter term final exams. Many felt that we did not need this exam and that the time was better spent devoted to in class work. However, there is not strong agreement with this proposal by a significant majority of the department. Since we are split on the issue, we will review the outcomes of this year's winter exam period.

2. Bill has agreed to contact the nine peer schools in the area to find out what they do at the end of the winter term with final exams.

3. At our next meeting, we will discuss the merits of using a final project or paper in lieu of an exam, as well as the possibility of giving take-home exams. Carol will be surveying the other academic departments to determine what "alternatives" to the traditional seated exam are in place.

4. Carol will also be in charge of taking the minutes for the next meeting which will be Wednesday morning December 13th.

Exhibit 8.6B

To: **Department**
From: **George Jones**
DATE: **February 9, 1995**
RE: This morning's discussion

Thank you all for such constructive feedback. We are all part of a team effort trying to make this school one of the best in the country, and I know that we can reach that goal only if we are all crawling, walking, and running in the same direction. So let this be a first step in clarifying that direction, if not the speed.

I completely agree with most of what you said this morning, and I've enclosed the following time-line for you to see what I have been charged to do and have attempted to get done. This time-line work plan is something the Head's Advisory Committee works out each August and is one measure by which we are evaluated at year's end. These time lines are published for the Board of Trustees, who also measure our productivity. Thus, it has been these issues (tasks) to which I have been paying attention. I have been quite pleased that several of the goals on this time-line have been reached.

The tasks numbered 1.1, 1.2, 1.3, and 1.4 all come from the Long Range Plan Document. There are items that are not on this time line such as departmental budget allotment and staffing reductions that have taken some of my time. I would hope that some of my "priority one" tasks are also yours. If not, then please help me determine which ones are yours, so that we can be working synergistically.

I've also enclosed a study I did about one specific budget item of concern to all of you—copying budget. I have not had time since January 19th to study this data, but I am ready and eager to work in the mode that you all have requested. Let us together study this raw data and determine what it means.

On Tuesday, I like us to determine in what specific areas, not limited to those that appear on my time-line sheet, you want to concentrate your and my efforts so that we can arrange our own time-line and goal dates.

---

istrators who have a need to know what might be happening in your department.

The follow-up document should be specific about the tasks that are to be done before the next meeting and who will accomplish those tasks. In addition, the follow-up document can note who will be doing what for the next meeting, e.g., timekeeper and recorder, etc.

Exhibits 8.6A and 8.6B show some typical follow-up memos from well-run meetings.

Other Helpful Hints

Striking a Balance

In the best meetings, there is a balance between working at solidarity (re-lationships) and completing the objective (tasks). When the members of a group balance personal traits such as intelligence and social ability, the group gets more done in a more productive manner. Not surprisingly, if there is one person who has overwhelming skill in one of these areas, the group may not function very well, because their working processes will be skewed toward the more gifted person. Robert Sternberg of Yale University has found that an important trait in successful group work is having group where most people in the group have similar levels of persuasiveness, ex-pressiveness, and aggressiveness. A group lacking such ability or over-loaded in such ability usually falters.

Harmony tends to lead toward creative and effective group functioning. However, you cannot invoke harmony or change the constituency of the group by inviting a new person into the department or asking a veteran to leave. But you can talk about the need for balance in the group and ask everyone to be alert if there seems to be a distinct lack of balance in an area.

Helping the Group to Engage in Talk

Using the same ideas about wait time and student responsiveness in a classroom, you should not be too anxious to fill in the dead time with leader talk. Let the group have time to process what you have posited or asked. The three–five second rule is a good one. Do not speak for at least five seconds once you have asked a question.

In many meetings, especially those that take place between only a few people, there is a tendency for the interaction to fall into a pattern where the respondent talks directly to the leader and not to the others in the group. You can help break this pattern by averting your eyes from the eyes of the re-spondent. If you look down and begin writing what the respondent is saying and do not look up until you feel his or her gaze move to another person, you will have forced that person to look elsewhere for eye contact. Once eye contact is established with others in the group, then you can look up.

The size of the group also influences the amount of talk that occurs. Clearly, when there is more opportunity for talk, there can be more partic-ipation. Research seems to support a minimum group size of five to six, if discussion is the purpose for the group getting together. In studies done with juries, it has been found that a jury of twelve takes longer to reach a decision than a jury of six, but the decisions that are made are nearly identical in both groups.

One suggestion Ava S. Butler makes in her book *Team Think* is to use toy eyeglasses as a prop to help people snap out of old thinking and old habits. Before the meeting you should provide everyone in the meeting with a pair of silly discount store eyeglasses. Cheap sunglasses with the lenses removed will do the trick. When you think the participants are going to have preconceived ideas about the agenda topic or when you want to stimulate a meeting where changes must be made, the glasses are distributed to every member. The participants are supposed to put the glasses on when they think they are falling into old ways of looking at things or when they think the speaker is falling into old ways of looking at things. Not only will the glasses serve a bit of humor and diversion, they will cause those speaking to really reflect upon their point of view.

Common Group Problems

It is common in groups for there to be competition among the participants to be the "unspoken" leader. This competition can be overt and usually takes the form of speaking sarcastically and negatively about the topic or about other people in the meeting. You must address this behavior immediately by asking the person who is being negative to consider that such comments are keeping the group from accomplishing its goals.

Silent disapproval takes many forms, but the outcome is the same—a lack of support for whatever is decided. When you see participants shaking their heads or rolling their eyes, you need to say, "I've got the feeling you don't agree with where we are headed, but we haven't heard from you. Can you help us understand what you're thinking about this issue?" Do not just ignore the silent disapprover, because he or she is not going to go away. Silent disapproval is going to become verbal disapproval, only it will be carried out behind your back.

A common meeting problem is the person who feels he must interrupt with a witty comment or pun every time the opportunity presents itself. While you should not run a meeting in an authoritarian model, you also cannot allow for such constant interruptions. Usually, this person means no harm and is trying to be helpful, feeling that humor will make a possibly dull meeting more bearable. You should mention that while the comments are humorous, they tend to take the group off on tangents and, given the limited amount of meeting time, you'd like to have everyone refrain from such behavior as much as possible. However, understand that sometimes there will be an overpowering force that must be submitted to.

Neutral agreement is a strange type of problem. Ordinarily, one would think that agreement is always good. But neutral agreement happens when no one really cares much about the issue at hand. Since there is little care, there is little investment in the outcome. It is easy to go along with any suggestion, no matter how problematic it might actually be. When this happens, you need to remind the group that they may be agreeing to something they will not want too support. In fact, it may be that no one really supports the decision or conclusion, but because the personal investment is

---

Exhibit 8.7A Post-Meeting Reaction to the Leader

Meeting:_____ Date:_____

	High Good Yes Positive						Low Bad No Negative
1. The leader's preparation	7	6	5	4	3	2	1
2. The leader's contribution of facts and explanations	7	6	5	4	3	2	1
3. The leader's contributions of personal opinions and justifications	7	6	5	4	3	2	1
4. The leader's crystallizing key substantive points	7	6	5	4	3	2	1
5. The leader's crystallizing points regarding the tone of the meeting	7	6	5	4	3	2	1
6. The leader's efforts to keep the discussion focused	7	6	5	4	3	2	1
7. The leader's introducing the discussion	7	6	5	4	3	2	1
8. The leader's closing the discussion	7	6	5	4	3	2	1
9. The leader's questions during the discussion	7	6	5	4	3	2	1
10. The leader's verbal support and encouragement of group members to participate	7	6	5	4	3	2	1
11. The leader's nonverbal support and encouragement of members to participate	7	6	5	4	3	2	1
12 The leader's avoidance of negative behaviors such as sarcasm, interrupting, and domination	7	6	5	4	3	2	1
13. The leader learned something on the topic: new information, insight, understanding	7	6	5	4	3	2	1
14. The overall quality of this meeting	7	6	5	4	3	2	1

From Ron Hyman, *Improving Discussion Leadership.* New York: Teachers College Press, 1980.

Exhibit 8.7B Post-Meeting Self Rating

Meeting:_____ Date:_____

	High Good Yes Positive					Low Bad No Negative	
1. My preparation	7	6	5	4	3	2	1
2. My contribution of facts and explanations	7	6	5	4	3	2	1
3. My contributions of personal opinions and justifications	7	6	5	4	3	2	1
4. My crystallizing key substantive points	7	6	5	4	3	2	1
5. My crystallizing points regarding the tone of the meeting	7	6	5	4	3	2	1
6. My efforts to keep the discussion focused	7	6	5	4	3	2	1
7. My introducing the discussion	7	6	5	4	3	2	1
8. My closing the discussion	7	6	5	4	3	2	1
9. My questions during the discussion	7	6	5	4	3	2	1
10. My verbal support and encouragement of group members to participate	7	6	5	4	3	2	1
11. My nonverbal support and encouragement of members to participate	7	6	5	4	3	2	1
12. My avoidance of negative behaviors such as sarcasm, interrupting, and domination	7	6	5	4	3	2	1
13. I learned something on the topic: new information, insight, understanding	7	6	5	4	3	2	1
14. The overall quality of this meeting	7	6	5	4	3	2	1

From Ron Hyman, *Improving Discussion Leadership.* New York: Teachers College Press, 1980.

so small, no one feels the need to disagree. However, once the policy or decision is in place and there is complete neutral feeling about the policy, there will be no support and it will be totally ineffective.

Get Feedback on Your Meeting

Exhibits 8.7A and 8.7B show possible post-meeting evaluation forms. If you want to improve your leadership of meetings, you must solicit feedback from the participants. As with any kind of evaluation, there will be a certain amount of fear in asking for this information. Most people are

Exhibit 8.8A Procedures for a Long Meeting

Meeting Procedures

1. Please expect meetings to begin promptly.
2. In the interests of efficient use of time, the Committee will use a version of parliamentary procedure:
   a. A quorum consists of a majority of the Committee present, and sessions will begin when a quorum exists.
   b. Motions are in order any time when in full session, and the Chair may invite a motion when he feels an appropriate juncture has been reached. Motions must be seconded. Amendments will be voted on and decided in the same manner as motions.
   c. A motion carries if it receives more affirmative than negative votes. Abstentions will be noted in the final tally, but they will have no weight in deciding a question. A motion fails to carry in the event of a tie vote.
   d. The Chair of all segments of meetings will have a vote.
3. Through mid-day, Monday June 19, a vote on a question is to determine if the motion will be carried forth to the beginning of the day of decision June 20th. If a motion on the floor fails to receive enough affirmative votes, the idea/proposal at the heart of that motion is discarded from the Committee's current considerations.
4. Jim F. has volunteered to take minutes and to coordinate the flow of paper from and to the Committee during the meetings. When indicated on the detailed agenda, a group or individual is responsible for giving Jim a written report, which he will funnel to the secretarial help for turnaround to the committee the following day after lunch.

Jim Fariman
Zach Goodstun
Reggie Bradstreet
Dave Phillipson

Agenda Subcommittee

Exhibit 8.8B Detailed Agenda for a Long Meeting

Standing Committee on Academic Life (SCAL)
Meeting and work agenda: June 12–16, 1995
All meetings in HB 201

Monday June 12

9:00–9:30 A.M.	Procedures and ground rules
9:30–10:30 A.M.	The Ten Questions: Deletions and amendments [vote]
10:30–10:45 A.M.	Break
10:45–12:15 P.M.	Subcommittees from SCAL finish reports
12:15–1:15 P.M.	Working Lunch
1:15–1:30 P.M.	Subcommittees assign task of presentation to the full committee

Subcommittee Reports

1:30–2:15 P.M.	"The Present Curriculum": V. Dans and D. Frun, capts.
2:15–3:00 P.M.	"Parent and Alumni Views": R. Stew and R. Bradstreet
3:00–3:15 P.M.	Break
3:15–4:00 P.M.	"College Perceptions": J. Edsel, S. O'Fallon

Tuesday June 13

9:00–9:45 A.M.	"Faculty Opinions": J. Davis and Z. Goodstun, capts.
9:45–10:15 A.M.	"Peer Schools": R. Stew and Z. Goodstun, capts.
10:15–10:30 A.M.	Break
10:30–12:00 P.M.	Brainstorming of ideas contained in Faculty-at-large proposals
12:00–1:45 P.M.	Working lunch (to be supplied). Expert groups of 2–3 people write "pro/con" and "questions" position papers to be presented to the full group.

At-Large-Proposals

1:45–2:30 P.M.	Gallagher Proposal
2:30–3:15 P.M.	Cobbett Proposal
3:15–3:30 P.M.	Break
3:30–4:15 P.M.	Davis Proposal

Wednesday June 14

9:00–9:45 A.M.	Goodstun Proposal
9:45–11:00 A.M.	"Expert" groups meet on department proposals/reports. Each member is part of a team of 2–3 who will write a "pro/con" and "questions" position paper for presentation to the full group.

Subject/Department Proposals

11:00–11:30 A.M.	Arts Proposal
11:30–12:00 P.M.	Science/Math Proposal
12:00–1:00 P.M.	Lunch break
1:00–2:00 P.M.	History and Social Sciences Proposal
2:00–2:15 P.M.	Break
2:15–4:00 P.M.	Motions, Amendments, and votes on proposals to take forward in the SCAL's final work. Motions must be presented in writing at the outset in this segment of the meeting and will be written on the Bulletin Board before voting. A written summary of these are the responsibility of J. Edsel to give to J. Davis at the close of business.

Thursday June 15

9:00–9:15 A.M.	Read over what we have decided to create up to this point.
9:15–9:45 A.M.	Motions in order
9:45–12:00 P.M.	Expert groups on "Ten Questions" (See June 12.) These now may be fewer than ten questions but they may not be more. Each member is part of a 2–3 person group and will write on the pros/cons & questions report on the questions assigned.
12:00–1:00 P.M.	Lunch
1:00–2:00 P.M.	Question #1 [vote]
2:00–3:00 P.M.	Question #2 [vote]
3:00–3:15 P.M.	Break
3:15–4:15 P.M.	Question #3 [vote]

Friday June 16

9:00 10:00 A.M.	Question #4 [vote]
10:00 11:00 A.M.	Question #5 [vote]
11:00–11:15 A.M.	Break
11:15–12:15 P.M.	Question #6 [vote]
12:15–1:15 P.M.	Lunch
1:15–2:15 P.M.	Question #7 [vote]
2:15–3:15 P.M.	Question #8 [vote]
Adjourn for the weekend	

Monday June 19

A.M.	Finish the Questions [votes]
12:00–1:00 P.M.	Lunch
P.M.	Buffer time for Question voting

Tuesday June 20

9:00–10:15 A.M.	Trouble in River City? Are there items to drop out now before we begin work on the final proposals?
10:15–10:30 A.M.	Break
10:30–1:30 P.M.	Three groups meet to produce three draft proposed reports by this committee. Working lunch
1:30–2:00 P.M.	Xeroxing or reports on different colored paper
2:00–4:00 P.M.	Green report presented

Wednesday June 21

9:00–11:00 A.M.	Red report presented
11:00–12:00 P.M.	Break and lunch
12:00–2:00 P.M.	Blue report presented
2:00–4:00 P.M.	Synthesis discussion

Thursday June 22

9:00 A.M.–end	Goal: Two proposals, including timetables of recommended implementation; discussion of each report and vote.

It is likely that a final "clean" version of each of the proposals will have to be drafted and circulated for comment in July. SCAL will reconvene in September with these two proposals in finished form, taking one meeting to discuss full faculty meeting presentational questions.

Agenda subcommittee: Z. Goodstun, R. Bradstreet, J. Davis

---

afraid of what they might find out. However, you must continue to remember the "Teflon Man" model of receiving information. If you treat the most disparaging evaluations as an attempt by the provider to help you, then even those negative reviews will not seem so bad. What you are more likely to discover is that you run fine meetings for the most part and could run even better ones with attention to the more subtle details.

Exhibits 8.8A and 8.8B show an agenda for an extended meeting. The detailed planning for this meeting led to a superior event for all participants.

References and Bibliography

Barnum, Carol M. (1994). Here's how to manage your meetings effectively. *Communications Briefings, 13,* (no. 6).

Butler, Ava S. (1996). *Team think: 72 ways to make good, smart, quick decisions in any meeting.* New York: McGraw -Hill.

Hyman, Ronald T. (1980). *Improving discussion leadership.* New York: Teachers College Press.

The 3M Meeting Management Team with Jeannie Drew (1994). *Mastering meetings: Discovering the hidden potential of effective business meetings.* New York: McGraw-Hill.

Quimby, Don (1994). "How to plan and manage effective meetings. *NASSP tips for principals.* (November).

Stone, Donald & Alice (1988). The Seat of Power. *Carnegie Mellon Magazine, 7* (no. 2).

Chapter 9

Creating a Learning Environment
Through Supervision and Evaluation

Before jumping into the theories and practices behind useful supervisory techniques, immersing yourself in a hypothetical supervisory relationship provides a context for the techniques that are going to be presented. At this point you should not make any assumptions about whether the following procedure is one that is being advocated or simply tested. Instead, you should proceed on the basis that this is what the school, Midstone High

---

Using Sandy's Case Study

Using the following supervision summary and based upon the information provided in the Sandy case, you are to create a numerical score for Sandy. Just as in real life, you are going to find that you wish you had more information about Sandy and more information about the high school. However, you must do your best with what you are given. The directions that precede the supervision document are the ones every department head at Midstone must use. You are to imagine you are the mathematics department head at Midstone and are to proceed with the evaluation. The Midstone supervision document has recently been developed by a faculty committee to replace the free form letters that had been the usual documents used in supervision. This new format will be the process by which all faculty are measured. The philosophy behind the one document and numerical scoring procedure is that it puts all faculty on an equal footing and prevents the personality of the supervisor from being a major factor if a dispute arises.

Instructions: At the end of the detailed sheet titled the Teacher Supervision Form, there is a shorter score sheet entitled the Summary Teacher Supervision Form. To use this form do the following. First,

---

rate Sandy in each of the categories listed on a score of one to five, with a 5 being a superior rating and a 1 being poor rating. Then, determine how much you think each category is worth, as a percentage of the teaching job. (The whole job represents 100 %.) Then multiply the % of worth by the rating to get a number of points in that category. When you have finished with the entire form, add up the number of points Sandy has earned. The highest possible number of points that a teacher can earn is 500. The faculty at Midstone has agreed that a teacher needs to earn 325 quality points to be retained.

As an example, you might rank Sandy's performance in *Planning and Preparation* superior and thus a 5, and you also feel that this behavior is worth 30% of the job. This nets Sandy 150 points (30 x 5 = 150). At the same time, you rank *Command of Subject Matter* a 3 and feel it constitutes the remainder of the job, or 70%. This nets Sandy 210 points. Sandy's total points is therefore 360 points and Sandy would be retained.

Included in **Sandy's Case** are a stream of consciousness narrative from the department head, two supervisory letters from the department head, and two supervisory letters from the athletic director.

The Case of Sandy Samuels

You are the mathematics department head at Midstone High School and have held that position for the last three years. Long an outstanding college preparatory institution and since 1918, a country day school with a small five-day boarding component, the high school bears the name of its first principal, Samuel S. Midstone. The unusually broad curriculum of Midstone High School offers students many opportunities for individual pursuits. Seven academic departments offer traditional core courses, as well as a variety of electives, honors and Advanced Placement courses. There are also a number of interdisciplinary courses. The school emphasizes a solid traditional education in preparing its students for college. The sense of community at the school is strengthened by its diverse array of students and faculty. Sports are offered in all major categories, and the school competes regularly with seven peer schools.

Sandy Samuels is a third-year teacher who came to teach at Midstone immediately after graduation as a mathematics major from Eastville State College. Sandy was hired to replace Robert, a senior member of the math department who moved to another school to assume the department headship. Robert was famous in the school for having the most demanding courses in the math department. In fact, during the last few years of his tenure, over 50% of the students in his classes earned grades of C or below. Robert's constant railing about his being the last of the true standard keepers in the school was not missed by many faculty or parents after his move. Sandy's warm personality was a welcome change and a key ingredient in being offered the job.

Presently, teacher Samuels teaches two Algebra I classes to ninth graders and two Geometry classes to sophomores. Colleagues feel Sandy is an average mathematics teacher who shows concern for students, but who is not especially talented or creative in the subject of mathematics. At your suggestion, Sandy attended the Regional Math Workshop last summer and found it a great help. Yet, when asked to participate voluntarily in the department-sponsored prep sessions for the State Mathematics Olympics, Sandy balked at the request and found excuses not to be part of the process. You know Sandy is dedicated to the classroom, hasn't missed a class in over three years, and would go the extra mile with any student. Sandy has the reputation for always being available for extra help for all students in any Algebra I section.

Students, when asked to fill out evaluation forms for Sandy's courses, use phrases ranging from "solid," "caring," and "the first teacher to really care about me," to "unexciting, but makes me learn," "not very clear," and "sometimes gets a bit confused at the blackboard, but makes up for it the next day." There has never been a disciplinary incident in any of Samuels' classes. Students have never complained about Samuels' courses to you, but other teachers in the school have made oblique comments about those courses being the ones their advisees count on to be easy.

In Sandy's personal life, you know that all isn't going smoothly. Like many mid-level executives, teacher Samuels' spouse has been laid-off from work, and the loss of that salary has made Sandy wonder aloud how they will manage to get along on one salary. The house they have recently purchased in Vernon has a substantial mortgage. Sandy was proud to have been able to purchase that home and has mentioned that it was a realization of a major life goal.

As the math department head, you have heard from students' advisers that Sandy's classes have the reputation of being "easier" than those of some others on your staff. And it seems as though those students who enter Algebra II from Sandy's classes almost always have trouble during the first month review of the Algebra I course. In addition, Sandy's student reports have been returned to you by advisers who have complained that they read like a psychologist's evaluation and not a teacher's academic report.

On your visits to Sandy's classroom you've noticed a predominance of what only can be called self-esteem building posters: "<u>YOU</u> are Important" and "I can do it and <u>I WILL</u>." In the classroom, you also observe that Samuels is keeping a bulletin board for newspaper clippings of articles relating to mathematics. Students often make contributions to this board, and you know they are discussed in class. You've watched Sandy work especially hard, but unsuccessfully, at individualizing class work during the last three weeks. Samuels told you that the idea for such individualization came from that Regional Workshop you suggested and expressed gratitude for your suggestion.

Recently, Sandy has become very involved in the school. But a support group Sandy recently formed for new students who were experiencing problems adjusting to the school has not sat well with the school counselors, who feel it is "meddling" and "outside the normal programs that the school offers." As the school's lacrosse coach, Sandy has been a breath of fresh air to a team uncharacteristically weak. Samuels even spent a week last summer running a free training camp for any players who wanted to attend. Some of the boarding students stayed at Sandy's house during the "camp" and were markedly improved thereafter in their general attitudes toward school.

Sandy has mentioned on more than one occasion that students need adult guidance in the area of moral choices. "We too often shirk our responsibility to help adolescents question and shape their moral behavior. Let's face it, this kind of knowledge is much more important than the quadratic equation."

Today, the Vice Principal for Academic Affairs has called you to the office to inform you that two sets of parents have written a joint letter complaining about Sandy's teaching. It seems that in Sandy's Algebra I section, students have been allowed to take re-tests until they are satisfied with their grade. The parents who've written, and whose children did very well on tests the first time they took them, feel this isn't fair, because their children are feeling that it is of no import to be prepared. They stress that everyone knows Sandy is too soft. Their letter claims that Sandy's teaching methods devalue the meaning of grades and foster the impression that there are no standards at the school.

All of this comes to mind as you open Sandy's faculty file. This is your first pass at a formal analysis of Sandy's work

Midstone High School
203-688-4944 • Walbury, Connecticut 06000

June 9, 1995   COACHING EVALUATION

First let me say that Sandy has been one of the most cooperative coaches to have hit the Midstone campus in quite some time. With Sandy, I have always felt comfortable in making sudden changes in venue, because I know that Sandy does whatever is needed. Sandy is no prima donna.

As a coach new to our school, Sandy has worked hard to fit in and has begun to develop a strong sense of teamwork with the varsity lacrosse team. It has not been easy, as that team has had two coaches during the last three years, and we were faced with the serious dilemma last spring of having no one on the faculty who was qualified or who wanted to coach that team. Sandy, though not having played since high school, eagerly volunteered.

This has presented a slight problem in that the players felt, and some still feel, that they should be coached by someone with more recent college experience. However, Sandy has handled this nicely. It would have been even easier to deal with if the team had been able to win more than three games, but this team has not ever been very strong, and it is my belief that they were probably lucky to do as well as they did.

As I've watched Sandy coach, I have noticed a tremendous amount of attention to sportsmanship and the principles of team play. "Work together" seems to be the constant echo from the lacrosse field. While concentrating on this aspect of our athletic philosophy is commendable, I have also noticed that practices have, at times, been somewhat ragged and I hope that next year Sandy will be able bring a bit more focus to those practices.

On no account, however, should this criticism of Sandy's work overshadow what I have seen—a clear desire to be successful and, through team sports, to help shape students into the leaders of tomorrow.

Dick Falston
Athletic Director

Midstone High School
203-688-4944 • Walbury, Connecticut 06000

June 12, 1996   <u>COACHING EVALUATION</u>

Sandy's second year as the Varsity lacrosse coach has to have been both rewarding and disappointing. Again, the team managed only three wins, but what they lacked in skill they more than made up for in spirit. It is unfortunate that several of the returning seniors decided not to play lacrosse, instead opting for the proverbial "lazy" senior spring. Those who did remain with the team had the opportunity to see a coach who never gave up, who always had faith in the players, and who focused on leadership and teamwork. Teamwork is one of the virtues we like to stress at Midstone, and Sandy is probably more tuned into this than most of our coaches.

Sandy has worked hard to develop a strong lacrosse program. The summer "free" lacrosse camp held during the last week of August was one concrete way that made it clear to all that developing a fine lacrosse program was an important part of Sandy's work here. I support such efforts and will continue to do so if Sandy decides upon running the same kind of camp this summer.

However, before this camp runs this August, I suggest that Sandy attend the New England Juniors' Lacrosse Coaching Camp for some training in the latest coaching methods, practice drills and game strategies. It's always good to have as large a repertoire of methods as possible. In addition, there have been several rule changes for next season and I want Sandy to be able to incorporate these into whatever strategies might be needed next year.

While there is still room for growth in one's coaching, I see no reason why Sandy shouldn't continue to coach this team for at least another year.

Dick Falston
Athletic Director

CHARTERED IN 1918   MIDSTONE HIGH SCHOOL   FOR BOYS AND GIRLS

Midstone High School
203-688-4944 • Walbury, Connecticut 06000

May 20, 1995   <u>CLASSROOM EVALUATION</u>

Sandy has taken giant steps in the year since being hired. Sandy came to our campus with the kind of limited experience that practice teaching provides, but with no experience in a school like ours. In the first year of teaching, last year, Sandy found the classroom a challenge, often a daunting and frustrating one. At times Sandy felt unprepared for the challenges, especially for the emotional tensions students can bring to the classroom. Sandy expended effort on the classroom work and went at the tasks with resolve and spirit. Sandy's mentor has remarked at the tenacity with which Sandy asked questions, sat in on classes, redoubled efforts, and did the intelligent thing: used the struggles of the first year as a challenge to learn.

The struggles have paid dividends. How much Sandy has gained in these nine months. I can see Sandy has gained considerable confidence and poise, is more knowledgeable in subject content, and is more at home with students. The classroom is a happier place and Sandy can feel more at ease there, more flexible, more ready to accept the challenges and surprises that students are capable of delivering.

There are still challenges to meet, however. They say the best way to learn all the material in a course is to teach it. I'm sure that Sandy felt this way after some early difficulties in Algebra One. We expect every teacher to have total command of the discipline and, while that is not presently the case, next year should be a markedly different story.

Sandy brings important personal qualities to teaching. There is a dedication to learning more about mathematics and there is a similar dedication to knowing the students. It is clear that Sandy works to know them and understand them and to make the classroom a stimulating place for them. Sandy has developed a helpful rapport with them both inside and outside the classroom.

By any measure of experience, Sandy is still a novice. But the growth I've seen in this brief time promises well for a future in teaching.

Michael G. Walsh
Mathematics Department Head

CHARTERED IN 1918   MIDSTONE HIGH SCHOOL   FOR BOYS AND GIRLS

Midstone High School
203-688-4944 • Walbury, Connecticut 06000

June 13, 1996   <u>CLASSROOM EVALUATION</u>

Your work in the classroom teaching mathematics is an extension of your highly personal, caring, and imaginative way of approaching work. This encourages the students to develop the same qualities of individualism and imagination in their studies as they see in your teaching. I hope the encouragement and support you give to students will help them blossom as mathematicians. Your enthusiasm for student creative effort is infectious. Students who have felt ungifted in math can find in your interest in their work a new sense of themselves as mathematical thinkers.

As you head off for the summer break, I hope you will take some time this summer to gather more expertise in inequalities, an area you mentioned to me in which you still feel somewhat unprepared and have had trouble teaching.

This year, while your work load of two sections of Algebra I and two sections of Geometry was the same as last year, you have been moving at a slightly faster pace and ended the year nearly in stride with other like sections.

I still see room for improvement in your understanding of basic subject matter as you can be confused, or maybe distracted is a better word, when you are at the blackboard. And since you are still a somewhat new teacher, I suggest you attend, this coming summer, the Regional Mathematics Workshop on Individualized Instruction. This will help you develop a more solid repertoire of teaching techniques.

Your stellar record for never missing class in two consecutive years is a remarkable accomplishment, and I commend such devotion. You've made an easy adjustment to department life, have worked well with colleagues and have continued to earn their respect and liking. (They would get to know you much more if you could join our prep sessions for the Math Olympiad each month.) My hope is that you will continue to learn the craft of excellent teaching during your time at Midstone.

Michael G. Walsh
Mathematics Department Head

CHARTERED IN 1918   MIDSTONE HIGH SCHOOL   FOR BOYS AND GIRLS

TEACHER SUPERVISION FORM

NAME: _____

The supervisor should use a five point scale in completing the following rating list, with a range of 5 to 1 points per item. The rating of "superior" earns 5 points, the rating "poor" earns 1 point. Circle the appropriate score against each item.

S u p e r i o r	A B o v e A v e	A v e r a g e	B e l o w A v c	P o o r

I. INSTRUCTIONAL COMPETENCE

A. Planning & Preparation:

sets long-range goals clearly recognizable by all, plans daily lesson to fit into larger year plans, plans show understanding of student needs, interests, abilities.   5   4   3   2   1

Comments:

Areas for Improvement:

B. Attention to Students' Social & Emotional Needs:

provides differentiated activities, assignments and counseling which takes account of differing s/e needs, is genuinely interested in each student as an individual, is concerned with moral values, en-

couraging students to examine values on which
decisions are based, demonstrates commitment to
students with particular academic and/or social
and emotional problems or crises.   5   4   3   2   1

Comments:

Areas for Improvement:

C. Students are Stimulated and Motivated by
    Teacher:

is alert and alive in the classroom presents the work
to students in an interesting and captivating manner. 5   4   3   2   1

Comments:

Areas for Improvement:

D. Classroom Atmosphere :

shows evidence of friendly and respectful
teacher-pupil relationship, maintains an orderly
and effective working atmosphere, shows concern
for   the
appearance of the classroom.   5   4   3   2   1

Comments:

Areas for Improvement:

E. Command of Subject Matter:

knowledge of subject matter shows depth and
breadth has kept informed about current methods
and materials in subject area, has consistently developed his knowledge of subject, presents subject
matter so that students can readily understand.   5   4   3   2   1

Comments:

Areas for Improvement:

F. Effective Teaching Methods are Employed:

methods are appropriate to the subject matter and
purposes of instruction, uses varied teaching and
learning procedures (discussion, group reporting,
individual study, lecturing, etc.), shows an understanding of and utilizes a variety of questioning
techniques to promote discussion and learning,
uses media to good advantage, shows respect and
commitment towards students of differing abilities
and interests.   5   4   3   2   1

Comments:

Areas for Improvement:

G. Knowledge of the Learning Process:

ensures pupils are engaged in learning that fosters
development of a variety of levels of cognitive
awareness and intellectual tools.   5   4   3   2   1

Comments:

Areas for Improvement:

H. Evaluation/ Testing:

provides adequate and frequent opportunities for students to demonstrate mastery of newly acquired concepts, teacher's periodic achievement tests cover the material of subject matter adequately and fairly, and show careful thought and preparation, uses varied approaches to evaluation, consistent with the range of indicators for the subject taught.   5   4   3   2   1

Comments:

Areas for Improvement:

II. TEACHER AS PROFESSIONAL STAFF MEMBER

A. Fulfillment of Professional Responsibilities:
carries out willingly, effectively, reliably and punctually such ancillary duties as may be assigned to him, consistently attends and constructively contributes to department and faculty meetings, complies with school and faculty policies, is available and willingly provides reasonable amounts of extra help to students who have academic or personal problems, uses discretion when speaking   of
colleagues.   5   4   3   2   1

Comments:

Areas for Improvement:

B. Teacher Uses Evaluation for Self-Improvement:

is not defensive when given constructive criticism, welcomes professional evaluation by those having responsibility for this task, encourages students to assess classroom learning activities and materials.   5   4   3   2   1

Comments:

Areas for Improvement:

C. Relations with Colleagues and Students:

gains the respect of pupils through fair and impartial actions, cooperates with colleague, keeps parents and appropriate colleagues advised of each student's progress, and works with them to resolve pertinent problems.   5   4   3   2   1

Comments:

Areas for Improvement:

III. PROFESSIONAL DEVELOPMENT

Continues professional study through advanced courses, travel, participation in workshops, etc. Strives to increase teaching skills, shows genuine interest in the profession by participation in curriculum writing or by giving talks, has stated career objectives, has a written self-development plan with concrete goals and criteria to measure progress.   5   4   3   2   1

Comments:

Areas for Improvement:

IV. COACHING

offers an organized experience around the goal of exercise, helps players learn about themselves and the game, follows the educational philosophy of the school(encourage diversity, discourage sexism, racism, and other forms of discrimination), emphasizes sportsmanship, uses appropriate motivational techniques, seeks to build character.   5   4   3   2   1

Comments:

Areas for Improvement:

V. Other

is involved with students outside the classroom offers time freely for non-classroom events.   5   4   3   2   1

Comments:

Areas for Improvement

SUMMARY TEACHER SUPERVISION FORM

Categories	Value (the worth to you as a %)	X	Score (from 5 to 1)	=	Evaluation Points
I. Instructional Competence					
A. Planning and Preparation	___		___		___
B. Social and Emotional	___		___		___
C. Stimulation-Motivation	___		___		___
D. Class Atmosphere	___		___		___
E. Subject Matter	___		___		___
F. Teaching Methods	___		___		___
G. Learning Process	___		___		___
H. Evaluation/ Testing	___		___		___
II. Teacher a Professional Staff Member					
A. Responsibilities	___		___		___
B. Self-Improvement	___		___		___
C. Colleague Relations	___		___		___
III. Professional Development	___		___		___
IV. Coaching	___		___		___
V. Other	___		___		___
Total	100%		xxxx		Total Points ___

School, follows, and that you represent the math department head of this school.

Now that you have finished the case study, you may have discovered that there were two ways to proceed. You could have made up your mind after reading the documents that Sandy did or did not belong at Midstone High School and concocted a score to total more or less than 325 points depending upon your inclination to rehire or not. Or you could have scored

Sandy, without regard to any final disposition, and been surprised at whatever the outcome might have been.

Either way, feeling agitated and somewhat uneasy while working with this case is entirely natural. Several hundred department heads have used this case in controlled seminars, and there has not been a time when the participants didn't say that they were having a hard time being quantitative about what they felt was such a subjective event as supervision. They then catch themselves and try to explain what they mean by subjective, since subjectivity is one of the last things the person being supervised wants as the basis of their performance review.

Many who read the case are somewhat angry at the department head, whose written letters seem to have contradictory and vague messages about Sandy's performance. His letters do not give much direction for future action to either Sandy or the acting department head and are, possibly, less than forthright. But often, what most bothers those who study this case, is the fact that in the real world such supervisory reports are all too common. When coupled with the fact that teachers are rarely informed about how much any behavior is worth to either the department head or the institution, the need for clear communication of important data in a systematic and thorough manner is paramount.

Finally, they recognize the greatest defect of this evaluation model. Where is the voice of the teacher? What is it that Sandy values? What are Sandy's goals and methods to reach those goals? Without some system for conversation and dialogue, this important voice in the supervision equation is absent.

Factors in Successful Supervision

There is only one reason to enter into the supervisory process. That reason must be to improve the quality of instruction in order to improve learning. If you, as the department head and team leader, enter into such a process with this as your primary goal, you will be asking yourself why you have been putting off such supervision for so long; why you have been fearful of this part of your job. In effective supervision, teachers discover those things for which they have skill and are allowed and helped to improve those things that need improvement.

Before proceeding, it must be made clear that the bulk of this chapter is concerned with **developmental supervision.** Developmental supervision is a process that should be used in the majority of all teacher reviews (Gleave, 1978; Siens, 1996). This is a process used to foster good teaching and to help the teacher improve performance. It is not to be used to determine if a teacher will be rehired or not. Such use for summative evaluation is treated at the end of this chapter. Summative evaluation is a specialized type of evaluation that is not entered into on a regular basis. Summative evaluation is connected with a clearly understood lack of success in past performance. Developmental supervision is an *ongoing process whereby the teacher and the department head work together to improve the quality of instruction and, hence, learning.* Teachers have the RIGHT to good developmental supervision; when teachers are not provided with a supervision system, they are being cheated out of one of the most powerful factors in career development. Teachers vary in ways that they relate to themselves, students, and peers. Knowing how to call upon a repertoire of actions and how to match strategy to situations, can be the result of developmental supervision.

In any successful supervision interaction, it is important that there be a merging of *what is present* with *what is wanted.* There should be a meshing of the teacher's goals with departmental goals and with school goals. The process by which the teacher reaches this unification of goals may be identical to the process of all other teachers in the institution. However, the substance and content of the supervision should be idiosyncratic to the teacher being evaluated. In any case, it must be clearly discernible that teachers must meet the departmental and school goals, whatever teaching methodology they might favor.

In order that such clarity of goal attainment and practice be accomplished, several factors need to be in place before any actual supervision takes place. McLaughlin and Pfeifer (1988) present several of these factors. Primary among them is trust and open communication. There is only one pathway to these two fundamentals. Constant predictable behavior by the department head and administration accompanied by continual conversation.

A trusting environment exists when a teacher does not have to fear for his or her job, but is open to suggestion, feels free to ask questions, can express disapproval of a policy or requirement, confess to a weakness, and intimately discuss those elements of the job of teaching that are admittedly difficult. If this kind of environment does not now exist in your department, you need to take charge and create it. You need to open the doors of conversation and true dialogue.

Other factors for successful supervision include active involvement of the person being supervised, effective feedback, flexible instruments of supervision, the integration of supervision and development, and finally accountability after the supervision takes place. Each of these factors works synergystically with the others to create a system for strong professional development and satisfaction. Brundage (1994) has noted that too often veteran teachers feel that supervision does not provide helpful feedback on practice and that the scope of such supervision is too narrow.

In Sandy's Case, you should note that not many of these elements were present. The instrument for supervision was rigid. Sandy was not actually involved in the design of the supervision nor in helping the supervisor come to an understanding of her teaching goals. The feedback Sandy received was not especially helpful, and there was no mention as to what Sandy might be held accountable. In short, the absence of these factors is one reason why case participants feel so agitated by the case. On the surface, there is a well thought out process and an instrument that obviously took a long time to create, but ultimately it doesn't work. However, there are useful pieces of this tool, so don't be too quick to discard it in its entirety.

The most common form of supervision has been called the clinical model. The father of such supervision is Robert Goldhammer (1969) and his texts from the late 1960s outline the basic components of such supervision. The term *clinical* does not mean "therapeutic," but rather "up-close." It means that the supervisor and the supervisee work closely together to discover something about teaching and learning that they didn't know before. One of the basic tenets of clinical supervision is that good teaching is a learned skill. By providing the teacher with objective data, the teacher learns to augment those portions of her or his work that are effective and reduce those that are not.

Presently, Nolan has identified five conditions to facilitate change in a teacher's thinking and behavior during the supervision period. These conditions are (1) the development of a supportive relationship, (2) continuity over time, (3) focused, descriptive records of actual teaching, (4) teacher control over the supervision products, (5) post-conference reflection by both partners.

But, above all, clinical supervision is a visible and cyclical process. The more common it is for teachers to be supervised, the less threatening it becomes. The more times that students and faculty see department heads working with all teachers on the team for the purpose of instructional improvement, the more positive they will be about the quality of the instruction they are receiving. When supervision is seen merely as a summative tool, whose main purpose is the retention or dismissal of a teacher, students will become skeptical about the level and expertise of the teaching they are receiving, while faculty will become secretive about what they actually do in a class. Students can lose confidence in the teacher and teachers can become hesitant in their work such that instruction is less effective. Thus, it is essential that supervision be a common event. It must be an event where the teacher can be very open with the class and with the department head about the nature and purpose of the supervision.

Creating a Developmental Process of Supervision

All teachers have personal theories of education. These theories serve as the underpinning of intentions, which lead to actions teachers take. The point of these actions is to reach high-level goals dealing with issues such as social justice, standards of behavior and respect, ethical and moral positions, as well as love of subject matter.

The problem is that these personal theories are sometimes not clear to the teacher. They may be able to talk about personal theories, but in fact the teacher often needs help in discovering exactly what those theories are. In this system of developmental evaluation, the department head or team leader will be an essential actor in bringing the teacher to a full realization of his or her theory of teaching and learning.

It is particularly helpful for the teacher to think about his or her teaching using the categories outlined by Charlotte Danielson (1996) in her excellent treatment of an ideal teaching framework. She describes four main domains and fleshes out each domain with components that should be present in the teachers work.

Exhibit 9.1 shows the essential portions of the supervision process. It is a cyclical structure, modeled on the typical five step clinical model: (1) Pre-Observation Conference, (2) Observation, (3) Analysis, (4) Post-Observation Conference, and (5) Cycle Evaluation. However, this model, which I have proposed, has substantial differences from the typical clinical model. These differences are embedded in the structure. The process is traditional only in that it is cyclical in nature and involves close work by the supervisor and the supervisee. Beyond that, this model focuses on a developmental theory of how adults learn.

Stage One: Self-Discovery

In the more typical clinical model, this is the stage where the supervisor and the teacher get together and talk about the essentials of the lesson that is going to be viewed. The supervisor wants to know what is going to be accomplished and how. The teacher tries to be clear about the methods that will be used and about what instructional goals will be reached via this lesson. There may be a discussion of the preparation that led to this particular approach.

Components of Professional Practice

Domain I: Planning and Preparation
             demonstrating knowledge of content and pedagogy
             demonstrating knowledge of students
             selecting instructional goals
             demonstrating knowledge of resources
             designing coherent instruction
             assessing student learning
Domain II: The Classroom Environment
             creating and environment of respect and rapport
             establishing a culture for learning
             managing classroom procedures
             managing student behavior
             organizing physical space
Domain III: Instruction
             communicating clearly and accurately
             using questioning and discussion techniques
             engaging students in learning
             providing feedback to students
             demonstrating flexibility and responsiveness
Domain IV: Professional Responsibilities
             reflecting on teaching
             maintaining accurate records
             communicating with families
             contributing to the school and district
             growing and developing professionally
             showing professionalism

Such a micro-approach seems too narrow in focus. Instead, the general thinking of the teacher needs to be explored. Teachers need to be aware of their unspoken, even unthought, motivations. Chris Argyris and Donald Schon (1989) have pointed out that tacit beliefs underlie our behavior, and often we cannot explain those beliefs or actions, no matter how hard we try.

For example, we are able to recognize a familiar face in a crowd of hundreds of people, and yet we would be hard pressed to explain exactly how we can do this. We understand the structures of correct speech, even though we do not know the formal structures and rules of grammar that underlie that understanding. It is what Michael Polanyi has called tacit

Exhibit 9.1 The Cycle of Developmental Supervision

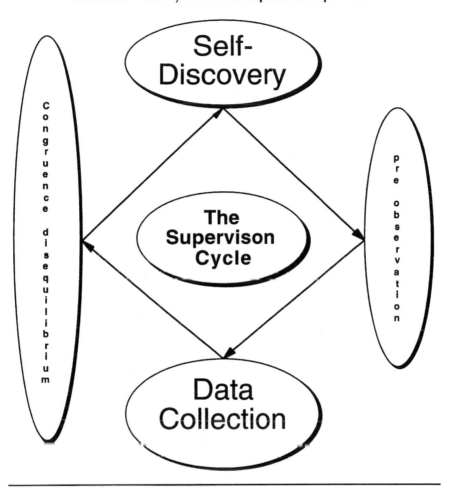

knowledge. It is this tacit knowledge that the teacher needs to discover to fully understand his or her work.

To do this, the supervisor, who in most cases should be the department head, needs to have an extended conversation with the teacher being supervised. This conversation should be recorded on video tape, which the teacher gets to keep. The teacher may decide to include all, some, or none of this tape as part of a portfolio of professional development. This conversation is one of the key events in the developmental supervision structure. It is also one of the most rewarding interactions between the department head

Exhibit 9.2 Argyris and Schon Model One and Two Behavior

Most people when interacting with other people behave in a **Model One** fashion so as to:

1. Unilaterally define goals and act to achieve them. In such interactions, the actor can appear secretive, defensive, and maintains a power relationship with others. It may, on the surface, look as if two people are working together, but closer inspection might point out that others have to guess at what is meant by the actor's statements and actions.

2. Maximize winning and minimize losing. In such interactions the actor isn't necessarily being helpful to others, unless it furthers his or her own cause. The actor can appear conciliatory on the surface, but that is only because his or her mind is already made up. This is a strategy of mystery and mastery.

3. Minimize the generation or expression of negative feelings. In this interaction, the actor will speak in generalities with little or no confirmable evidence. True feelings about the situation will be suppressed and blaming will predominate. The actor will also be blind to the impact such actions have upon others.

4. Above all be rational. The main reason is to protect others from being hurt. In such an interaction, there will be little exchange of real information. Rules will be created to govern behavior and to censor information. Another action that also characterizes this stage of interaction is that there will be more and more clandestine meetings between only a few members of the group.

On the other hand **Model Two** behavior looks like this:
Individuals act so as to:

1. Design situations where participants can access valid information. It is not necessarily second-hand information. In fact, these interactions are often designed so that the participants are the source of much of the information.

2. Allow the task to be jointly controlled. In so doing, the participants learn not only how to describe the environment, but also how to completely change the environment.

3. Develop an internal commitment to the choice of action and monitor its survival. It is through internal commitment that true growth can occur. The ultimate in professional development is for such development to be completely internally focused.

4. Bilaterally protect one another. There is no more unilaterally action and one-upsmanship. Rather there is teamwork and the realization that success, outside of team success, is actually a form of failure.

and the teacher. Creating the context for this conversation takes some planning as well as some understanding of the basic models of human behavior.

In Exhibit 9.2 I have outlined two models of human behavior as described by Argyris and Schon. It is the department head's job to move the conversation beyond the Model One stage and into the Model Two stage. Knowing that most human interaction takes place on a Model One plane puts the department head in a strong position to make breakthroughs in the relationship between him or herself and the teacher.

In conducting an open conversation with the teacher, the department head hopes to establish the groundwork for breaking out of the unilaterally defined actions of Model One behavior. In terms of personal behavior, such understanding can inform the department head about his or her own actions. The reflective and, thus, effective department head wants to test hypotheses, not hide them.

For example, if a teacher repeatedly says that he or she does not want to attend the next department meeting, it only seems logical to find out why. Yet many a department head will quietly fume. Such a department head may even think, "That teacher probably thinks I'm not a very good leader, that I run terrible meetings. Well, to heck with him. He's not too bright himself."

But a department head who is willing to test his or her beliefs and hypotheses by clearly asking a pointed question can interact with that teacher. "I've noticed that this is not the first time that you haven't been able to attend the department meeting. I'm wondering if these meetings serve a useful purpose for you. I want them to be important and not waste your time." The teacher's answer will either help the department head understand his or her meetings in a new light or find out that there is a personal need that must be met and which requires the teacher to be absent from important department business. To be told that the teacher has a regular doctor's appointment, which conflicts with the meeting time may, indeed, be the simple answer. In any case, open and clear testing of assumptions will be a major breakthrough in developing closer relationships with the departmental staff.

The most common element of Model One behavior is this lack of testing of assumptions about another's behavior. In supervision, this can be a serious error. In Sandy's case, you might have noticed that Sandy did not participate in the Math Olympiad training sessions. What did you think about this at the time? You probably ascribed one of several reasons for this behavior: (1) Sandy isn't a good enough mathematician to be able to do that kind of math; (2) Sandy doesn't really like the other members of the department; (3) Sandy is afraid she'd be embarrassed by the smartest math students in the school. On and on it could go. None of these reasons may be true, or they all may be true, but until they are confirmed by Sandy, they are not helpful conjectures.

Thus, in the developmental supervision stage of self-discovery the conversation is one that constantly attends to the public testing of assumptions. In so doing, there is a higher likelihood that true learning can occur. This is why the conversation should be captured on video tape, or at the very least, audio tape. This allows both participants to go back to certain segments for the purpose of asking further follow-up questions. It allows both of the participants to hear not only what was said, but to explore the reasons behind what was said.

Exhibit 9.3 lists questions to begin such conversations about a teacher's work. They are common questions and are modeled after the ones Dan Lortie (1975) used in his landmark sociological study *Schoolteacher*. Usually, this initial session takes about an hour to an hour and one half. After the conversation, the teacher can take the tape home to view and to listen to what was said about teaching. The teacher should develop several statements of his or her theory of teaching. Argyris and Shon call these The Espoused Theories of teaching. They are what we say we do and what we say we think about teaching. When the teacher is finished with the tape, The department head should take the tape and do the same. When finished, both sit down together and watch the tape again.

In understanding how knowledge about the world is created, there are often two ways to view its creation: rules-based knowledge and context-based knowledge (Duffy, 1995). Rules-based knowledge follows procedures that yield one correct answer to a specific question. This type of knowledge occurs in the study of subjects such as physics or language where the rules for problem solving are such that in playing by them, the one correct answer will be discovered.

Context-based knowledge takes the form of wisdom, experience, and stories—not rules. It varies with the context of the problem being addressed. Thus, this kind of knowledge is more typical of that found in teaching. There certainly is not one right answer to a pedagogical problem, and the situations that teachers find themselves in are messy. To understand such situations, there must be a contextual story that gives meaning to that particular event or events. In telling the story, the teacher can make sense of that event. In holding a conversation, the teacher is more likely to rely upon the complexity of relationships and social discourse in making sense and, hence, understanding his or her work.

Exhibit 9.3 Some Selected Questions

1. When did you first decide to be a teacher?
2. What were the biggest factors in your decision?
3. What was it about teaching that attracted you?
4. Did you try any other careers?
5. Why did you choose independent schools (public schools)?
6. Was it important to you that you be in a boarding school (day school)?
7. What was the attitude of your friends and parents when you told them you were going to be working in a prep school (public school)?
8. How do you describe your line of work to strangers or people you've just met say at a cocktail party?
9. At the time you went into teaching what qualities did you think you possessed that would make you a successful teacher?
10. Can you remember having any real doubts that you would "make it" as a teacher?
11. I want you to describe your overall job to me?
12. Describe your typical day from beginning to end.
13. Is there a particular age group you prefer to teach?
14. Of all the things you do here, which do you consider the most important? Which are the most challenging?
15. What do you think others value most in your work here?
16. Many teachers feel there isn't enough time in the day to do everything. Do you feel that way?
17. How do you manage this situation?
18. If you were told you would be able to concentrate on one aspect of your job next year and eliminate all others, what would you choose to spend your time doing?
19. I'm interested in how you view other teachers. Is there a teacher you've had who you've felt was especially outstanding? Can you describe what it was that made him or her outstanding?
20. Where might you place yourself relative to these very best teachers?
21. Every once in a while I'll hear a teacher say "Wow! I had a really great class today." Can you tell me how you feel when you come out of a class like that? What was it that made such a class so good?
22. From time to time I hear a teacher say "If I just could get through to _____." Do you have students like that in your class? What is difficult about them? Can you give me an example of how you would deal with one of them?
23. Can you recall an occasion when you've been especially pleased with your work?
24. Overall in your job here, what are your main goals? What is it you're trying to accomplish?

25. When you ask yourself the question "How am I doing?" what kinds of things do you pay attention to? In other words how do you know you're being an effective teacher?
26. If things weren't going very well in your class, to whom would you turn?
27. Do any of the satisfactions you derive from teaching come as a surprise to you?
28. What is especially satisfying about teaching here?
29. What is especially frustrating about working here?
30. Every teacher seems to recognize that certain influences were very important in the development of his or her own teaching style. What experiences do you think were most important to you as you learned to teach?
31. What kinds of knowledge must a teacher have in order to be successful in the kind of teaching you do?
32. What are the specific skills or know-how, in a practical sense, that a teacher must have in order to "make it" in the kind of teaching you do?
33. Can you describe any point in your career when you said to yourself, "I've made it now. I'm really a good teacher."
34. Most teachers adopt a certain set of "rules" in their classrooms. Do you have such a set? Can you describe them?
35. Every teacher, I suppose, acquires a "reputation" with students, a kind of shorthand a student uses when describing a teacher to another student. What kind of reputation would you like to have?
36. What kind of qualities must a teacher have to be successful with students?
37. What kinds of qualities do you think make a teacher a really good colleague?
38. What do you think the major challenges facing you as a teacher in the next ten years are going to be?
39. What would you like to be doing professionally five or ten years from now?
40. If you had it to do all over again, what occupation would you choose?
41. Tell me how you have felt about this chat we've been having.

Stage Two: Pre-Observation

In this stage the department head and the teacher discuss the findings of the videotaped conversation and try to discover and clarify the personal teaching theories of the teacher. The discussion can be even more effective if a third person also participates and acts as the general questioner in the debriefing of the videotaped conversation. However, this process can work quite well with only two participants. During this phase, the teacher might stop the tape to elaborate upon a point or ask what the questioner was trying to get at by the question. The teacher might want to know if the response given was adequate. New thoughts might occur to both of the participants. All of this goes to embellish and more clearly define the espoused theories of teaching. It is these espoused theories that are crucial.

Once the espoused theories seem to be clear, the teacher and the department head share lists and discuss those theories. After thorough probing, to make sure the proposed theories are in fact true theories and beliefs, the discussion can turn to what the ideal model of exceptional teaching might look like, given this set of personal theories. If the ideal model can be defined, then when actual practice is observed, there will be a standard reference to which to compare the actual behavior.

It seems appropriate that such authentic assessment might be as popular among faculty members as it is within the new models of student assessment. If a teacher's espoused theories denote that he or she is a strong supporter of collaborative learning, then the ideal to which the teacher must aspire must be of the great collaborative teacher. It may be that the espoused theory points to a lecture/recitation model, or to group discussion, or to an individual-support model. Whatever the model might be that is most congruent with the teacher's espoused theories, it is essential that there be a detailed understanding of the paradigm for that style. Exhibit 9.4 outlines some teacher behaviors that characterize good teaching in general. These can be translated into specifics for a particular espoused theory a teacher might describe. Shapiro (1996) and Haymes (1995) provide summaries of standards for effective portfolios.

Exhibit 9.5A shows a verbatim conversation between a department head and a twenty-year veteran . Exhibit 9-5B teacher shows how a selected dialogue can be derived and the espoused theories clarified as they arose from that discussion. (Exhibit 9.5C). You can see that these discussions can be quite emotional, but the beauty of these conversations is that they strike to the heart of teaching. These discussions also tend to bring out doubts and fears, and the department head should be prepared to deal with them. Because the task of teaching is not simply an assembly line process, the backgrounds, aspirations, frustrations, joys, and sorrows of the teacher affect every day's work and the work of his or her colleagues. As the department head, you must be willing to tackle such "messy" subjects. Chap-

Exhibit 9.4 General Characteristics of Good Teaching

1. *Knowledge of Subject Matter.* The teacher must have a breadth of command of the subject at the level that is appropriate for the students being taught. This means that not all teachers must have the same level of expertise in a particular department unless the goal is for everyone to be able to teach every class. It means that teachers should not be thought less able if they are teaching junior high math and do not know the ins and outs of multivariable calculus.

2. *Intellectual Ability and Problem Solving Skill.* An excellent teacher must be able to improvise and act spontaneously, depending upon the situation at hand. There must be a wide repertoire of behaviors available to be used. The excellent teacher can adapt to new technology, new learning research, new materials. The excellent teacher is always seeking a better way to do things and rarely does the same thing in exactly the same way twice.

3. *Pedagogical Skills.* Excellent teachers have high expectations for themselves and their students. They seek high levels of student involvement and monitor the effectiveness of their teaching. They seek out the best curricular materials available and make their own when not able to find those that satisfy their needs. They search for the most expedient ways to get things done. They are clear and correct in their teaching.

4. *Curriculum Knowledge, Insight, and Skill.* Excellent teachers appreciate the many different ways of teaching. They experiment with more than one style of teaching. They know that there is no one right way to teach.

5. *Knowledge of Learners and Learning.* Excellent teachers know that students learn in many ways, and they provide the opportunity for all learners to learn. They are continually searching for new ways to illustrate their subject. They focus their efforts on what students need. They take time to analyze how each of their students learns and then provide experiences for that student to make use of their learning strength.

6. *Exhibit Appropriate Attitude and Disposition.* The excellent teacher is not a whiner. The excellent teacher loves children. They take pride in their own and their students' accomplishments. They are committed to their peers and are eager and willing to share their expertise. They do not gossip or denigrate their colleagues. They devote as much time as possible to their work and do not consider such devotion a drag.

Exhibit 9.5A   Verbatim of a Veteran Teacher

May 30, 1996

Q: Sam, when did you know you wanted to go into teaching?

A: Well, I wanted to become a teacher right out of college. I'd had many many fine teachers in college and also a few here in high school. When I was a student, John Burdess was an individual I admired very very much. In college, you start getting images of you being able to teach or sort of mirror the type of teaching of your college professors, so I was attracted to the profession right then. In fact, I was very close to a philosophy professor who lived down in Redondo Beach, California, and he used to invite some students down and we'd play volley ball and we'd do some readings together—just informally—because he . . . he just brought people into his life and his family's life and this became very appealing to me.

Q: So you liked the uh . . . You saw what they were doing and you said this looks like a pretty good life style . . .

A: Nope, it wasn't just attractive. I felt like I was learning something. I felt like I could continue to learn.

Q: Um . . . When you're in a cocktail party situation, you know, when there are a lot of strangers around, how do you describe to them what you do?

A: A lot of it is just "Freddy wants to buy a computer and what do you recommend?" Formerly, when I taught in college, because I was dealing so much with problems that high school students . . . learning to read or having any type of educational problem at all . . . I was involved with assessment of profound learning problems, and if I just came out with that at a cocktail party, someone would always want to talk about their child and the type of problems he was having. But here I try to talk about what we're trying to do. I try to talk about what students are learning, what the faculty are learning, and I think people don't have any insight into how computers are used other than to think you put software into them. They think it's like putting a CD into a CD player. They don't think about the ways that you're trying to change the way students think about knowledge, and it's hard for them to grapple with it. They never had an experience like that in their own education.

Q: When I think about teaching, I'm often thinking about what qualities people think are connected with good teaching. Or often they're our own qualities. When you went into teaching, what did you think about yourself? I mean you say I have this and I have that, they're part of me. So could you talk about those attributes you see in yourself that make you a good teacher.

A: Well, I was always very service oriented all throughout my life. I just feel you're not having a leg up on life unless you're giving to people. In that mode, in high school during the summers, I volunteered in hospitals . . . working in hospitals for kids with special surgery in New York . . . Uh . . . kids who were leading lives completely different from mine. The seed got planted there when I learned how to interact with other people. I learned that by the time I was fifteen or sixteen . . . that you could make a difference one on one with the children. Then I had these experiences in college working with Fresh Air camps outside of Los Angeles. When I had a number of service activities serving the University of Southern California. So that by the time I came out, I had found that as an individual I had quite a bit to give out to other individuals. I found out that I had quite a love of learning. I had no idea how that was to play out. It was only the kind of interactions that I had with others and the responses that I'd gotten back that led me to understand I could become a teacher. That I could work at many different age levels with many different types of people.

Q: It's interesting given what I know about your background, that you ended up teaching here as our Director of Academic computing. Your background was in English, in reading, in liberal arts, not in computers. You didn't follow the typical path of mathematics and using computers for computing and not using computers to handle alternative ways of learning.

A: It is interesting! I was more or less channeled into the humanities out of the type of schooling that I had. But also out of the kind of self-education. After I was about age of eight, I was always involved in pretty technical things. I remember going to my father's office, and they were using thermal copiers. I remember the secretary pushing this special paper through. I had the top off that thing so fast the minute the secretary was gone. I remember her being upset, because I had taken the top off, something that she herself had never done, because I wanted to see how the thing worked. By the time I was fifteen, I can remember building radios, crystal radios, and staying up half the night trying to get them to work. I could rarely get them to work, and I'd have to go and get help. In college, I was also getting interested in computers. I knew some professors who were using them and I also had a great deal of luck . . . a stroke of luck of working with George Lucas at USC when I was a sophomore. He was a graduate student and TA of a course I took, and he changed everything about the way I thought about images. These weren't just cartoons we were working with, but that you could use them to make a deep impact on people's learning.

Q: All teachers have an issue with time in their day. There's never enough time. How do you make time to do what you want?

A: (Laughter) Time as a resource is something you just have to struggle with. I make lists and then don't so much as rank them according to what's the most important to do but rather what do I really feel like doing that day. That's important to me as I try to get . . . I try to get a lot of things out of the way that I don't want to have to think about anymore. So I can get into that kind of mode also.

I can also get into the mood where I have great ideas, and I have got to work with just those. And then people start letting me know pretty quickly what things I have to get done. So I can sometimes also get those things done. There's no real science to it. I try to make my time work for me. I'm also the type of person who works excessively . . . sixty or seventy hours. So why do I do it? It's because I like the teachers I'm working with.

Q: Does this setting of priorities to do what you like bleed over into your teaching? Some teachers will have a syllabus, and this is what they'll do . . . on May 15th they know exactly what they're doing because it the May 15 date. Other teachers are much more free form. They have a holistic view, saying well I want to do Chapter 7 this week, but I don't know what the assignments will be until I can see what it is the students know and don't know. Which side do you see your self on?

A: When I was a college teacher I was told I had the most elaborate syllabi of any of my colleagues because I would have worked on them. I would go to . . . I believe in self-learning. It's not what the teacher is going to teach in class. So I always had reserve reading that applied to the specific concepts. I can tell you I had a lot of discussion with the librarians, and I would tell my class that if you didn't come to the class, but you had done these readings and they had brought certain experiences with them and you could come to my office and demonstrate that you knew the material, that was fine. But if you're a person that doesn't have that way of learning, you need to be here. So I like alternative ways of learning. In my own teaching, I tend to set out a train of assignments. I try to do it by date, but I'm always way behind. But what I try to pick up upon when I teach is an interest in my students. As soon as I detect this, I dive into that more. I try to let them explore it and extend the learning in that area, rather than trying to cover every single character and plot development in a story. I want them to think about literature and how the author is crafting the work.

Q: When you come out of a class . . . I want to follow up more on the idea of diving into an area . . . and you say to yourself, "Wow, that was a great class." What was going on in your head that allowed you to think that?

A: It has less to do with what I did, than with what happened internally within the students. You usually try to get all students to participate and understand the major ideas I'm trying to elicit on that date. More importantly I'm trying to get them to follow up and make connections to other learning we have done in class. I try to get them to think of the larger picture. They just . . .

Q: You mean they're too immersed in the story?

A: Right they can't see the forest for the trees. And suddenly they begin making connections that roll all the way back to the fall, two terms ago. The world of literature begins opening up to them and that's very exciting. That's what's happening. Sometimes the discussions go so fast that after forty minutes they have to leave and they can't believe it was so quick.

Q: Do you ever follow any tactics, say such as Mortimer Adler suggests. He wrote a book called *How to Read a Book,* and in it he says that reading a book in isolation, which is what a lot of us do when pleasure reading, isn't truly reading a book. Reading a book always involves discussion. Do you have to spend time with your class teaching them how to read a book?

A: You do. You have to teach them how read and how to think about characters. I read Moby Dick in tenth grade and I thought it was an adventure story. If you let them go their natural inclination, they'll all tell you they were born reading. I think what they are reading now is very challenging. It matches their level at the fifth-form level, the eleventh-grade level. Actually, what they are reading isn't difficult. It's written in a dry documentary style by Daniel Defoe. So what I'm always trying to get them to do is to connect across books the same themes so they can see how authors . . . so they can see how authors really work. When an author sits down and puts pen to paper, there was a plan. The author was deliberately writing something in there and . . . and they are missing the whole point if they don't see what that plan was and that that author began that chapter with.

Q: So you're not buying into deconstruction?

A: No. I find that interesting in the same way I find experimental theater interesting. I like to talk about it, but as far as deconstructive theories applied to this level, I think it would be kind of irrelevant.

Q: So If I could break down some of your main goals. One of them is connecting . . . getting students to connect themes of literature across times and genres?

A: Yes.

Q: What other kinds of goals . . . If you were to answer the following, "What am I trying to accomplish with my students?" what would you say?

A: Well I think it would be a range from very low levels such as being able to look at what is good writing, what makes a good sentence . . . as I try to have them read poetry or good prose all the way up to very high levels of, for example how Coleridge in his beliefs about Romanticism, why he wrote as he wrote? What did Romanticism truly mean to that genre of . . . those poets.

Q: And, of course, they didn't know that they were the Romantic poets.

A: No, they . . . they're really blind to it. So that when you look at how those Romanticists are consistent in their approach to treatment of nature, a very good example, or their strange and unusual characters, not heroic characters or epic type, but strange and funny idio-syncratic characters, that changes their awareness of literature. So what I am trying to do is give them a deep appreciation and love for the kind of weirdness of literature . . . trying to understand in that way that it's not bland. It may be hard, but it's not bland. There are always three or four meanings from the literal to . . . um . . . the highly symbolic language of different meaning. I try to come at it like a crossword puzzle. It's supposed to be fun and I try to show them that there's no one right answer. For some students, they are relieved, but in others it creates some anxiety. They don't want to think about it. Damn it, they want to get the high grade, and that bothers them.

Q: What is it you'd like me to think?

A: Just tell us what it is we're supposed to know, and I'll give it back to you. And I won't do that for them.

Q: To be a really good teacher is there any special type of knowledge that you have to have?

A: Well, you get better as you go along. Right from the beginning, if you had some good models and you're aware of where you want to go. In writing . . . I've had some . . . the . . . and we have to work on it all the time, but not specialized knowledge. When I'm reading the Bible as literature. The guidelines for tenth-grade English are simply to read one of the Gospels. I decided to use Luke because it's less commonly used, uh, and I found that you can't read that unless you've read Genesis and Noah's floods. I wanted to get into Mosaic law and over vacation I read the Gospel again, and I found a huge amount of information that was inexplicable, and it had to do with Mary Magdalene. And so I went and bought a book about her to try and get a grip on a very complicated relationship with Christ, and I realized I was into such a small area of scholarship that I couldn't spend a week on this with my students but just for myself I, uh, presented a lot of information that made my students wonder why the major images of women within that Gospel range between virgin and whore and why these extreme forms and models of women. I then followed that in the other literature Often you get extreme presentations of women's roles. It's really interesting.

Q: So for example when you do *Macbeth*, you have Lady Macbeth in some very extreme roles.

A: Yes she's extreme. She says she would just as soon pluck a smiling infant from her nipple and bash his brains upon a rock in order to prove her resolve. So absolutely extreme she wants to absolutely prove that she can hold forth with these plans that she and her husband have. So you get extreme roles for a women.

Q: Yes, think about when she tells Macbeth to " hang thy courage to the sticking place."

A: So looking at literature from a biblical perspective and reading the Bible that way for me myself, I still feel like a beginner at it. There's a lifetime of scholarship that could be brought out.

Q: So your use of the Bible is not a Christian device . . .

A: Right.

Q: But more a . . . that this book shapes early literature

A: Yes, how literature parallels similar themes in the Bible. That um . . . we're rooted in them. Western literature . . . that those roots are long and deep and that that's one way to begin to see . . . it takes a least a term or two for students to see these parallels.

Q: I want to turn the discussion in another way. When things . . . we've been talking about when things are going well. There are two things. You get the feeling that things aren't going well. Now somehow you have to be monitoring what's going on so how do you when you ask yourself "how am I doing?" how do you answer that? And then, if the answer to that is "not so well right now," what do you do?

A: OK . . . well you are constantly monitoring the environment. For example, is it too cold, too hot? Two people who are talking and being distracting. I'm always looking at what's going on. They may be upset from a test. Usually, I'm trying to know about this and assess it before class.

Q: You mean as you enter the room?

A: Yes. There is a person in the class who has a problem with geometry. and it reflects her behavior into my class. I can tell almost right away who's prepared, and I can go to those who aren't right after class to ask what's going on? I feel like you're not participating. If they are getting drowsy, I get more active I might walk around the class and that almost always starts stirring them up. I vary the type of questions, make them more complicated to make them have to listen more intently, and then I turn kind of rapid fire and move through each student and ask them to agree with other kids. I play a sort of point/counter point.

Q: So you're trying to make them be active?

A: I write things often on the board but it's . . . I always turn to that if things aren't going well. Then I'll ask students to go to the board and add to the diagram. If I think the work isn't going well. If the whole class hasn't done their homework, you simply have to . . . you don't drop back ten yards and punt . . . you do drop back and read a passage You have someone read. I do that enough anyway that they wouldn't notice things weren't going well. Now after a page or two, we have a common experience and to get at what I really want.

Q: So you can still have a productive class and urge them on their leaving that tonight they really must do the reading.

A: I'll tell them specific things I want them to be able to pull out of the reading for the next night. So I use a variety of strategies uh . . . I don't think when I'm doing things badly, does it have anything do with my preparation or lack of preparation. I usually do my major readings a month or so ahead, and I take huge numbers of notes. I usually go over the notes to remember what major points I'm trying to elicit.

Q: Many teachers have a set of rules in their classes. Do you have such rules?

A: No chewing gum. Sit up in the seat. Be there on time . . . and . . .

Q: Some people have specific rules such as not turning in papers that have been torn from a spiral notebook with those curlies hanging off . . .

A: No, I don't do that. Beyond those I really don't have any rules. Other than I expect them to participate. I do have a participation grade. In my conferences with them, I remind them of that, and I point out ways that they can participate. You see I'm always trying to figure out what they know, and I'm doing that in a way, using a sort of series of inductive questions. I'm trying to ferret out whether it's a reluctance, or whether they truly don't know. At any rate, I try to let every one of them know I value their response, and we try to develop a composite of responses as we try to develop a framework to understand the work. So I'm trying to work hard at my questions and the questioning process.

Q: Do you set up the questions beforehand. Do you say, "I'm going to open up with a series of factual questions that call for low level and them move to inductive questions at the middle to see if they can appreciate the abstract"?

A: You know, I really don't know the answer to that. I know what the major themes are, and I always have a list of the pages and everything underlined in the book so I can always turn to a page . . . uh . . . to be able to have a starting place. But where I go . . . I try to thread through their responses I'm getting. If they signal I can go up a level in inductive or down a level um . . . I listen to a couple in the class, and for a couple, even after eight months, it's still a risk for them. It's not their style. They would be perfectly content to sit there and get good grades on tests. They would do all the work, but having to say something in front of the class is still hard. One on one, they're great so I know they can do it. There are other people . . . there's one who dominates, and I try to send the discussion away from that person. But in truth I don't know, sometimes I'll write out a couple of questions, especially if they deal with a lot of detail . . . but it's one thing to know where I want to be at the end of a lesson and how I get there is mapped into all my understanding as a teacher.

Q: But one trait of good teaching is the ability to be spontaneous. From what you been saying, I hear that notion in your work. Can you give me any other examples of this spontaneous teaching style?

A: Oh completely. I thought their writing was going horribly by mid-fall. They were looking at it as a paint by numbers approach. They had to have complete sentences and double checked for comma splices, but they still didn't know anything about how to write for character. How to write a lead into a story, how to initiate conflict. Boarding school life is not your average life. There really isn't a lot of conflict. I mean there can be, but usually there is not. Their needs are all met. I found a pattern I didn't like. I didn't know how to get rolling, so I took them all down to the downtown and to all the different cafes near the train station and told them for the next twenty-five minutes imagine yourself working here and get a grip on the characters here. I want you to be able to tell me how the cafes are decorated. You know that's a pretty seedy part of town. The characters who are down there are pretty amazing . . .

Two boys were sitting in the cafe, and a homeless fellow came in, and they had an amazing conversation. So there was an irritant that I discovered when they weren't willing to do the learning themselves. So I could see that in their writing. I want them to think it through all by themselves. After that, their writing became almost transformed. Almost everything after that was exactly what I wanted them to do, There was some threshold that had been passed.

Q: Let me ask you what characteristics in a teacher make for good colleagueship?

A: You know it's funny. Teaching is a funny profession because it's very private situation. You get into that classroom, and you could go twenty years without an interaction in your classroom. I have known department heads for twenty years, and they don't want to intrude. Unless you show up drunk for heavens sake. It really . . . this is thought to be something you are trusted with, and I've always wondered why. I've worked in other areas where you work shoulder to shoulder and are always talking about tricks of the trade. But educators don't do this. They don't talk about what they are doing . . . feeling. Especially with twenty-year-olds. They need to know the world. Try to get them to have a few calluses about this. So try to disarm fear is something a good colleague does by talking and visiting. It's a bit foreign, but I don't know why. Of course, we don't have time to enroll in each others' classes, but it would be immensely popular if we could. I've heard of faculty here who are sort of like Peter Abelard, people would follow through the Alps to listen to them lecture. I know that a good portion of . . . if the headmaster wanted to form a small liberal arts college, he would have a good core faculty right here. And we don't celebrate this teaching. We intrinsically feel the love and power of the profession by what we do and therefore don't need recognition. You don't get many rewards in teaching. You know external outward rewards. Most people say, Who needs it? But getting respect of colleagues is enough . . . and you get that at lunch The issue is respect and listening and talking freely about writing—your own or your students. If mine's not working for me, I ask one person I trust who will tell me what is wrong. It's unfair to always say it's only time.

In the supervisory relationship I always hope the colleague will learn by watching someone show his or her talent. Maybe I could be some help. For that person to be a better teacher. You have to look at the fact that every teacher wants to improve, and the supervisor is key for this.

Q: Let me ask you a final question. How have you felt during this half-hour to forty minutes of conversation?

A: I've started thinking about two or three articles I want to write. I didn't realize I had these thoughts so worked out. I thought about an article or two. This is a real mystery to me . . . about being a great teacher. Most are modest about ability. If they had more time to read and share together because this allows you to grow. There is nothing like academia to let you develop yourself as an individual.

Exhibit 9.5B Selected Verbatim Responses: Responses from a Boarding School Science Teacher with Twenty-Five Years of Experience

"This department is made up of people interested in teaching and in teaching 'good science.' It's a dynamic department. We support each other. We're continually consulting with each other . . . trying to create new ways to add to our teaching. We visit one another. The administration knows when to leave us alone and when to support us when we need it."

"I like teaching kids who are willing to take a chance . . . willing to be committed to something . . . open to being motivated . . . eager to learn. Kids who are feisty . . . can respond to me and the interest, uh . . . excitement, and enthusiasm I provide. I'm not interested in only the creme de la creme. They're somewhat like automatons, running with the ball. I like kids who need my help to see that they can get to another level. The kids I like most are the ones who walk into Chemistry and say, 'I can't do chemistry.' There are some kids who surrender the first week. They think it's the hump they're never going to get over. I like those kids the most."

I'm absolutely interested in building kids' self-esteem. There are enough kids who tell me, even though they're never going to do chemistry, they can understand it and feel confident they can do the work. By working together, we can build their self-esteem and perhaps my own self-esteem but . . . many who feel this was going to be the worst year of their life but it wasn't."

"I like to have a lot of fun. I'm very serious about what I do, but I don't take myself seriously. I like lots of give and take in my class. Jokes. Kids enjoying each other, the subject and me. I'm animated, silly at times, and I hope demanding. I'm having fun. Kids also need to see learning is fun, even if it can be demanding."

"A dynamite class for me is one where everyone walks out of the class still talking about it."

"I'm satisfied with my ability to . . . my . . . what I think is the environment I create in my chemistry classes. People are comfortable asking me questions and learning, and people feel good about themselves. I'm satisfied with the academic and the personal parts."

There are areas I'm still weak in and am dissatisfied with. The chaos of ninth graders, their inability to take notes, the apathy, was driving me crazy . . . and the relationships with ninth graders are harder to establish than with Juniors or Seniors. It was too anxiety-producing to work with them. Older students . . . I enjoy my relationship with them much more."

"I spend time getting reluctant students to feel engaged and part of the group. Then, I shoot for the middle . . . but there's not as much enrichment for the top end as I'd like."

"My perspectives on teaching have changed as I've gotten older, in that my understanding of the process of learning . . . the environment that it takes to be a good learner. At first I was really busy trying to show how competent I was in my subject area, and I still feel strongly about that, but now I understand much more about how kids feel. That even bright kids need to be 'set up' to learn. So if I can facilitate classroom dynamics, so kids feel good about themselves, support each other, and feel they can take risks, then I feel we're all set. As I get older, I see more and more other aspects besides the technical information that I'm giving that I feel are important and so I work on those things."

"I don't fear parents coming to talk. I don't fear Parents' Day. It's real fun. It used to be a chore."

"I don't know if as I get older if I don't feel I can continue to do it. What happens in fifteen years? I don't know if I'll be excited. I can relate to kids now, I don't know if when I'm fifteen years older they'll see me as so far apart from them that they don't include me, and I feel included right now. They ask for advice. They're friendly. But right now I feel the next ten years are going to be fine and I feel terrific about that."

Exhibit 9.5C Agreed Upon Espoused Theories of Teaching

1. I enjoy collaborating with other teachers. This is important for me to feel professional.
2. I need to feel helpful to students. I like their appreciation. I am most stimulated by those who think they can't do it.
3. I teach to build student self-esteem. I also look at my own self-esteem while I'm working.
4. I manage the classroom environment such that students support one another. I also make sure that all students learn. I specifically arrange work so that students will be successful.
5. I create an atmosphere of joy and fun in my class. Students joke with me and others. It is important for me that there is a lot of give and take. I organize my questioning so that students feel comfortable asking questions.
6. I feel I relate well to my students on a personal level. My students confide in me and that's important. I think the kids are then willing to go the extra mile for me in the classroom.
7. I'd like for there to be more enrichment for the most able students.
8. I'd rather teach older students. Younger students don't respond well to or appreciate my style.
9. I'm confident in my ability to be an exciting teacher for the near future. I don't know about the long haul.

---

ter 4 "Effective Communication" has some worthwhile tips on how to be involved as an active listener.

In Exhibit 9.5A, notice how spontaneous the responses are in bringing the theory of teaching to light. These statements would more than likely be missing if the process were a less conversational and more formal introspection. When a teacher is asked to write out his or her theory of teaching, what often emerges is ponderous, weighty, and bears little resemblance to what is actually held deeply. When teachers are asked to put pen to paper in such a formal manner, the unspoken expectation is that the ideas must be more structured. And some of the ideas, while genuine and sincere, don't seem to be as important as others. Certainly, they might not seem as important as the formal discussions of teaching that can be found in educational texts. Thus, important insights into the desires and motives of the teacher are lost or, at the very least, unspoken.

In addition, conversations create serendipitous insights into the mind of the teacher. "By working together we can build their self esteem, *and perhaps my own self-esteem*." What exactly did the teacher mean by that?

Having the conversation on video tape allows the department head to go back over any portion of the conversation to find out more. In this case, it was discovered that the teacher meant that he also felt more competent when the students felt the same way.

But what is most important is that the details of the conversation produce the substance of what should be viewed when conducting the next phase of the process.

Stage Three: The Class "Visit"

Just as it was crucial to hold the initial phases of the developmental evaluative process in front of a video camera, it is also important to use video tape as the primary tool in class visitation. The teacher is asked to put a video camera in his or her class for a week or so and to tape as many classes as desired. Then the teacher submits for viewing about five classes worth of tape.

The purpose of letting teachers be completely in control of the tapes that exhibit his or her "best work" is to allow them to be in charge of as much of the process as possible. As the supervisor, one of the purposes of this type of supervision is to capture examples of the teacher's best work and to discuss how to improve practice. It is too easy for the teacher to feel somewhat cheated when classroom observation happens to be conducted during the two or three classes that just didn't work well. By making the teacher responsible for showing his or her best work, the department head has the opportunity to praise good behaviors. Behaviorists have maintained that a more effective means of changing behavior is to "catch them being good, rather than bad." It is easier to strengthen good habits, through praise, than to eliminate bad habits through disapproval.

In addition, five hours of tape probably come from twice that much total taping. This means that the teacher has made some decisions and has thought about his or her work. They have self-selected what they choose to exhibit, based upon some internal standard, which is another example of bringing forth espoused theories of teaching. Also, the more often a teacher can view himself or herself in the process of teaching, the more likely he or she will be able to make adjustments and refinements in methodology and pedagogy to fit the model of good teaching held in his or her head.

Because the classes are on tape, there can be no "filter" to inhibit the conversation between the department head and the teacher. When there is no taped record, all subsequent discussions are filtered by what the department head purportedly saw and heard. The teacher, being too engaged in

Exhibit 9.6 Teacher Student Interchange

Each interaction is recorded for a typical class. The class was an English class focused on discussion of a short story. The symbols represent the following: Q = question; A = answer; S = statement; E = explanation. Note that the students adjacent to the teacher and directly across from the teacher are not active in the discussion.

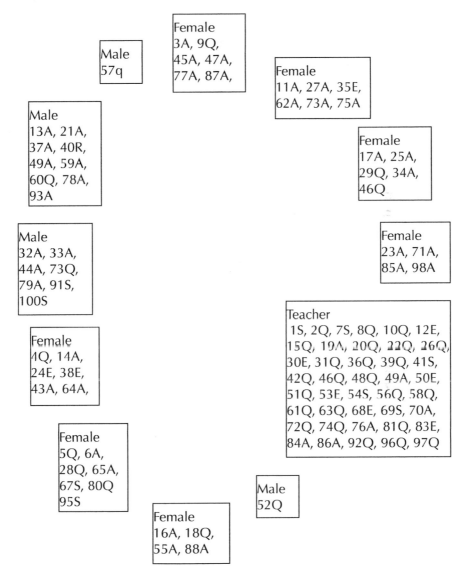

Exhibit 9.7 Time on Task Analysis

Every two minutes the observer records what each student is doing according to the categories below:

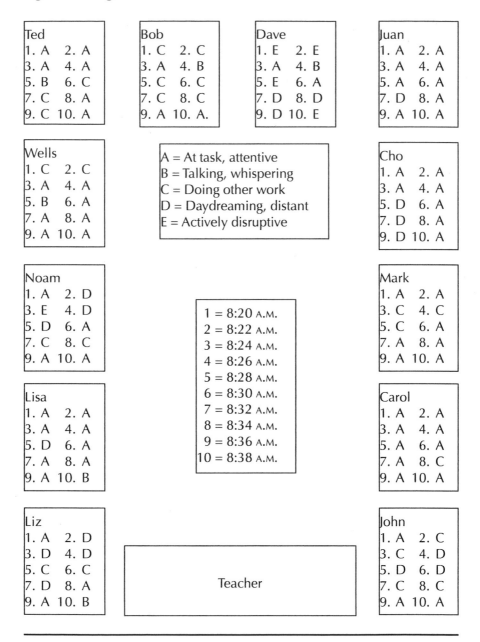

Ted
1. A   2. A
3. A   4. A
5. B   6. C
7. C   8. A
9. C   10. A

Bob
1. C   2. C
3. A   4. B
5. C   6. C
7. C   8. C
9. A   10. A.

Dave
1. E   2. E
3. A   4. B
5. E   6. A
7. D   8. D
9. D   10. E

Juan
1. A   2. A
3. A   4. A
5. A   6. A
7. D   8. A
9. A   10. A

Wells
1. C   2. C
3. A   4. A
5. B   6. A
7. A   8. A
9. A   10. A

A = At task, attentive
B = Talking, whispering
C = Doing other work
D = Daydreaming, distant
E = Actively disruptive

Cho
1. A   2. A
3. A   4. A
5. D   6. A
7. D   8. A
9. D   10. A

Noam
1. A   2. D
3. E   4. D
5. D   6. A
7. C   8. C
9. A   10. A

1 = 8:20 A.M.
2 = 8:22 A.M.
3 = 8:24 A.M.
4 = 8:26 A.M.
5 = 8:28 A.M.
6 = 8:30 A.M.
7 = 8:32 A.M.
8 = 8:34 A.M.
9 = 8:36 A.M.
10 = 8:38 A.M.

Mark
1. A   2. A
3. C   4. C
5. C   6. A
7. A   8. A
9. A   10. A

Lisa
1. A   2. A
3. A   4. A
5. D   6. A
7. A   8. A
9. A   10. B

Carol
1. A   2. A
3. A   4. A
5. A   6. A
7. A   8. C
9. A   10. A

Liz
1. A   2. D
3. D   4. D
5. C   6. C
7. D   8. A
9. A   10. B

Teacher

John
1. A   2. C
3. C   4. D
5. D   6. D
7. C   8. C
9. A   10. A

Exhibit 9.8 Time on Task Analysis

	8:20	8:22	8:24	8:26	8:28	8:30	8:32	8:34	8:36	8:38	total	%
A	9	6	8	7	2	7	6	6	8	9	68	57
B	0	0	0	2	2	0	0	0	0	2	6	5
C	2	3	2	1	3	3	3	4	2	0	23	19
D	0	2	1	2	4	2	3	2	2	0	18	15
E	1	1	1	0	1	0	0	0	0	1	6	4

Twelve students observed individually 10 times.
Total number of student observations = 12 x 10= 120

Behavior key
A = At task
B = Talking, whispering
C = Doing other work
D = Day-dreaming
E = Actively disruptive

the actual act of teaching, will not be able to recall the incidents in exactly the same way as the department head might have. In fact, the teacher may have viewed particular incidents in exactly opposite terms from those of the supervisor. Taping eliminates this problem. Having a record on tape also allows more than one kind of analysis to take place. Exhibits 9.6 to 9.10 are some examples of common methods of classroom interaction analysis, which can be quite helpful at creating the conditions for an excellent dialogue between the department head and the teacher.

Finally, having a taped record of the classes can serve as an important ongoing file of teacher growth. Imagine how useful it would be to one's career to have a series of tapes of classroom teaching. Such artifacts would serve as a fundamental component of a teacher portfolio. A portfolio can also be viewed as an essential set of documents to help teachers make sense of their work and make plans for improvement. Exhibit 9.12 shows some possible portfolio contents. Wolf (1996) and Blake (1995) give detailed instructions for creating effective teacher portfolios.

While this method emphasizes the use of video tape, this is not to say that spending time sitting in the teacher's classroom isn't important. Certainly, it is important to get the feel of the classroom atmosphere, but do

Exhibit 9.9 Verbal Flow

Similar to the other record-keeping methods, but now the observer is recording positive and negative response from the teacher. In this case, the teacher wanted to know if she was favoring one of the genders more than the other when giving praise.

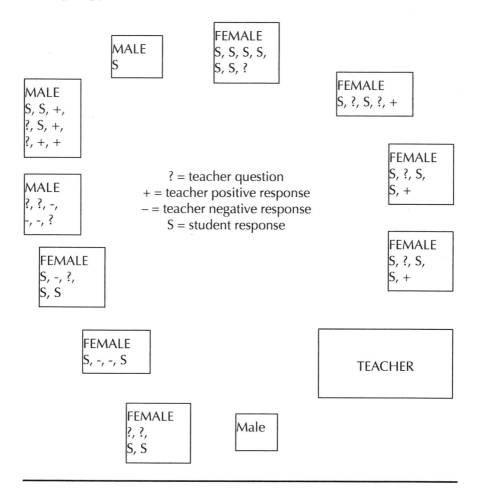

not take notes or write anything down while visiting. Any post-visit discussion with the teacher should be totally focused on the classroom ethos and not on any aspect of the teacher's performance. If these personal visits are to get a feeling for the atmosphere of the classroom, then they must not be contaminated by selective filtering, which is what will happen when

Exhibit 9.10 Verbal Flow Analysis

Analysis of the responses shown in Exhibit 9-9.

	Number of students	% of questions
Females	7	64
Males	4	36
Total students	11	

	Teacher questions to students%	
Females	11	64
Males	6	36
Totals	17	

	Positive teacher response	%
Females	4	50
Males	4	50
Total	8	

	Negative teacher response	%
Females	3	60
Males	2	40
Total	5	

Exhibit 9.11 National Board for Professional Teaching Standards: Five Core Propositions

"The National Board for Professional Teaching Standards seeks to identify and recognize teachers who effectively enhance student learning and demonstrate the high level of knowledge, skills, dispositions and commitments reflected in the following five core propositions."

1. Teachers are committed to students and their learning.

Board-certified teachers are dedicated to making knowledge accessible to all students. They act on the belief that all students can learn. They treat students equitably, recognizing individual differences in their practice. They adjust their practice, as appropriate, based upon observation and knowledge of their students' interests, abilities, skills, knowledge, family circumstances, and peer relationships.

Accomplished teachers understand how students develop and learn. They act on the belief that all students develop and learn. They incorporate the prevailing theories of cognition and intelligence into their practice. They are aware of the influence of context and culture on behavior. They develop students' cognitive capacity and respect for learning. Equally important, they foster students' self-esteem, motivation, character, civic responsibility, and their respect for individual cultural, religious, and racial differences.

2. Teachers know the subjects they teach and how to teach those subjects to students.

Board-certified teachers have a rich understanding of the subject(s) they teach and appreciate how knowledge in their subject is created, organized, linked to other disciplines and applied to real-world settings. While faithfully representing the collected wisdom of our culture and upholding the value of disciplinary knowledge, they also develop the critical and analytical abilities of their students.

Accomplished teachers command specialized knowledge of how to convey and reveal subject matter to students. They are aware of the preconceptions and background knowledge the students typically bring to each subject and of strategies and instructional materials that can be of assistance. They understand where difficulties are likely to arise and modify their practice accordingly. Their instructional repertoire allows them to create multiple paths to the subjects they teach, and they are adept at teaching students how to pose and solve their own problems.

3. Teachers are responsible for managing and monitoring student learning.

Board-certified teachers create, enrich, maintain, and alter instructional settings to capture and sustain the interest of their students and to make the most effective use of time. They are also adept at engaging students and adults to assist their teaching and at enlisting their colleagues' knowledge and expertise to complement their own.

Accomplished teachers command a range of generic instructional techniques, know when each is appropriate, and can implement them as needed. They are as aware of ineffectual or damaging practice as they are devoted to elegant practice. They know how to engage groups of students to ensure a disciplined learning environment, and how to organize instruction to allow the school's goals for students to be met. They are adept at setting norms for social interaction among students and teachers. They understand how to motivate students to learn and maintain their interest even in the face of failure.

Board-certified teachers can assess the progress of individual students, as well as that of the class as a whole. They employ multiple methods for measuring student growth and understanding and can clearly explain student performance to parents.

4. Teachers think systematically about their practice and learn from experience.

Board-certified teachers are models of educated persons, exemplifying the virtues they seek to inspire in students . . . curiosity, tolerance, honesty, fairness, respect for diversity, and appreciation for cultural differences . . . and the capacities that are prerequisites for intellectual growth . . . the ability to reason and take multiple perspectives, to be creative and take risks, and to adopt an experimental and problem-solving orientation.

Accomplished teachers draw on their knowledge of human development, subject matter, and instruction, and their understanding of their students to make principled judgments about sound practice. Their decisions are not only grounded in the literature, but also in their experience. They engage in lifelong learning, which they seek to encourage in their students.

Striving to strengthen their teaching, board-certified teachers critically examine their practice, seek to expand their repertoire, deepen their knowledge, sharpen their judgment, and adapt their teaching to new findings, ideas, and theories.

5. Teachers are members of learning communities.

Board-certified teachers contribute to the effectiveness of the school by working collaboratively with other professionals on instructional policy, curriculum development, and staff development. They can evaluate school progress and allocation of school resources in light of their understanding of state and local objectives. They are knowledgeable about specialized school and community resources that can be engaged for their students' benefit, and are skilled at employing such resources as needed.

Accomplished teachers find ways to work collaboratively and creatively with parents, engaging them productively in the work of the school.

From *Toward High and Rigorous Standards for the Teaching Profession*, 1989. Published by the National Board for Professional Teaching Standards, 26555 Evergreen Road, Suite 400, Southfield, MI 48076

recording through writing. A video tape, with excellent sound quality, can perform just as fine a job at conveying classroom atmosphere, as does sitting in a classroom seat.

The issue of taping quality is an important one. In many video cameras, the omni-directional microphone will pick up a lot of ambient sound and amplify it to a large degree. Using a separate, high quality microphone will vastly improve the sound quality. However, careful placement of the camera in the room can also minimize the distracting background noise.

The "Post-Observation" Conference

When the taping is finally finished, the teacher views the tapes with an eye towards showing concrete instances of his or her espoused theories of

---

Exhibit 9.12 Portfolio Contents

1. Statement of teaching responsibilities;
2. Statement of espoused theories of teaching;
3. Syllabi, reading lists, assignments, exams, and handouts from courses taught;
4. Description of efforts to improve teaching;
5. Peer evaluation of teaching and teaching skills;
6. Formal evaluations from the department head;
7. Videotapes of instruction;
8. Measures of student achievement (Graded samples of work, National test scores of students, awards that students have won);
9. Other evidence of good teaching (letters from students, parents or alumni. Letters of thanks from colleagues for developing or sharing instructional material);
10. Future teaching goals.

Peter Seldin, *The Teaching Portfolio: A Practical Guide to Improved Performance and Promotion/Tenure Decisions,* Bolton, MA: Anker Publishing Company, Inc., 1991

teaching. The supervisor also views the tape(s) and tries to do the same. The purpose is to confirm that there is congruence between what the teacher thinks he or she is doing (the espoused theories of teaching) and what is actually being done (the theory in action). In addition, by using the process of questioning and story-telling, the teacher and supervisor are setting up a situation where the highest levels in Maslow's hierarchy of needs can be approached. The need for self-mastery and providing a sense of real meaning to the events in one's life is the highest niche in this schema. See Figure 1.1. Because the prior use of the taped conversation provides the background and underlying theories of work, the likelihood that such sense-making will occur is greatly increased over the typical form of clinical supervision, which is more localized and focused.

As the espoused theories of one teacher, as shown in Exhibit 9.5C, are compared with actual classroom performance, the teacher is placed in a state of either congruence or disequilibrium. Being in such a mental state allows true learning in the teacher to occur. This process of seeing one's self in the act of doing has been a key component of the athlete's repertoire of improvement techniques for some time now. There is no doubt that this technique can be equally effective in the teaching profession. Piaget has described the learning process in children and adolescents in exactly this fashion. Being placed in a state of disequilibrium forces the child to come to grips with reality and, in so doing, learn. There is no reason to believe the learning process is radically different for adults.

Often, what the teacher and the supervisor discover is that the espoused theories are, in fact, completely congruent with the teacher's practice. In this case, the supervisor can note this fact and provide the appropriate praise. It is crucial, in this phase, to broaden the discussion to encompass both the departmental and school goals. If the teacher's practice and espoused theories mesh, but are opposed to the departmental educational goals or the school's philosophical mission, then the teacher may be personally effective, but institutionally ineffective. The department head needs to help the teacher focus, not only on personal effectiveness, but also on institutional effectiveness.

For example, an English teacher may hold, as an espoused theory, that the most important element in literature analysis is a combination of a close textual reading and a subsequent wrestling with that text in order to understand what it means. In this teacher's eyes, the use of secondary critical works is not useful to the student's progress. When the department head views the tapes of the classes and holds the interview with the teacher, it is clear that students never use secondary sources. They work hard to decipher the complexities of the text and how it has made sense to them. This is clear evidence of congruence between the teacher's espoused theory and his or her actual practice.

However, what if one of the goals of the department is to help students understand modern theories of criticism and how classic works of literature are constantly viewed through new approaches. The student is supposed to emerge from his or her study of literature with an appreciation for the great human themes that such classics present and to understand why some works remain interesting through the ages and some do not. If the student is not allowed to confront modern literary criticism and interpretation through secondary readings, this important goal will not be achieved. While this may not point out any flaw in the teacher's pedagogical theory, it does point out noncongruence with departmental policy. The teacher has failed to achieve a departmental goal, which was, no doubt, designed carefully to ensure that students leave with a particular standard of achievement.

In addition, the school mission statement might state that students are to leave the school fully prepared to meet the challenges of college study. If the student does not understand how to use secondary sources to write a critical paper, that student will be at a severe disadvantage compared to those students who do. So the teacher's classroom emphasis and approach have also not been directed to fulfill a major, overarching school goal. The department head must now work to help that teacher bring his or her practice into closer congruence with both of these larger institutional goals. If the teacher cannot or will not, then there might be a serious conversation about the advisability of future employment in the school.

More often than not, the discussion of the tapes unearths a truth that was not a part of the teacher's espoused theories. In this case, the discovery allows the department head to point out the fact that there is an element of practice that has not been consciously recognized as an espoused theory. Holding such tacit beliefs is common to all teachers and perhaps to all professions (Schon, 1987). What is important here is that the department head help the teacher translate this behavior into words. The interpretation of action via written statements is important in helping the teacher develop a well-rounded sense of practice.

For example, a physics teacher who continually moved away from the stated lesson plan, when there seemed to be some interest on the part of the class in a question or discussion that was somewhat peripheral or even wildly divorced from the specific topic, can clearly be wasting precious class minutes. In order to follow such a pedagogy, the teacher had to leave the room for several minutes to find a particular piece of apparatus to demonstrate what had been brought up in the classroom discussion. Before viewing the classroom tapes, this pedagogical behavior would not have been discovered. However, upon viewing these tapes, both the supervisor and the teacher agreed that this behavior was not in the best interests of the students.

The teacher, in the subsequent discussions, made it clear that he internally believed in the "teachable moment" school of pedagogy. When students appeared interested in a topic, the teacher's duty is to follow that thread of student interest. This taped discovery allowed the department head and the teacher to add another espoused theory to the list that had been developed during the initial conversational phase of the supervision. This espoused theory stated that students learn best when they are interested in a topic and the teacher's job is to be aware of and build upon these times of interest.

While this might be commendable in some schools, it might not be for this particular department. It meant that when students were faced with the common examinations, which were part of the ethos of the department, this teacher's students were at a marked disadvantage. They had not spent the same amount of time on the commonly agreed upon topics for that period of learning. This espoused theory might be at odds with another of the teacher's espoused theories that stated that all students should be taught so that they have the same intellectual footing as all other students. The teacher had stated that he felt that all students can be successful in his sub-ject, and his practice should focus on helping students be successful.

In this case, the teacher discovered why his students were not doing as well as the other teachers' students on the common exam. He had always thought that it was due to a personal lack of skill relative to the other teach-ers in the department. However, he had not wanted to bring such a matter up to the teaching team because of the obvious threat to his ego and, pos-sibly, to his position. This teacher, who was quite skilled at teaching, was losing valuable teaching time devoted to side-bar topics. When such topics were completed, there was no follow-up with reading or problem assign-ments. They occurred at the moment and in isolation from reinforcement exercises. They were often very interesting, but they did not allow the teacher to fulfill his duty with the departmental and school context.

The teacher agreed that this was the case and was able to alter, signifi-cantly, his practice by keeping such meanderings short and then moving the class back to the material at hand. Again, this shows that what is im-portant is not that there is a particular right method of teaching or wrong method of teaching. Rather, there is teaching practice that allows for the at-tainment of goals and the teacher must focus his or her practice in such a manner to make the attainment of those common goals a reality.

When such nonverbalized and nonproductive espoused theories are discovered, they should be added to the list. The teacher should use further video taping to discover if his or her practice has changed to increase like-lihood of reaching departmental goals. When this happens, a teacher can be said to be more effective than when such goals were not being attained.

Additional "Post-Observational" Analysis

While the videotapes form the basis for concrete information about teach-ing practice, there are other materials that can also support the search for congruence between espoused theories and practice. Such materials can be collected to form a portfolio of teaching practice.

In this phase of the process, the department head and the teacher should concentrate on the important question of "How do I now determine if my approach has been effective in helping students learn?" After all, this is the prize and the purpose for developmental supervision. It is in this analysis phase that the most beneficial learning takes place. This is the phase where the teacher hopefully moves from the "what is" phase to the "what ought to be" phase.

Yet, holding these final sessions can be the most difficult of all the phases in the developmental process. Whenever two people meet, the chances for miscommunication and misunderstanding are great. It is crucial that the post-observation conversation be as open as possible. The supervisor and the teacher must both agree that what is important is to discover what is working well and to make concrete plans for how there can be improvement, no matter how well things are going. But, because there is always some amount of power differential involved, simply because of the nature of the supervisor/supervisee relationship, the discussion can be difficult.

Most often, the greatest difficulty lies in the probability that when bad news has to be given, the giver of that news will want not to give it. And, of course, it is the rare receiver of information who welcomes bad news. The department head might wish that the interaction would be easy. An easy interaction for the department head can be thought of as one where the task to be accomplished is easily defined, where the department head feels especially competent, where the teacher to be given the bad news is passive, willing and strives to avoid conflict. In these situations, the department head has no fear of rejection.

However, there will be times when none of these characteristics are present. In such cases, what is the department head to do? Basically the answer is not to let fear of negativity overcome your ability to act. It is the department head's duty to be as straight-forward in delivering all news, whether it be good or bad.

In the letters of supervision for Sandy Samuels at the beginning of this chapter, the department head has so diluted the real message to Sandy about weak teaching, that it is nearly impossible to discover. Sandy will have no idea that there is a problem until several years later when the department head will reach a breaking point and try to dismiss Sandy. The department head will, no doubt, then point to the letters of supervision and the interpretation that there is criticism involved—in fact, even positive criticism—upon which Sandy did not act. Or a new department head will have to deal with years of non-useful supervision and be faced with dealing with a less than capable, yet veteran, mathematics teacher.

Thus, it is fundamental that the supervision communication, whether verbal or written, be as clear and factual as possible. If seven families have complained about the teacher's work, that should be stated. If, at the same time, seven families have praised the teacher that should be stated also. If the teacher finished the year three units ahead of everyone else, this needs to be stated. At the same time, if the teacher finished the year three units behind everyone else, this needs to be stated. Pulling punches will not be helpful.

That being said, it is also true that the final conversations must be well-structured. Hold them in a private place. Do so at the end of the day and the end of the week. Place as much in writing as possible, but do not send the report to the teacher. Rather, have the teacher read your report at the beginning of the meeting. Let the teacher know at the outset what importance the supervisory report has. Does the report imply that there are serious problems or does it mean that there are no problems. Does it mean the teacher needs to be working under a provisional contract the next year? Does it mean that the teacher is doing a great job and should be helping others to develop the same level of teaching expertise? Being clear about such issues will defuse the potential for anxiety.

A key pitfall to avoid is discussion of the teacher's work in light of what YOU would do if you were that teacher. The final conversation should be focused on what the teacher will do over the long run. Having the teacher address the question of long-term plans for teaching is one good way to help structure this portion of the conversation.

Difficult Conversations

It is not always the case that the teacher is receptive to your suggestions in these conversations. Whenever someone is asked to change, the level of anxiety can rise. The key here is to help the teacher maintain self-esteem. There are always good practices that every teacher performs. Be sure to seek them out and give praise where praise is due. However, you must be sure to give all the feedback that you planned to. If you listen carefully, the teacher will often give you an opening for the delivery of what you might be considering as bad news. Again, remember that what we might think is bad news may not be so for the recipient.

You need to check for commitment and understanding from the teacher as the conference proceeds. The questions you ask can set the tone here. For example, "If you were to summarize what we've covered so far what would you say?" "Can you tell me the one or two things that most made an impression on you in our discussion so far?" "Is this something you're interested in pursuing?" "Would you like me to get more involved in this aspect of your work?" "Would it help to have another follow-up talk next week?"

Gender Issues

As the supervisor, it is important to also understand the possible interaction dynamics when supervising members of the opposite gender. Some interesting results have come from studies of interactions between males and females versus similar gender interactions. (Shakeshaft, 1991).

Several popular books have pointed out the different needs of men and women, even at a time when the differences between men and women, especially in the area of professionalism, are certainly being actively reduced. In an educational setting, parity and equality are the norms for behavior. But there is also the reality that some differences still remain, if in less overt manifestations than twenty years ago. One of her more interesting findings is that women tend to receive less feedback than men do. Men receive more positive and negative feedback, while women receive neutral feedback. Such neutrality results in decreased ability to adequately understand the seriousness of any situation and clearly discern the strength or weakness being commented upon.

The Written Report

It is important that you be comfortable with the format for the written report. If you return to the Sandy's Case teacher supervision form, you can see that by removing the actual rating numbers, many good teacher characteristics can be commented upon. In fact, there is even space for that to happen. But many department heads will be uncomfortable with the kind of standardized evaluation form that this document represents. The department head should feel comfortable in creating his or her own document. The important factor is that all pertinent areas of skill and areas for improvement and attention are covered.

The written report should emphasize the developmental aspects of the process. The supervisory report is a road map for the teacher to see where he or she has been and, hopefully, blazed an exceptional swath and where he or she needs to go to fully explore the landscape of learning. The supervisors task is to keep the supervision document clear and selective.

It is much better to focus on one, two, or even three aspects of the teacher's work. Creating a globally focused document will be overwhelming for you to prepare and overwhelming for the teacher to receive. Rather, the report should concentrate on a small number of issues for which the teacher has immediate understanding. In selecting items for attention, be sure to balance the positive and the negative. As academicians, we have been trained (all too well) to be critical. The department head must find the "good" and spend a good deal of time commenting upon this area.

But again, the watchword is balance. A supervisory report that does not give the teacher some feedback on where there are weaknesses and how those weaknesses might be addressed is not helpful. Above all, teachers want the evaluation process to result in something valuable. It must lead the teacher to the self-realization that there are ways to improve student learning.

Since these reports will be ongoing in a developmental supervisory process, it is important for the supervisor to link past reports to the present and to foreshadow future reports and how they will be referenced to this present report. Such referencing helps the teacher recognize the growth in

---

Exhibit 9.14 A Sample Teacher Supervisory Report

Margaret Stanley   Third Year Evaluation

Margaret's teaching load this year is the same as last year, two sections of earth science and two of physical science. She is reasonably happy about the way both of these courses are running. In earth science, a new edition of the text has caused some problems and, in actuality, the new text is not as useful or effective a resource as the older version. The result is that the students need more extra help than in the other years, and that kind of time takes its toll on Margaret. The seventh-period class for which Meg gave me video tape is clearly an exciting class with a terrific group of students. They are bright, have good skills and are actively interested in the course. Margaret is looking for more ways to get demonstrations into the class, but that requires more preparation time than she feels she can devote to that effort.

In terms of course mechanics, Margaret collects written homework three times per week, which is fine, but the real paper-grading burden in this course is the lab notebooks. Margaret has stated that "hands-on work is crucial, if the child is going to make connections between the real world and the world of theory." She has noted that one of her espoused theories is that "real learning must have a real world component to it." From the tapes it is clear that this theory is definitely turned into action.

In the laboratory, the students are getting better and better at working with the computers, which are so integral to the program. In general, the lab is directed by Tom Smith, the course leader, but Margaret is happy to follow his lead. She and he are working well together, this being her third year. One minor area where Meg might be a bit more attentive is in terms of doing all she can to maintain the kind of order and cleanliness that Tom insists upon in the classroom and lab. His standards are very high, as he has let Margaret know on several occasions.

In Physical Science, again, the text book posed some problems. It was new this year and quite simply did not work out as we had expected. Next year, we will be looking for a new text. The class itself was quite small, and Margaret showed skillful use of that venue. She and the students formed a tightly knit group, all pulling in the same direction. The hand-outs for lab exercises were excellent, as you might expect for a teacher who places a high degree of emphasis upon the actual doing of science. She included a fair amount of independent project work this year in those two classes, and it has served as a model for some of the veteran teachers who are also interested in this kind of approach. She also created a very successful new field trip. The students spent some time at the local amusement part studying elementary physics principles. The trip was well-organized and thought out. Margaret hopes to expand this trip next year.

The observations we made of her classes confirmed that Margaret had worked on some of the minor criticisms I offered last year. Her style is much more relaxed and nonthreatening these days. She comes across as caring and happy, yet organized and firm. Her work at the blackboard has become the model, which I only hope to be half as good at. She has a natural ability to use the board at just the right time and in the perfect manner to illustrate a point without having the students feel that they have to write everything down as quickly as possible.

She manages to include all the students in discussions, engaging them in effective dialogue, rather than just "jumping" around the room with quick questions to students. This is something we talked about last year, and I can see a big positive difference in her handling of the discussions now.

In terms of professional growth, Margaret does feel a bit frustrated that rather than really "enhancing" her teaching, she is just keeping up, "treading water," so to speak. She describes herself, somewhat frustratingly, as a "jack of all trades, and master of none." She would like to be able to concentrate on some of the subject matter in which she specialized in college, and build upon that by offering a new course, perhaps in geology. She toyed with applying for a special summer fellowship, but realized that finances wouldn't work at this time. Pedagogically, she is interested in the fundamental question of student retention of material and in incorporating some of the newer discoveries in this area into her teaching.

Use of computer technology in science classes continues to be on the rise here and Margaret has helped us with our general program by agreeing to be the liaison between the science department and the technology services department. She has found them to be more and more helpful in trouble shooting. It is important at this point, however, to realize that a person in this liaison position may be asked in the future to take on more and more responsibility, especially considering the upgrading of the science building's computer center and the need for more supervision there. She is interested in doing more in this area, but not unless there is recognition that such an assignment cannot simply be an "add-on."

Finally, it is clear to me that Margaret is a teacher who is making a difference in the lives of our students, who cares deeply about those students, who remains knowledgeable about current pedagogy and who is experimenting and changing in all the correct ways. We should be very pleased with her work.

his or her practice. No veteran teacher wants to be formally recognized as being the same teacher now that he or she was fifteen years before. No young teacher wants to think there is no room for further growth.

The most effective reports tend to be written in somewhat of a "letter" voice. They should be written directly to the teacher and not to some unknown third-person. However, you must feel comfortable with any format you choose. If this is not your style of writing, then by all means do not try to write in this style. Do what suits your strengths. Exhibit 9.14 shows an example of an excellent department head report.

When Supervision Fails

Inevitably there will be instances where the teacher's style, level of subject competence or performance will not match the needs of the institution. If, after being afforded the opportunity to alter his or her work, there has been no improvement, the institution has no course to follow except termination of the contract. In such cases it is essential to make sure the following practices have been followed. (This list is adapted from Karin O'Neil, Association of Independent Schools of New England Leadership Conference, 1997)

1. Be sure the school has clearly stated expectations for ethical conduct and professional standards and that these have been communicated well to the entire faculty.
2. Communicate promptly with any teacher who fails to meet standards of performance that are required by the school. When there is reason to believe a teacher's continuation is in question, that should be communicated to the teacher along with indications of what can be done to remedy the situation.
3. Be certain to allow a reasonable length of time for growth and progress to occur. Offer and provide assistance consistent with the school's existing policies and practices.
4. Document specifically the ways in which the teacher's work has not met acceptable standards, what the teacher can do to meet those standards, what efforts the supervisor and the school will make to provide assistance to the teacher. Be certain that a record is kept of any efforts the supervisor or the school make.
5. Recognize with humility and clarity the point at which you conclude that further supervisory efforts are unlikely to yield sufficient progress to bring the teacher's performance up to acceptable standards.

6. Communicate clearly with others in the school (such as the Head, Principal, Vice-Principal , Division Head, etc.) who have supervisory responsibility and from whom you will need support and backing. Discuss who should play what role in counseling the teacher or letting the teacher go. Consultation with the school's attorney may be advisable in some situations.
7. Know state laws that apply to teacher employment and dismissals. Make sure you follow all of the union guidelines.
8. Follow the general constitutional principles of fundamental fairness and due process.

Summary

The focus of developmental supervision is to help all teachers develop the skills that can directly influence student learning. The process outlined in this chapter, is one where the input of the teacher is a valued resource. The strength of the process is that it allows the uniqueness of a teacher to shine forth. While all institutions publish their common goals in the form of a mission or vision statement, the way to achieve that goal is through valued and varied teaching styles. In developmental supervision, good teaching can be recognized and improved in a manner that is satisfying to both the supervisor and the supervisee.

Whether the teacher is primarily a technician, a planner, a talker, a doer, a conceptualizer, an advocate, a standard bearer, an emotional fount, or a stolid problem solver, the best of such behaviors and styles can be improved and recognized as being of value to the school. Developmental supervision, as described, allows for the separation of facts from feelings. It can create a strong bond between the department head and the teacher. Research tells us that teachers prefer a collaborative and nondirective supervisory style (Whistler and Wallace, 1984). This method has as its underlying structure a collaborative approach. In addition, this method gives credibility to the expertise of the teacher as well as the supervisor.

Finally, this method allows the supervisor to show an openness to ideas of the teacher and stresses the desire to problem-solve together. It allows the supervisor to give advice and encouragement, as opposed to directions. The method keeps the lines of communication open and signals the fact that improvement of teaching is an ongoing, never-ending process.

References and Bibliography

Argyris, Chris and Schon, Donald (1989). *Theory in practice: Increasing professional effectiveness.* San Francisco: Jossey-Bass.

Cogan, Morris L. (1973). *Clinical supervision.* Boston: Houghton Mifflin.

Danielson, Charlotte (1996). *Enhancing professional practice: A framework for teaching.* Alexandria, VA : Association for Supervision and Curriculum Development.

Glickman, Carl D. (1969). *Developmental supervision.* Alexandria, VA: ASCD.

Goldhammer. Robert (1969). *Clinical supervision: Special methods for the supervision of teachers.* New York: Holt, Rinehart and Winston.

Hoy, Wayne K., and Forsyth, Patrick B. (1986). *Effective supervision: Theory into practice.* New York: McGraw-Hill.

Jackson, Philip W. (1986). *The practice of teaching.* New York: Teachers College Press.

Joyce, Bruce, and Showers, Beverly (1988). *Student achievement through staff development.* New York: Longman, Inc.

Lortie, Dan C. (1975). *Schoolteacher.* Chicago: University of Chicago Press.

McLaughlin, Milbrey, and Pfeifer, R. Scott (1988). *Teacher evaluation: Improvement, accountability and effective learning.* New York: Teachers College Press.

Ryan, Joseph, and Kuhs, Therese (1993). "Assessment of Preservice Teachers and the Use of Portfolios." *Theory into practice.* Columbus, Ohio: The Ohio State University, College of Education, Spring.

Rubin, Louis J. (1991). *Artistry in teaching.* New York: Random House.

Schon, Donald (1983). *The reflective practitioner: How professionals think in action.* New York: Basic Books.

Schon, Donald (1987). *Educating the reflective practitioner.* San Francisco: Jossey-Bass Publishers.

Seldin, Peter (1991). *The Teaching portfolio.* Bolton, MA: Anker Publishing Company.

Articles

Blake, J. et al. (1995). A portfolio-based assessment model for teachers: Encouraging professional growth. *NASSP Bulletin, 79* (Oct.), pgs 37–46.

Brundage, Sara E. (1997). What kind of supervision do veteran teachers need? An invitation to expand collegial dialogue and research. *J. Curriculum and Supervision, 12* (No. 1), 98–94.

Duffy, Francis M. (1995). Supervising knowledge work: A different kind of supervision. *NASSP Bulletin* (Oct.), 56–66.

Gleave, Doug. (1997). Bifocals for teacher development and appraisal. *J. Curriculum and Supervision, 12* (Spring), 269–281.

Haymes, David (1995). One teacher's experience with national board assessment. *Ed. Leadership, 52* (March), 58–60.

Nolan, J. (1993). Case studies: Windows onto clinical supervision. *Ed. Leadership, 51* (No. 2), 52–56.

Norris, Cynthia, J. (1991). Supervising with style. *Theory Into Practice, 30* (Spring), 128–133.

Shakeshaft, C., et al. (1991). Gender and supervision. *Theory Into Practice, 30* (Spring), 134–139.

Shapiro, Barbara (1995). The NBPTS sets standards for accomplished teaching. *Ed. Leadership, 52* (March), 55–57.

Siens, Cathrean, and Ebmeirer, Howard (1996). Developmental supervision and the reflective thinking of teachers. *J. Curriculum and Supervision, 11* (Summer), 299–319.

Whisteler, N. L., and Wallace, N. E. (1984). How teachers view their supervision. *Catalyst for Change, 14*, 26–29.

Wolf, Kenneth (1996). Developing an effective teaching portfolio. *Ed. Leadership, 53* (No. 6), 34–37.

Chapter 10

Putting It All Together

The preceding nine chapters have been aimed at helping you develop specific skills to manage your department or team in order to fulfill the mission of each team member within the context of departmental and school goals. But, before any of that can happen, you must be willing to follow the advice of Sophocles, "One learns by doing the thing; for though you think you know it, you have no certainty until you try." The task of creating a collaborative atmosphere where, in the words of Judith Warren Little (1982, 325–340), "Teachers teach each other the practice of teaching." can be daunting. And schools do not readily provide a context for socially cohesive communities. More often, they appear to be "shopping malls" (Powell et al., 1982) or possess "fractionated" curriculum and staff relationships (Sizer, 1984).

It is the department head and team leader who is the prime mover in altering the forces that work to drive teachers into increased isolation, repetitive response, and closed communication. Of all the roles that the department head must play in the organizational, administrative, educational, and supervisory arenas, the most important one is the supervisory role. Building a healthy climate through teamwork, creating the context for learning and change, resolving conflict through openness and honesty, making decisions through collaboration and consensus, all demand essential "people" skills. While it is important for the department head or team leader to understand the subject matter of the department and to have been, and continue to be, an effective teacher, the ability to organize activities and practices that help your department members become more committed to education is of primary importance. Ginty (1995) promotes three areas of understanding for the successful school leader: (1) understanding yourself, (2) understanding people and then using that understanding to manage them (3) understanding the environment, and using inquiry to make decisions.

In Lortie's classic work (1975), he discovered that while teaching is a very isolating profession, with teachers not sharing much of a common technical culture, there was also a paradox. He observed that [teachers] turn to one another for assistance and consider peer help their most important source of assistance." As the leader of teachers, it is up to the department head to do all in his or her power to provide such assistance.

Earlier I mentioned the aphorism made popular by Burt Nannus and Warren Bennis, "Managers do things right; leaders do the right thing." Notice the emphasis on "doing." The department head must be a doer—and quite often this means acting in ways that might not feel completely comfortable. But if the department is to improve, there is no other starting point than action by the department head.

What might be the "right things" a department head should do? The following is a short list of some of those things. You will certainly have your own specific actions that are idiosyncratic to your team to add to this list.

Show confidence in your faculty. Having a high regard for their ability to do well, for their capacity to change, for their willingness to work together must be your outlook. Encouraging them to discuss important things about the job with you will allow them to develop attitudes that are empowering and energizing. It is up to you to seek teachers' ideas and to make use of them. This is an active role that you must play if you wish to create an exceptional department.

Build positive attitudes toward the school and the department. There is a tendency in teachers to look on the dark side of the world. It may stem from the intellectual training that underlies most academic disciplines. We have been taught to be critical, to question, to accept nothing at face value; we spend our days "correcting" others. All of this can lead to a pretty depressing atmosphere. Many of you will remember Spiro Agnew's plaintive cry about the news media as "nattering nabobs of negativism." This can easily become the ethos of the department if you do not take action to prevent it. The effective department head works to generate favorable and cooperative attitudes towards other department members, other departments, and school administration. This is no easy task. To do so might mean halting years of negativity as a way of being. But to have an exceptional department means you must act.

Help teachers feel important, needed, useful, proud and respected. Because the work that teachers do is often unappreciated and because the profession is extremely isolating, your active support for the emotional well-being of your team is an important facet of your work. No one knows the day-to-day struggles and heroism of teachers better than you do. You can use this knowledge to inform other administrators of particularly exemplary work, so that administrator can acknowledge that work. Often, what teachers want most is for someone to recognize that that they are making a difference in the lives of their students. Additionally, you will always have teachers of varying abilities on your staff. Helping everyone stretch a bit to be more effective than they thought they could be, helping those who are less able to become better teachers and be proud of their progress as teachers, is something only the team leader can do with constancy and immediacy.

Remind everyone that the main responsibility of a school is to serve students. Too often, teachers lose sight of this fact. It becomes easy to think about how the school must be organized to serve their own personal needs. Because departments play the central role in the social and political world of a school, a particular group think can emerge that has a kind of twisted logic. This logic says that the best teachers are those who are contented with their work and their environment. Making sure such contentedness exists is actually a service to the students. Therefore, the school should always act in ways that will bring increasing levels of contentedness to the teacher. This means policies and practices that are followed and adopted, which might not be in the best interest of the student, should not be questioned if they keep the teachers happy. In the long run, such practices are in the best interest of the student.

Your role as the leader in preventing such thinking cannot be overstated. You must continually bring your team back to reality by emphasizing that the primary mission of the school is to serve students. If both students and teachers can benefit from a particular practice, then all the better. But practices simply for teacher satisfaction are not the best to follow.

Realize that teachers prefer meaningful work to idleness and idleness to busywork. For example, there is nothing more frustrating to a teacher than to have to attend a meeting where nothing happens. No decisions are made, no important issues are discussed, no opportunity to influence major school issues is provided. Or to be in a situation where the department is called upon to make a study of some particular aspect of curriculum and nothing happens to the report when finished. If you and your department have carefully crafted the departmental mission, then all work that is done in the department should reference this mission. This will ensure that when teachers are asked to spend time on a project, it will not be wasted. Your constant awareness and referencing of that mission and acting within the spirit of that mission will ensure that teachers' time is put to good use.

Do not be shy about acknowledging departmental differences.
Siskin (1994) clearly points out that "departments are more than simple dividing lines in a school." Certainly, they create boundaries of expertise and knowledge bases. Often, departments are physically separated by floor or wing of a building or may have their own building. Physical separation emphasizes the epistemological separation that makes one department differ from another.

Departments think of themselves as groups with common norms and understandings. Science teachers understand each other in tacit ways and are less likely to understand the needs and practices of subject departments unlike theirs. As an example, it is common for science teachers to point out to other departments that they must teach laboratory sections, which feel like separate courses, in addition to the regular class. To them, this feels like added work, and science teachers often want reduced loads or extra pay to account for this perceived increased workload. However, English teachers feel that they have just as much additional work because of the volume of writing they have to correct. Often, the writing assignments take students into areas not clearly linked to the particular lesson at hand. Both sets of teachers have legitimate concerns and, yet they do not truly understand each other. Both think that the other teachers are involved in work that is nothing more than the work normal to that discipline, not work that calls for extra recognition.

So while there are legitimate differences between departments, the leader can act to transform these differences into strengths for the school. By acknowledging that the approach to learning might be different, department heads and team leaders can encourage innovative teaching techniques, which when taken as a whole create a collective commitment to students.

When math teachers obsess about "placement" of students, they are trying to be helpful. When English teachers complain about the number of students they teach, they are following a similar pattern to those math teachers. Both want the policies of the school to reflect their needs. Both are focused on the needs of the students. It is the task of the leaders to make sure that these underlying commonalties are not discarded or misunderstood.

The entire school benefits from the diversity of approach and content that each department fosters. By working with the other department heads in the school, you can be the instrument that transforms learning. By acting with an understanding that all departments cannot be treated the same, you will be acting in the best interests of the students. It will be your mission to help everyone in the department realize that the nature of the discipline might call for one department to have a teacher/student ratio much lower than another. It will be your job to help teachers move away from the generic approach to teaching.

Final Words of Advice

Finally, this brings me to the last words of advice for a department head or team leader. What can you specifically do that will make a difference? Here is a list of ten principles that I have found to be most useful for a department head to hold near and dear as he or she strives to be effective, admired, and respected.

1. Have a vision. Put that vision into writing, and live it everyday. Don't try to force that vision onto the department, but rather let it wash over the group, as waves continually wash the shoreline smoothing the beach and allowing for new footprints to make their mark on the sands.

2. Let people see how they can contribute to that vision. This will create the group identity for which you are striving. Remember that the memory of how a team worked well together lasts much longer than the memory of the details of the project. When you delegate and create meaningful roles for people to play in the department, you draw each and every person into that vision.

3. Be the calm at the center of the storm. Let the winds of turmoil, when they blow, swirl around you. Don't be afraid to repair someone else's damage. You can display your energy by focusing it in helpful and constructive ways.

4. Help people reach their goals. This means you must know their goals. You must talk with your team. Know them. Use whatever means you have at your disposal to do this. Ask questions. Listen to the grapevine. Give people your time. Always pay attention when they make a request for you to listen.

5. Promote people. This does not mean giving them a new title. It means using sincere praise and sharing the credit for work well done. It means knowing what people do, while helping them feel confident and powerful. Be a part of their dreams.

6. Give yourself permission to lead. In the words of Blanchard and Hersey, "sell, don't tell." Follow through on your ideas. Be open. Do what you think is "right." Do not hesitate to act. It is easier to ask for forgiveness than to receive permission, so be a doing person.

7. Give yourself time to lead. You will have to make choices. The task at hand is large and must be approached with the long-term vision in mind. Incremental progress can be incredibly powerful. Don't try to do it all the first month or even the first year.

8. Be a communicator. Don't be a fact hog. People want information. Give them as much as you can. Be around them, and listen to them. Use group communication systems such as common bulletin boards or electronic conference sites. Ask questions. Investigate. Probe. Be tentative in your approach to new practices.

9. Be decisive, yet flexible. Try to develop consensus, but don't worry about mistakes. To work at the edge of great success is also to work at the edge of great failure. In reality, there is no such thing as trial and error. It is really trial and learning.

10. Expect excellence. Do this both for yourself and for them. Work on those areas of weakness in the team. Focus on quality by helping everyone see what the "possible" might be. This will take time so do not be impatient, but excellence is a lofty goal and an inspiration to everyone.

As I have said elsewhere in this book, there is no more important position in the school than that of department head or team leader. Your leadership at the grassroots level will make or break a department or school. Hopefully, you now have some new ways of acting and some methods for developing your department and team. Follow the words of Goethe as you move forward. "Knowing is not enough; we must apply. Willing is not enough; we must do."

Putting It All Together

Lortie, Dan (1975). *Schoolteacher.* Chicago: Chicago University Press.

Powell, A. G., Farrar, E. and Cohen,D. C. (1985). *The shopping mall high school.* Boston: Houghton Mifflin.

Roberts, Wess (1997). *Protect your Achilles heel.* Kansas City: Andrews and McMell.

Sergiovanni, Thomas (1996). *Leadership for the schoolhouse.* San Francisco: Jossey-Bass.

Siskin, Leslie Santee (1994). *Realms of knowledge: Academic departments in secondary schools.* Washington, D.C.: Falmer Press.

Sizer, Ted R. (1994). *Horace's compromise: The dilemma of the American high school.* Boston: Houghton Mifflin.

Articles

Ginty, Edwin F. (1995). Supporting the success of the aspiring and beginning school leader. *NASSP Bulletin*, *79* (Dec.) 34–41.

Little, Judith Warren (1982). Norms of collegiality and experimentation:Workplace conditions of school success. *American Educational Research Journal*, *19*, 325–340.

Schmoker, Mike (1997). Setting goals in turbulent times. *ASCD 1997 Year Book*. Ed. Andy Hargreaves. Alexandria, VA: ASCD, 128–148.

About the Author

Rodney LaBrecque has been a teacher, administrator, coach, and dormitory supervisor for thirty years and has served as a science department head for twelve years. Mr. LaBrecque has directed the Leadership Workshop for Department Heads and Team Leaders for the last eighteen years. He recently spent five years on start-up independent high schools in the San Francisco Bay area and is now Head of School at Wilbraham and Monson Academy in Wilbraham, Massachusetts. He has served as an educational consultant to over seventy-five schools in the United States and Canada.

Subject Index

Author Index

Argyris, Chris, 88, 94, 119, 250, 253, 256
Ash, Mary Kay, 74

Bass, Bernard, 198
Blake, J., 289
Blanchard, Kenneth, 44–46, 295
Bolman, Lee, 188
Bolton, Robert, 120
Brundage, Sara, 248
Burns, James MacGregor, 40, 188
Butler, Ava, 221

Coleridge, Samuel Taylor, 94
Conner, Daryl, 183, 192
Covey, Stephen, 1, 34, 173
Csikszentmihalyi, Mihaly, 79, 151

Danielson, Charlotte, 249
Deal, Terrance, 188
Depree, Max, 40, 74
Deutsch, Morton, 72
Dickens, Charles, 157

Elgin, Suzette Haden, 125
Emerson, Ralph Waldo, 158
Evans, Robert, 185, 189, 192

Frost, Robert, 187
Fulwiler, Toby, 158

Ginty, Edwin, 291

Goethe, Johann Wolfgang von, 296
Goldhammer, Robert, 248
Greenleaf, Robert, 19

Hackman, J. R., 99
Haynes, David, 257
Hersey, Paul, 44–46, 295
Hyman, Ron, 218

Jentz, Barry, 122

Leavitt, H., 78
Lewin, Kurt, 43
Lightman, Alan, 143, 145
Lipman-Blumen, J., 78
Little, Judith Warren, 291
Lortie, Dan, 23, 256, 291

Machiavelli, Niccolo, 177
MacKenzie, Alec, 164
Maeroff, Gene, 79
Maslow, Abraham, 14, 66, 198, 277
Mayo, Elton, 65
McLaughlin, Milbrey, 247
Morris, P., 189

Nolan, J., 248

Oldham, G., 99
O'Neil, Karin, 287

Pawlas, George, 106